conceptualization and measurement
in the social sciences

conceptualization and measurement in the social sciences

Hubert M. Blalock, Jr.

SAGE PUBLICATIONS
Beverly Hills / London / New Delhi

For information address:

SAGE Publications, Inc.
275 South Beverly Drive
Beverly Hills, California 90212

SAGE Publications India Pvt. Ltd.
C-236 Defence Colony
New Delhi 110 024, India

SAGE Publications Ltd
28 Banner Street
London EC1Y 8QE, England

Printed in the United States of America

Library of Congress Cataloging in Publication Data

Blalock, Hubert M.
  Conceptualization and measurement in the social sciences.

  Includes bibliographical references and index.
  1. Social sciences—Methodology. 2. Social sciences—Statistical methods. I. Title.

H61.B5758   300'.724   81-23269
ISBN 0-8039-1804-6   AACR2

SECOND PRINTING, 1983

CONTENTS

PREFACE   7

Chapter 1   Introduction   11

            The Indirectness of Measurement   20

            The Tradeoff Among Generalizability, Simplicity,
              and Precision   27

Chapter 2   Fundamental Measurement, Scaling, and
            Dimensionality Issues   33

            Extensive Measurement   35

            Dimensionality, Information, and Error   46

Chapter 3   The Comparability of Measures   57

            The Use of Common Indicators in Multiple-
              Indicator Analyses   76

            Noncomparability with Respect to Slopes
              and Intercepts   85

            Noncomparability with Respect to Complexity
              of Settings   94

            A Caution on Biases   106

Chapter 4   Categorical Variables, Conceptualization,
            and Comparability   109

            Noncomparability Due to Multidimensionality
              of Concrete Situations   110

            Interpreting Categorical Data   115

            Collapsing Decisions and Marginal Distributions   120

Constraints Imposed by Social Definitions and
    Data Collectors   127

Predicting Choice Behaviors: An Illustration   130

Linking General Experience Dimensions with
    Background Variables   135

**Chapter 5   Some Implications of Omitting Variables from
Causal Explanations**   147

The Omission of Intervening Variables   148

The Omission of Variables Relating to Past
    Experiences   176

Concluding Remarks   194

**Chapter 6   The Confounding of Variables and Oversimplified
Interpretations**   197

The Confounding of Measured and Unmeasured
    Variables: The Example of Social Status   198

Background Variables and Experiences Involving
    Differences or Comparisons   226

**Chapter 7   Aggregation and Measurement Error in
Macro-Analyses**   237

Aggregating Effect Indicators   240

Aggregating Cause Indicators   247

Aggregating by Geographic Proximity   252

Aggregating Samples of Variables from Blocks   260

Concluding Remarks   263

APPENDIX   Assessing Comparability with Multiple Indicators 265

REFERENCES   273

INDEX   281

ABOUT THE AUTHOR   285

PREFACE

The opening sentence of my son's college physics text (Sears et al., 1980, p. 1) reads: "Physics has been called the science of measurement." The text then goes on to quote Lord Kelvin as follows: "I often say that when you can measure what you are speaking about, and express it in numbers, you know something about it; but when you cannot express it in numbers, your knowledge is of a meagre and unsatisfactory kind; it may be the beginning of knowledge, but you have scarcely, in your thoughts, advanced to the state of Science, whatever the matter may be."

Physics is also recognized to be a science that is strong in theory, perhaps being the one academic discipline that most closely approximates the ideal of a deductively closed system of thought, though one that also has obviously arrived at this deductive theory through a very long series of meanderings, out-and-out failures, exceedingly patient efforts to collect empirical data and improve measuring instruments, and its fair share of theoretical debates and fruitless controversies. Social scientists are far from agreed on the desirability of holding up physics as an ideal model to be emulated. Indeed, as we shall see, the social sciences are faced with a host of difficulties that vary considerably, at least in complexity, from those encountered in the physical sciences. Nevertheless, there is a sufficient number of commonalities so that we can hardly afford to throw away whatever success models may be available to us.

The social sciences also vary among themselves with respect to two important criteria: the degree to which their most important theories are stated precisely enough to lend themselves to mathematical formalization, and the degree to which

they have been concerned with conceptualization and measurement problems. Economics is obviously the most formal-
ized of the social sciences, whereas psychologists have contributed most importantly to our knowledge of the measurement-
conceptualization process. Sociologists and political scientists,
however, have been profiting from developments in economics
and psychology and have begun to make important contributions of their own. In many respects, sociologists and political
scientists seem to be facing the worst problems of all: we share
with economists the inability to experiment and the necessity
of dealing with both very micro and very macro social processes, and we share with psychologists the problems connected
with highly indirect measurements and the need to collect our
own data with very meager resources.

The writer is a sociologist with some degree of acquaintance
with the political science literature. It is my distinct impression
that the conceptualization and measurement problems faced in
these two fields are almost identical in nature, although the
specific variables that we use may differ. But there are also
sufficient similarities across the several social sciences that I
believe make it reasonable to consider the measurement-
conceptualization problems faced in the social sciences as
though they were nearly identical in nature, though perhaps
relevant to varying degrees across disciplines and subdisciplines.
Therefore, the title of this work refers to the social sciences as a
whole, while the illustrations I shall use are drawn primarily
from sociology.

This is not a book that deals with specific measurement
techniques, such as Guttman scaling, factor analysis, latent
structure analysis, multidimensional scaling, or index construction. Rather, it is addressed to a series of more general issues
that seem to me to be of a very fundamental nature and that
refer more specifically to the *relationship* between theory and
research, or between our theoretically defined constructs and
our measurement procedures. In particular, we shall be very
much concerned with the problem of generalizability and the
comparability of one's measurements across diverse settings. We

shall also be very much interested in the implications of indirect measurement and the omission of important variables from empirical data analyses, and how these most necessary expedients affect our ability to generalize across settings. Such issues obviously crosscut the social sciences and have certain parallels with measurement problems faced in the physical sciences.

In focusing on these very general types of problems, it is my assumption that one of the major reasons for the current lack of consensus that exists within the social sciences, as well as the frustrating slowness of genuine knowledge accumulation in these fields, stems from our failure to face up to some very difficult and fundamental issues that are inherent in the scientific method, broadly interpreted. But these highly general issues, which will be addressed in the first two chapters, appear to imply far greater complexities and uncertainties in the social sciences than in the physical and biological sciences. Therefore, social scientists must become much more self-consciously aware of them in order to develop rational strategies of attack. It will be a major thesis of the book that certain complications must be directly faced, hidden assumptions brought out into the open, and complex "auxiliary measurement theories" constructed in order to deal simultaneously with the objectives of achieving greater generalizability along with increased precision.

The message of the book is therefore likely to be a discouraging one, especially for the beginning student or for those who like to take a highly pragmatic, research-oriented approach to the social sciences. The view taken is that unless very careful attention is paid to one's *theoretical* assumptions and conceptual apparatus, no array of statistical techniques will suffice. Nor can a series of ad hoc empirical studies produce truly cumulative knowledge, except in the sense of producing dated and situation-specific findings of immediate practical significance. The basic message is that theoretical and methodological concerns must go hand-in-hand. Progress in the one area without similar advances in the other cannot be more than minimal. In the words of Kelvin, we will have only the "beginnings of knowledge," with no obvious way of building systematically upon these beginnings.

Another major message that I wish to convey is that the conceptual-measurement issues we face in common throughout the social sciences are *both* technical and theoretical in nature. No "tricks of the trade" will suffice to overcome them. Indeed, they are worthy of our best thinking and immediate and continued attention, and they will be resolved, if at all, only very gradually.

It is assumed that the reader already has a reasonable degree of familiarity with topics in multivariate analysis, including causal modeling and path analysis, along with at least a rudimentary acquaintance with certain standard topics such as scaling, factor analysis, and the use of multiple-indicator models. A technical knowledge of these topics is not required, however, as the primary focus of this work will be on more general issues involving the relationships between some of these rather technical approaches and the "slippery issues" produced by a combination of real-world complexities and the looseness of our conceptual-theoretical apparatus. The interested reader may then return to some of these technical bodies of literature with, I hope, a greater awareness of some of the larger and more theoretical issues that also need to be addressed.

–H.M.B.

CHAPTER 1

INTRODUCTION

This book is concerned with the twin topics of conceptualization and measurement and with how sociologists and other social scientists can develop more effective strategies for integrating these two distinct processes so that theory building and theory testing can be carried out on a more systematic basis.

Conceptualization involves a series of processes by which theoretical constructs, ideas, and concepts are clarified, distinguished, and given definitions that make it possible to reach a reasonable degree of consensus and understanding of the theoretical ideas we are trying to express. This does not mean, of course, that we will necessarily agree on the truth values of specific assumptions or propositions, or the extent to which they may safely be generalized. But it does imply that others will understand what each of us is trying to say, including the logical structure of the arguments being advanced.

By measurement, we refer to the general process through which numbers are assigned to objects in such a fashion that it is also understood just what kinds of mathematical operations can legitimately be used, given the nature of the physical operations that have been used to justify or rationalize this assignment of numbers to objects. Thus, conceptualization refers to the theoretical process by which we move from ideas or constructs to suggesting appropriate research operations, whereas measurement refers to the linkage process between these physical operations, on the one hand, and a mathematical language on the other. The complete process involves a triple linkage among theoretical constructs, physical measurement operations, and mathematical symbols and operations.

Because of the fact that ambiguities and erroneous assumptions may occur at any point in these twin processes, we recognize that the slippage between theory and the interpretation of empirical relationships can be considerable and that our understanding of what is going on at any given stage can be very inadequate. My aim in the present work is to examine a sufficient number of potential points of ambiguity to attempt to point the way toward a more complete understanding of these complex processes as they apply to the social sciences in general, and to sociology in particular.

It is now recognized that on a very general level, many of the thought processes that have proved most valuable in the physical and biological sciences can be applied to the social sciences as well, though not without considerable modification and—in many instances—serious complications. Those who reject the position that the social sciences should follow a "positivistic" path will undoubtedly also reject the idea that measurement constitutes an absolutely essential part of the social scientist's task. But even those who reject measurement as neither necessary nor even possible within the social sciences must, at base, agree that a minimal amount of communication is necessary, and this of course implies the need to pay careful attention to matters of conceptualization. If I mean by "apple" what another person means by "warfare" and still another by "capitalism," we are obviously going to talk past one another.

I believe that it is the consensus among those who adhere to the goal of attaining a reasonable approximation to "objectivity" that it will be to our advantage to define concepts as clearly and concisely as we can, to attempt to assess the degree to which a common vocabulary has been attained, and to press for additional clarification as soon as ambiguities arise or further distinctions need to be made. Therefore, I will take it as a working assumption that those who subscribe to the goal of making the social sciences as "scientific" as possible are also those who will agree upon the objectives of clarifying our basic concepts as carefully as seems reasonable at any given stage of our knowledge development, and of reaching a high degree of consensus on a working vocabulary of such concepts.

There is often a fine line between perfectionism and defeatism, as well as one between honesty in reporting measurement inadequacies and ignoring them, thus leaving research projects so wide open to criticism that they are not taken seriously. The only way out of the implied dilemmas seems to require a frank recognition of the inherent difficulties one may expect to encounter in both theory construction and empirical research. Once these difficulties are more adequately understood, both researchers and their potential critics may come to a more realistic understanding of the limitations that may be anticipated in any specific piece of research, as well as the difficulties encountered in "adding up" the results of diverse studies using different measuring instruments appropriate to settings that are each somewhat unique.

At the outset, it is necessary to convince many social scientists that careful attention to measurement and conceptualization issues is worth the effort. A very common stance that may be taken—one that is certainly based on a degree of realism about the current state of our knowledge—is that our theories are at present so tentative and our research so exploratory that it is premature to pay too much attention to careful conceptualization or precise measurement until we have discovered a reasonably small set of explanatory variables on which we may pin our hopes. The disclaimer that "this study is purely exploratory" is often a very honest one. But the conclusion that is sometimes drawn from this, that "therefore, anything goes," is hardly justifiable, especially when a claim is made that the investigation supports or refutes a particular theoretical position, or that it suggests the superiority of one policy alternative over another. Yet it would also be foolish to claim that a concern for measurement precision is equally necessary in all studies or that all pieces of research are equally exploratory in nature or equally easily linked to social science theory.

One way to get hold of an issue such as this is to examine it from the standpoint of what we know about the implications of random measurement error in an independent variable in a multiple regression equation. If, say, a dependent variable Y is related to two independent variables X_1 and X_2 according to the very simple linear equation

$$Y = a + b_1 X_1 + b_2 X_2 + e$$

we know that random measurement error in X_1 will attenuate the slope coefficient b_1 toward zero, and that the *degree* of attenuation will depend upon the ratio of the true variance in X_1 relative to the measurement error variance in that variable.[1] Furthermore, we also know that the estimate b_2 of the true regression coefficient of the *other* independent variable (assumed to be perfectly measured) will depend upon the (true) correlation between the two independent variables X_1 and X_2. To the degree that these variables are highly correlated, random measurement errors in X_1 will produce an *over*estimate of the effects of X_2, thereby in effect giving the perfectly measured variable credit for the effects of the poorly measured one.

What do these simple facts imply in terms of strategic considerations for measurement? First, we may conclude that accuracy of measurement is much less crucial whenever we are dealing with situations in which there is considerable variation in each of our independent variables relative to (random) measurement error. Thus, if one is comparing eight or ten widely divergent societies for which there is little question that differences, say, in level of economic development or political stability are very substantial, then it is much less necessary to obtain precise measures of these phenomena than in instances where the differences are much less pronounced. In contrast, if one is dealing with change data for which the amount of change is rather small relative to presumed measurement errors, one must find ways of shrinking these measurement errors considerably before one has any faith that the findings are not due primarily to unreliability rather than real changes. The more homogeneous a population is with respect to any variable we are attempting to measure, the more concerned we need to be about measurement accuracy.

Second, and perhaps less obviously, the greater our concern about disentangling the effects of even moderately intercorrelated independent variables, the more precise our measurement of *all* these variables must be. If we measure some with considerable accuracy but use only rough indicators of others, we may expect to find that the former "look good" relative to the others, since there will be a double process at work. The coefficients of the latter will be attenuated, but the coefficients of the former may well be amplified, although this may also depend upon the signs as well as the magnitudes of the intercorrelations in most multivariate situations of any degree of complexity. In other words, we can easily be misled to the degree that our explanatory variables are intercorrelated. We must also remember that to the degree that there are measurement errors in each of these variables, we will not even be able to obtain accurate estimates of these intercorrelations, since the "true values" will be unknown.

We may distinguish several different kinds of situations involving this multicollinearity problem.[2] Sometimes these intercorrelations will be so high, and the "web" of interconnections among indicators so complex, that we may recognize the situation as empirically hopeless. Suppose, for example, that we construct eight indicators of "industrialization" and find their intercorrelations to be of the order of magnitude of .8 or higher. Lacking a clear-cut conceptualization of industrialization, we may not be able to decide which of these indicators comes closest, conceptually, to what we have in mind. In situations such as this, we will probably reach the conclusion that our indicators need to be combined into a single "variable" called "industrialization," and that it would be empirically hopeless to try to test a causal model in which all eight were treated as distinct. Someone wishing to disentangle them would have to obtain both a very large sample and much better measures of all variables.

At the other extreme, where all independent variables are expected to be only very weakly intercorrelated, although it will remain the case that the effects of each poorly measured variable will be affected—being underestimated in the case of random measurement errors—this will not lead the investigator to overestimate the effects of the others, except in relative terms. The intermediate case, however, is by far the most frequent one. There will be moderate intercorrelations among subsets of independent variables, and this is very likely to lead to a confusing picture empirically, as well as a difficult decision-making process in interpreting the results of one's findings. It is also one that is wide open to debate and differing interpretations based on ideological or disciplinary biases.

Very common in this connection are discussions that run along the following lines. The investigator points to inadequacies in previous research, which has found only weak to moderate relationships between a dependent variable and explanatory factors that the investigator wishes to dismiss. An "alternative" explanation is advanced, the relevant variables imperfectly measured, controls for one's opponent's variables introduced (with these variables also being imperfectly measured), and then some conclusions reached that usually favor the investigator's preferred explanation. Often, however, the differences in explanatory power are slight and easily accounted for on the basis of a combination of sampling and measurement errors. The latter, however, are usually ignored and tests are made only for the former. The reader is then left with an uncomfortable feeling that neither theory is very satisfactory.

It is precisely in situations such as these that the need for careful conceptualization and measurement is greatest. Yet these situations are frequently the subjects of serious theoretical debates in which the most extreme partisans are the least interested in so-called "objective" research. What are the most important causes of racism or of inequalities in income, occupation, or education? What are the factors most responsible for delaying economic development? What are the causes of crime and delinquency? What are the factors that affect decision-making processes in urban communities? We commonly encounter intercorrelated sets of independent variables such that one's empirical results can be very much affected by considerations of measurement. Often, the reasonably straightforward problem of assessing the reliability of each measure is compounded by theoretical ambiguities in the conceptualization, so that the empirically inclined social scientist must make a series of measurement decisions that appear to be arbitrary and that most certainly will be challenged whenever the findings do not appear compatible with whatever theoretical position is being espoused. The claim will be made that a "true test" has not been made, and this claim will be a correct one, although not necessarily because the researcher is at fault.

What can we do in situations such as these, which are indeed frequent in sociology as well as the other social sciences? In most general terms, the resolution is an obvious one. We take such disputes and ambiguous results as starting points or as signs that a much more careful theoretical reformulation is needed. We try to make a series of distinctions and conceptual clarifications that suggest how a more definitive empirical study can be made. Furthermore, we assess whether the theories under consideration should be posed as "alternatives," in the sense that they imply at least some incompatible conclusions capable of being tested, or whether they can be reformulated into a more inclusive theory that will usually be of a more complex nature. We expect, of course, that such a more complex reformulation will be opposed by those who prefer to take an uncompromising position, for whatever reason, and by those who favor parsimony at the expense of completeness or explanatory power.

There is another type of difficulty that also has profound implications for measurement-conceptualization issues. Many of the variables of greatest interest to us are extremely difficult to measure, even where they have been defined with great precision. Some would require extremely expensive data collection operations. Suppose, for example, one wanted to compare a set of norms in five different societies where these norms were defined in terms of some average set of expectations. In other instances, the data are simply lost in history. We will never be able to assess accurately just how unhappy a given set of peasants were in 17th century England, though perhaps we may try to infer this on the basis of reported uprisings that appear in selected documents. Still other variables cannot be measured because to do so would involve unethical procedures or ones that would encounter too much political resistance. Social scientists simply do not have the power to conduct experiments on elites, and thus settle for very brief experiments with their introductory students or those willing to accept small payments in return for their cooperation. What can we do in all of these instances? And what general kinds of stances toward measurement are likely to result from this state of affairs?

One such stance is that of rejecting the goal of measurement as both ideologically and politically biased and naive because of the fact that the data we are able to collect are likely to be subject to constraints that are not politically or ideologically neutral. Thus, if it is more difficult to study elites than relatively powerless individuals, a strong emphasis on quantification may result in an overemphasis on one set of substantive problems at the expense of others; for instance, we may be financed to study those whose behaviors the sponsoring agencies would like to control. This stance very naturally leads to an anti-science ideological position that also challenges the objective of "value-free" social science research. But quite aside from the ideological issues involved, it must be admitted that there is a very serious methodological problem as well, namely that of missing information and unmeasured variables. Furthermore, the nature of the variables that do not get measured is clearly based on a nonrandom process. We include only a subset of the theoretically relevant variables, and our choice is often a matter of convenience or, as some would say, opportunism.

A second stance, which is nearly the opposite, involves a measurement-by-fiat approach through which the investigator selects whatever remotely connected indicators he or she can locate and then merely announces that these will serve as measures of some highly abstract theoretical construct. The presumed rationale is that since the concept is difficult to measure, almost any indicators will do. This very appealing practice apparently enables the researcher to deal with important theoretical questions while, at the same time, trying to develop empirical tests of hypotheses that are related to these theoretical ideas.

The difficulty lies, in this instance, in how one can ever criticize the methodology in a constructive fashion, aside from pointing to the arbitrary way in which the concepts have been measured. The assumptions made in moving from the theoretical construct to the operational measure are simply left unstated, the justification being that readily available indicators are better than none at all. This may be true, but carried too far this stance turns opportunism and convenience into matters of principle and affords little motivation toward improvement of the measurement process. Furthermore, it makes the assessment of comparability almost impossible or implies that the comparability question is a strictly operational one of deciding upon nearly identical measures across settings. In the next chapter we shall have more to say about such an approach.

A third stance is essentially that of sidestepping the theoretical issue as being one that cannot be resolved by empirical means, turning instead to questions that can be handled in terms of much more direct measurement. To some extent this position, too, is reasonable in that we must admit that many kinds of interesting theoretical questions cannot be resolved empirically because of a lack of data. But pushed to the extreme, this third stance may encourage investigators to confine their attention to questions that are theoretically unimportant, rather than to begin the arduous task of improving on both the conceptualization and measurement of the most important variables contained in the theory. In the extreme, this path leads either toward blind empiricism or toward the practice of selecting problems according to matters of data availability rather than substantive importance.

The only constructive stance that I can suggest is one that admits to the nature of the problem, distinguishes between those theoretically defined variables that have and have not been associated with operational measures, attempts to state explicitly the assumptions required to link the former theoretical constructs with their indicators, and then proceeds to specify just which propositions can and cannot be tested with the data at hand. This stance basically admits that data collection constraints will mean that certain important variables cannot be measured, but it retains these variables in the model as unmeasured variables and thus permits the statement of a number of theoretical propositions that themselves cannot be tested with the data. It also requires the admission that certain of the linkages between constructs and indicators will be tenuous and involves as well the effort to specify the assumptions necessary to justify these linkages.

Finally, it forces on us the admission that only certain parts of the total theory can be tested by any one study, or even a single program of studies. But it also makes it painfully obvious that since the theory has been only partially tested, subsequent efforts must be made to fill in the remainder of the picture by paying greater attention to those variables that, for the time being, have not been measured. This includes a specification of how the variables might be measured under close-to-ideal conditions, as well as a search for research settings within which approximations to these ideal conditions might be feasible. Illustrations of what this implies will be provided in subsequent chapters.

THE INDIRECTNESS OF MEASUREMENT

Certain ways of perceiving and thinking about the world appear to be common enough to provide a starting point for our discussion. First, there is general agreement that the real world can only be examined through our own perceptions of it, and in particular our reliance on one or more of our human senses or extensions of these senses. We rely on observations or mechanical devices to improve this observation: cameras, telescopes, microscopes, and so forth. We "weigh" objects by lifting them and sensing muscle strain, or perhaps we substitute a balance scale or spring balance to provide a more precise pointer reading. We "feel" heat or infer an increase in temperature by looking at a thermometer, and so forth. But we can never directly answer through such observation any questions that refer to ontological "reality."

We do not know what electricity is "really," although we may develop models in which we postulate certain processes operating among objects with assumed properties, and we may then ask a series of verifiable questions about the implications of these processes for our senses or measuring devices. For instance, we may imagine tiny particles with masses, electrical charges, and spins. We may then state certain "laws" that enable us to predict how these imagined particles interact, and we may ask whether or not these interactions may be expected to have observable consequences. If our sensory apparatuses then tell us that in fact we are experiencing just what would be predicted— say, the expected trace pattern in a bubble chamber or a previously unnoticed point of light in a telescopic photograph, we can have more confidence in the theoretical model. If, however, the trace does not occur as predicted, we go back to the drawing boards and reformulate the theory, or perhaps we look a bit harder or attempt to improve our measuring device. Thus, all of our evidence is highly indirect, but the degree of faith we have in our theory depends upon its ability to provide consistently accurate predictions that would otherwise have been unexpected, or in its adequacy to tie together previously unexplained observations as instances of a single, inclusive scientific law.

It is important to stress this indirectness of the verification process and its dependence upon the human sensory apparatus or its extensions, so as to admit from the outset that we can

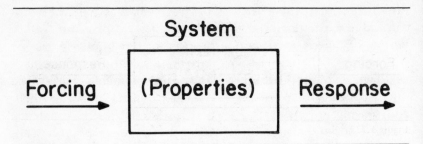

Figure 1.1

hardly expect more of the social sciences. Indeed, we shall have to expect considerably less because of the much greater complexities of the "laws" that connect whatever it is that we believe is occurring in the real world and those few consequences that are observable in this sense. As all social scientists are aware, the considerable indeterminacy and multivariate nature of our "laws" in the social sciences means that our predictions will be much less precise, the conditions under which they are expected to hold will be much more difficult to specify, and our measurement procedures much more subject to error than occurs in the physical sciences. Yet we also know that predictions are also very imprecise and insecure in sciences such as meteorology, geology, and medicine for much the same reasons. Therefore, we are separated from these sciences in terms of factors that vary by degree rather than by differences of a totally disparate nature.

System Properties, Stimuli, and Responses

We also recognize the commonness of a certain mode of thought that involves the tendency to perceive the world in terms of "somethings" that are operated upon by other "somethings," with the former "somethings" in turn responding. Furthermore, each of these "somethings" is thought of as having "properties" that may also influence the responses. Some such "somethings" may be composed of still smaller "somethings" as elements, with interactions among these latter ele-

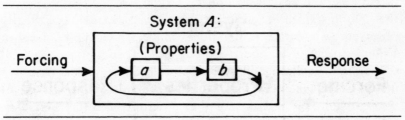

Figure 1.2

ments constituting some of the properties of the larger "some-things." Trimmer (1950) has diagrammed these processes as in Figure 1.1. The term "system" is commonly used as a generic concept to represent whatever one chooses to delineate as the "something" represented diagrammatically within the boxes. Trimmer's term "forcing" is usually referred to as a "stimulus" in social science terminology, but the term "response" is a familiar one to social scientists. Trimmer uses the term "law" to refer to descriptive statements interrelating these forcings, prop-erties of systems, and responses.

Another cross-disciplinary mode of thought involves the no-tion that systems can be composed of other systems as ele-ments, with these latter micro-level systems responding to one another as suggested by Figure 1.2. Thus, the properties of the macro-system A may consist not only of summarizing measures of properties of the micro-systems a and b, but also their *interactions*.

Insofar as this very general mode of thinking characterizes theory construction efforts in many different sciences, we see that there will be a necessity of dealing with cross-level situa-tions in which certain concepts or laws may concern themselves with micro-systems (such as systems a and b) that are them-selves elements of larger macro-systems (such as system A). This then leads to problems of obtaining measures pertaining, say, to the more macro-level system that may be based on the stimuli, properties, or responses of micro-level systems. It also requires us to be careful in distinguishing among concepts at the two (or more) different levels.

Within any given level (say, where the focus is on system a) it will also be necessary to distinguish among stimulus variables, properties, and responses and to decide whether or not—given the circumstances—each of these can be reasonably directly observed. We often find, for example, that many kinds of system properties cannot be observed, and sometimes we treat the system as though it were an inscrutable "black box." In many other instances, however, we postulate unobserved or unobservable properties and then attempt to infer their existence indirectly by predicting specific responses to particular stimuli.

The essential point in this connection is that the basic concepts or variables in any science need to be specified with sufficient clarity such that (1) we know the "system" or unit to which they are intended to refer; (2) we know how to distinguish them from other stimuli, properties, or responses with which they are likely to be confounded; and (3) we have also specified how concepts that refer to one type of system (e.g., System A) are related, definitionally or by some presumed causal law, to at least some concepts that refer to any other systems that are also expected to play important roles in our substantive theories. This last type of specification implies, of course, that it will often be desirable to use information provided at one level of analysis (say, about individual behaviors) to support, refute, or clarify theories formulated at other levels.

There is, in addition, a pervasive and extremely perplexing problem one encounters in the social sciences that will occupy a good deal of our attention in later chapters. This is the question of how one goes about formulating reasonably *general* propositions, which contain concepts or variables that are appropriate to a wide variety of circumstances, and which at the same time are sufficiently precise to be rejectable. Put another way, given the extremely wide variety of stimuli, properties, and behaviors that are described or assumed in ordinary discourse about human interactions, how can we categorize, conceptualize, and measure them in such a way that reasonably general propositions can be teased out of the morass of extremely specific descriptive statements and research findings that are available to us? Can we ever hope to achieve a closed set of important variables or concepts around which a reasonably tight and inclusive theoretical system can be built?

It does not appear as though the very extensive literature on the philosophy of science will be of much help in enabling us to define our basic concepts so as to achieve these objectives. Indeed, my own readings of the discussions of this literature that have appeared in the sociological journals and books on sociological theory have led me to conclude that as often as not, this philosophy of science literature has been used, ideologically, to support one or another "school" of social thought, rather than in a more constructive way to help provide insights as to how to proceed. This is in contrast with the scaling and measurement literature, developed primarily by psychologists, that has been much more effectively integrated among the working tools of empirically minded investigators. Unfortunately, the result is an imbalance in both our rate of actual progress and in our training programs, in the sense that measurement has come to occupy much more of our attention than has conceptualization.

Auxiliary Measurement Theories and Conceptualization

Some years ago (Blalock, 1968) I introduced the concept of "auxiliary measurement theories" to emphasize the point that the process of measurement requires a set of theoretical assumptions, many of which must remain untested in any given piece of research, and that therefore the processes of theory construction and measurement cannot be seen as distinctly different. Furthermore, when we come to actual "tests" of our theories— which ordinarily take the form of goodness-of-fit comparisons between predicted and actual empirical relationships—we discover that in any given instance, the substantive and auxiliary measurement theories will be confounded together. This means that if we obtain a poor fit, we will not know whether it is the substantive theory, the auxiliary measurement theory, or both, that is at fault. I also argued that this auxiliary theory will usually contain a number of causal assumptions connecting theoretically defined concepts and their measured indicators, and therefore such causal models can be conceptualized in much the same way that causal models among substantive variables can be constructed. However, the auxiliary measurement theory will of necessity contain at least some unmeasured variables and thus will involve added complications because of a substantial proportion of unknowns. Some of the points made in this connection can be briefly summarized, whereas others will occupy our attention in later chapters.

Many "property" variables that are associated with systems, of whatever nature, will be difficult to perceive directly in terms of any of our human senses or of the instruments that we may have constructed to serve as more accurate recording devices. Instead, we often infer these properties in terms of their presumed effects or sometimes their causes or the stimuli we assume produce them. Thus, we do not observe hunger directly but infer it on the basis of food deprivation or certain behavioral responses. We do not "see" a person's "loyalty" or a group's "solidarity," but we infer these by watching the individual or group respond to various stimuli. The physicist postulates a number of elementary particles having certain electrical charges, masses, and spins and then checks up on these assumptions by theorizing how these particles will behave when subjected to various stimuli and how these behaviors, in turn, may impact on other phenomena that may be observed, say, in a bubble chamber. Heat energy is measured in terms of its effects on a column of mercury, and mass is inferred on the basis of pointer readings produced by placing a number of weights on a balance at or near the surface of the earth.

In all of these instances, then, a causal theory is needed to link up the postulated property with some indicator that we can observe in a fashion we are willing to refer to as "direct." Even so, we admit to the possibility of measurement error attributed to the operation of other forces on the balance, the observer's misreading of the pointer reading, or perhaps an imperfection in the measuring instrument. Thus our causal model connecting the postulated property and the actual outcome of the measurement (as a number recorded by the scientist) may become somewhat complex, although we usually rely on very careful instrumentation and replications to make this auxiliary theory as simple as possible. When it becomes so simple that we are willing to take the research operations for granted, we begin to think of the measurement as direct and no longer pay any attention to it—until something goes wrong or until a greater level of precision is needed.

But what about the measurement of stimuli and responses? Aren't these direct in a much more straightforward sense? Suppose we do something to a child and the child responds by hitting or biting us. Certainly we may experience this behavior "directly" by feeling its impact. Or we hear someone say something or witness an interaction between two persons on a street corner. Here our difficulty is of another sort, but one that introduces causal assumptions via the back door, so to speak. There will be a need to *categorize* stimuli or behavioral responses. That is, we will need to aggregate "similar" behaviors, since even all acts of hitting or biting are not alike. Sometimes this can be done strictly on the basis of manifest similarities, as for example striking a blow with one's fists. But as we attempt to use more abstract concepts, such as the notion of aggression, we find it desirable to aggregate or classify behaviors that are manifestly different but presumed to be motivated by the same cause, say a desire to injure another party. Thus, many forms of behavior get defined either in terms of their presumed motivation (intent) or their actual consequences (Blalock, 1979b). In either case, causal assumptions will become part and parcel of the auxiliary measurement theory.

THE TRADEOFF AMONG GENERALIZABILITY, SIMPLICITY, AND PRECISION

We conclude this introductory chapter by posing what appears to be a fundamental dilemma for the social scientist. Although it is obviously desirable, in the abstract, to strive for theories that are simultaneously parsimonious, highly general, and therefore applicable to a wide range of phenomena, yet precise enough to imply rejectable hypotheses, it does not appear possible within the social sciences to achieve simultaneously all three of these ideal characteristics.[3] If so, we shall need to make some difficult choices. As will become apparent in the remaining chapters, my own position is that interests of realism dictate that, of the three, parsimony is the most expendable, whereas both generalizability and precision seem absolutely essential to the advancement of sociology and the other social sciences. Although this position will be elaborated throughout the remainder of the book, let us briefly consider why the dilemma exists and also note some of its practical implications for theory building and theory testing.

Without detracting from the efforts and ingenuity of physical scientists in achieving a remarkable rate of progress in improving measurement accuracy beyond what could have been imagined even a half-century ago, it is obvious that these improvements in instrumentation have depended on extensive governmental support that cannot be expected for the social sciences. But more importantly from a fundamental point of view, these gains in precision have been dependent on *homogeneity* properties of physical substances that can safely be assumed to hold up over numerous replications and under a variety of conditions. Also, where there has been indirect measurement of postulated properties (such as mass or electrical charge), the physical laws relating these properties to the indicators on the measuring instruments have been highly precise and usually deterministic. Where they have been probabilistic, their accuracy has been assessable through replication. As will be discussed in Chapter 2, these rather simple laws, when combined with homogeneity properties, have made it both possible and fruitful to define a large number of important variables in terms of a very small number of fundamentally measured ones. It seems extremely unlikely that we will ever be in this very fortunate position in the social sciences.

Precision can often be attained within the social sciences at the expense of generalizability. One way to accomplish this is to construct very simple social settings, often in so-called laboratory experiments in which small numbers of individuals (usually student volunteers or paid subjects) are given rather simple tasks and asked to repeat them a sufficient number of times so that reasonably reliable numerical counts can be recorded. Another way of obtaining precision is to work with very large populations and to "count heads" with respect to manifestly observable or easily recordable properties or responses—such things as when they were born, where they live, whether or not they are employed, how many children they have had, how many rooms they occupy, whether they are single, married, or divorced, and so forth. Even for such simple variables there will, of course, be response and recording errors, as well as imperfections in the sampling design or refusals to cooperate. But the measurement operations involved will be relatively straightforward and subject to correction and improvement.

Our problems arise, however, whenever one then attempts to relate these rather simple operational procedures to more general abstract theoretical concepts such as aggression, cooperation, domination, status, alienation, marital stability, and so forth. Here we encounter the twin problems of *generalizability*, which usually refers to a property of one's theoretical arguments, and *comparability*, which refers to a property of the measuring instruments. If we want our theories to be generalizable across a variety of settings or with respect to a variety of phenomena (say, different forms of aggression), then we obviously need to conceptualize our variables in such a way that propositions that contain these variables can be applied across such settings and diverse phenomena. This then forces us to ask whether we can assess the comparability of measurement operations across such situations. In what sense can we say that a measure of "aggression" in a laboratory setting—for example, the number of times a subject pushes a green button—is comparable to "aggression" in a natural setting, say, the shooting of American Indians by white settlers?

One very fundamental problem encountered in coming to grips with this type of issue is the fact that whenever research operations must change from one setting to the next, we need to assess what this change in operations implies for our tests of the theory. In the physical sciences, the fundamental measurement of quantities such as length, time, and mass either remains constant from one setting to the next or, if not, the relationships among the different measurement operations are well understood and given theoretical underpinnings. As we shall discuss at some length in Chapter 3, this is hardly the case in the social sciences, so that the assessment of measurement comparability becomes both highly complex and, unfortunately, wide open to controversy and ambiguity.

The general point that needs to be stressed is that whenever measurement comparability is in doubt, so is the issue of the generalizability of the corresponding theory. Although one may *state* a theory in a sufficiently general form that it may be applied in diverse settings, *tests* of this theory will require an assessment of measurement comparability. If the theory succeeds in one setting but fails in another, and if measurement comparability is in doubt, one will be in the unfortunate position of not knowing whether the theory needs to be modified, whether the reason for the differences lies in the measurement-conceptualization process, or both.

As we shall note in a variety of ways in subsequent chapters, the parsimony question also enters the picture at several points. Given the fact that all of our empirical studies will necessarily involve missing data and less-than-ideal methods of data collection and measurement, simplifying assumptions will have to be made at numerous points. Yet, if these assumptions become too simple, they will also be unrealistic in view of the complex nature of social reality. Sometimes, too, there will be a tradeoff between the complexity of our substantive and auxiliary measurement theories such that if we make the one overly simplistic we may need to build complications into the other, especially if we wish to increase the level of generality of the theory.

Although this highly abstract assertion cannot have much meaning until we have examined a number of illustrative examples, there is one extremely important point that can be made at the outset. If genuine progress is to be made in linking together our theoretical constructs and research operations, we must learn to make our assumptions as explicit as possible, painful though this process may be. We must learn to avoid and be highly critical of measurement by fiat, exemplified by lengthy discussions of a theoretical idea accompanied by a simple assertion that we have decided to measure a given variable in a certain way because it is most convenient. Instead, we must become accustomed to the much more tedious process of trying to make as precise theoretical distinctions as we can, and examining carefully what each of these implies about measurement. We then must learn to state explicitly just what assumptions are required in going from the theoretical constructs to operational procedures, the conditions under which these assumptions are most likely to be realistic, and the modifications that may be needed to extend the measurement to other settings.

In short, we must become much more attentive to the need for stating explicit auxiliary measurement theories and for examining comparability of measurement, just as we must also be concerned about the generalizability of our substantive theories. If we wish to test these latter theories and somehow assess their generalizability, then these matters of the explicitness of our auxiliary theories and the comparability of our specific measures must be given equal attention. If either process lags too far behind the other, we shall find ourselves stymied.

NOTES

1. By random measurement errors, I mean that if X_i is replaced by an indicator $X_i' = X_i + u_i$, then not only is $E(u_i) = 0$ and $Cov(X_i u_i) = 0$, but the error component u_i is serially uncorrelated over all observations and also uncorrelated with all other variables in the equation system, including measurement errors in these other variables.

2. The term "multicollinearity" refers to situations involving extremely high correlations among independent variables. Although the correlations must be of the order of .8 or larger before sampling errors become substantial, the effects of multicollinearity in the presence of measurement errors is less well understood. See Gordon (1968) for an excellent discussion of this problem.

3. This argument is developed more completely in Blalock (1979a).

CHAPTER 2

FUNDAMENTAL MEASUREMENT, SCALING, AND DIMENSIONALITY ISSUES

A number of highly important issues have been raised in the very extensive body of literature dealing with scaling theory and the foundations of measurement. Although this literature is far too diverse and technical to be summarized in a simple fashion, there are several basic issues that are essential to our own subsequent discussion. One of these revolves around the problem of deciding on the level of measurement yielded by any given research instrument or scaling procedure. Another is concerned with strategy and the tradeoff between the desirability of obtaining redundant information needed to check on the properties of any given measurement procedure and the extent to which the social scientist is willing to impose simplifying assumptions on the measurement model in order to reduce the extent of the research effort. A third related issue concerns the assessment of dimensionality and the tradeoff between the goal of parsimony and that of achieving a satisfying degree of fit between one's measurement model and one's data.

All of the issues that will be discussed in this chapter relate to the problem of linking one's research operations with mathematical representations in such a fashion that the use of specific mathematical operations, such as addition or multiplication, can be legitimated in terms of some sort of correspondence between the real-world operations and their mathematical counterparts. Although questions relating to generalizability and the indirectness of measurement arise tangentially in these considerations, they do not occupy center stage. For the most part, therefore, we shall not be concerned in the present chapter with issues of conceptualization or the linkage between theoretical constructs or concepts, on the one hand, and research operations on the other. We shall see, however, that a concern for conceptualization often motivates or helps to rationalize many of the more technical discussions oriented toward providing a formal or axiomatic foundation for measurement decisions.

Many treatments and courses on scaling deal with procedural "nuts and bolts" questions, so much so that the philosophical and theoretical underpinnings are often neglected or at least not raised to a sufficient level of consciousness that a concern for theory has been evident. Yet, those who have been most active in developing these techniques—persons such as L. L. Thurstone, Paul Lazarsfeld, Louis Guttman, Clyde Coombs, Roger Shepard, Patrick Suppes, Duncan Luce, Amos Tversky, and David Krantz—have also been very much interested in the problem of linkage between theoretically defined constructs and operational procedures, though they may have defined the problem in different ways. Thus, Guttman (1944) conceived of the problem in sampling terms, that of selecting items from a universe of content. Thurstone (1947), in developing a rationale for rotating axes in factor analysis, focused on the criterion of parsimony in his emphasis on "simple structure." Lazarsfeld (1954) conceived the matter in terms of latent classes, within which response patterns are essentially random. And Coombs (1964), in developing the rationale for his "unfolding" technique, conceptualized response patterns in terms of an individual's ideal point along an underlying continuum.

The point that needs to be stressed at the outset is that theoretical conceptualizations that are ambiguous, vague, or multidimensional can often be sharpened and improved through a series of exploratory applications of these quantitative scaling approaches. The more carefully delineated one's set of theoretical concepts, the more explicit the underlying assumptions, and the more attentive the theorist is to important distinctions and clarifications, the easier it will be not only to agree upon operational procedures but also, equally important, the more readily others can agree on the adequacy of the additional assumptions that will be needed to relate these research operations to a mathematical measurement model. Although measurement can be rather simply defined as the process of attaching numbers to objects, it will become clear from the ensuing discussion that this process is by no means routine.

EXTENSIVE MEASUREMENT

Earlier accounts stemming from analyses of measurement in physics have raised a number of critical issues regarding the processes by which physical operations are associated with numbers so that the customary arithmetical operations can be legitimated. Indeed, we usually take these measurement operations so much for granted that it seldom occurs to us that there may be something rather unique about this process. Consider the length of a body or its mass. When we lay a ruler end-to-end to measure the length of a carpet, or when we place several standard weights on one side of a balance and a body with an unknown mass on the other, there is a kind of physical "adding" operation that justifies our assigning numerical scores to represent the carpet's length or the body's mass. Krantz et al. (1971, ch. 3) refer to this physical operation as "concatenation." They, and others before them (e.g., Campbell, 1928; and Cohen and Nagel, 1934), point out that unless there is some such physical counterpart to "addition," as a mathematical operation, then there is no guarantee that the mathematical operation of addition (or multiplication) will yield interpretable conclusions about the real world to which the assigned numbers are supposed to correspond. Let us look more closely at what is involved, considering the measurement of length as perhaps the simplest of physical measurement operations.

One can compare the *relative* lengths of two bodies by laying them side by side, aligning one of their endpoints, and then noting which body extends beyond the other. Calling the bodies a and b, we may then determine which of three possibilities holds: a may extend beyond b (written a ⊱ b); b may extend beyond a (written b ⊱ a); or we may not be able to decide which extends beyond the other (written a $\sim$ b). These physical comparisons permit us to say that one body is longer than the other or that they are approximately equal in length, and thus this method of comparison permits us to substitute the mathematical operation "$>$" for the physical comparison "⊱," and the mathematical notion of "=" for the symbol "$\sim$."

Furthermore, one may observe in the case of three bodies a, b, and c, that if a extends beyond b (a ⊱ b), and if b extends beyond c (b ⊱ c), then it will empirically be true that a also extends beyond c (a ⊱ c). Thus, transitivity holds in terms of these measurement operations, just as it holds in the case of the assigned numbers. There is therefore a homomorphism between transitivity in terms of the research operations and transitivity in terms of the assigned numbers. In effect, we may assign an arbitrary value to the length of c, say 15. As long as we select a number greater than this, say 18, for b, we are not constrained as to what that value must be. Similarly, as long as we select a number greater than 18 to be associated with a, we may again be arbitrary. Any triplet of numbers satisfying this transitivity property will suffice, nor will any given triplet be superior to any other, except in the sense perhaps of being a simpler set of numbers with which to operate.

This kind of measurement process yields what we refer to as an ordinal scale and, strictly speaking, only a very restrictive set of mathematical operations can be applied to such ordinal scales, at least if we hold to our objective of making the operations and symbols of the mathematician correspond to some real-world counterpart. Put another way, we may arbitrarily transform one set of numerical scores into another, provided only that we preserve the numerical order among them. Given this extreme flexibility in making transformations, we cannot expect very "powerful" mathematical conclusions to result. In other words, the mathematics cannot be expected to carry us anywhere near as far as would be the case if greater restrictions had been imposed.

Now consider the possibility of concatenation. Suppose we begin with a body of length a and are able to find a copy in the form of a body of length $a' \sim a$ such that when we lay the bodies side by side, both their endpoints appear to line up almost exactly. We then "concatenate" by laying these bodies *end to end* and compare their total length with a body of length b. Referring to the concatenation of these first two bodies as (a ∘ a'), we must have either b ⊢ (a ∘ a'), (a ∘ a') ⊢ b, or b ∼ (a ∘ a'). If the last of these holds, then we assert that b has twice the length of a. To justify this claim mathematically, we need to equate the physical notion of concatenation (here, laying the bodies end-to-end) with that of the mathematical operation of addition. The physical combination (a ∘ a') becomes represented by the mathematical expression a + a = 2a. Likewise, if we can locate a third copy of a, namely a'', and if (a ∘ a' ∘ a'') ∼ c, we may represent the length of c as a + a + a = 3a.

Operations that have this "additive" property are referred to as involving "extensive" measurement, in contrast with "intensive" measurement that does not involve any such concatenation operation. One example of an intensive measurement process is that by which the relative densities of several liquids might be obtained by finding out which liquids float on the surfaces of others. Thus, if water floats on mercury, and gasoline floats on water, then the densities of the three liquids have a transitive property, in that if gasoline floats on water, and if water floats on mercury, then gasoline will float on mercury. But we cannot "add" the densities of gasoline and water in any meaningful sense. Similarly, we do not add the temperatures of two bodies in the sense that two pans of tepid water produce a pan of boiling water. We may, however, concatenate two weights by placing them on the same side of a balance to see whether or not they balance an unknown weight on the other side.

A closer look at what is going on here suggests that the distinction between extensive and intensive measurement is not that simple. Densities are not in fact "measured" in the way we have suggested. Instead, we first obtain extensive measures of "mass" and "length" and then *define* density to be mass per unit of volume, or mass divided by length cubed. Thus "density" becomes a *derived* concept that is completely defined in terms of two other concepts that have been extensively measured. Density thus defined possesses all of the desirable properties of a ratio scale, and indeed, the limiting value of "zero density" makes sense conceptually in that we can actually locate materials that have extremely small densities, and we can approximate the condition of a perfect vacuum in which the density of gaseous materials would be very close to zero.

Krantz et al. (1971, ch. 10) point out that although it may appear as though derived concepts such as density can be defined almost arbitrarily, only a few such concepts will turn out to be scientifically useful. Furthermore, the derived concepts that make sense seem to depend upon *homogeneity properties* or empirical constants that play very important roles in the measurement process. Thus, for any chemically pure substance, density is a constant, which of course means that *for that substance* one cannot vary the mass and volume independently. If one doubles the volume, the mass must also be doubled. The utility of the concept "density," as contrasted, say, with a concept defined as mass squared divided by surface area, depends on this homogeneity property. Similarly, each metal is characterized by a (roughly) constant coefficient of expansion such that a unit increment of heat energy applied to the metal will result in a constant expansion of its length (over some limited interval). We use this fact, of course, to obtain indirect measures of temperature by looking at the length of a mercury column or noting the pointer reading of a thermostat.

Cohen and Nagel (1934), among others, noted that the remarkable progress achieved in the measurement of physical phenomena has involved the process of substituting a large number of such derived measures for possible "intensive" measurement operations that would yield ordinal properties at best. In fact, it has been pointed out (see Krantz et al., 1971, ch. 10) that over a hundred basic variables in physics can all be defined in terms of six "fundamental" measures, or variables whose measurement operations involve independent procedures based on one or another form of a concatenating or physical adding operation. These fundamentally measured quantities in physics are: length, mass, time, temperature, charge, and angle. Furthermore, the important derived measures take the form of some *multiplicative* function of the fundamentally measured quantities, with small positive or negative integer exponents. For instance, density = mass/length^3; velocity = distance/time; acceleration = velocity/time = distance/time^2; and force = mass $\times$ acceleration = mass $\times$ distance/time^2, and so forth. This is a truly remarkable property of nature; a number of very simple but basic laws of nature make it possible to define theoretically useful concepts in this fashion.

As suggested in the examples of the concept of density and also the ways that we (as laymen) measure temperature, homogeneity properties often play an important role in physical measurement. We may also illustrate in terms of the indirect measurement of mass, which is inferred on the basis of assumed forces operating on a balance or, say, a spring scale. In the presence of the earth's gravitational force, which is for all practical purposes a constant at sea level, we "measure" the mass of a body through a concatenation operation that depends upon this gravitational force. Thus, if we place a standard object a on one pan, placing a copy weight a′ on that same pan, we may refer to this as a concatenation operation (a ○ a′). If this then balances a weight b, we conclude that the measure of b's mass is 2a. However, this depends upon the simplifying assumption that the mutual attraction between the two weights a and a′ is negligible, so that placing them close together has absolutely no effect on the downward force that is being compared with that produced by b, acting at virtually the same distance from the earth's center. The "adding" of the two weights is thus justified because of an underlying theory to the effect that no forces are operative other than gravitational attraction between the earth and each separate weight (Coleman, 1964). For this reason, the concatenation operation is justified only under rather limited circumstances. Put another way, extensive measurement is made possible by a rare set of circumstances that we cannot expect to hold in the case of most types of social measurements. Similarly, Krantz et al. (1971, ch. 3) note that the extensive measurement of time usually involves some reliance on periodicity, as for example the movements of a pendulum or the circulation of the earth about the sun.

Coleman (1964) also notes another important characteristic of extensive measurement, namely that the consistency of the measurement assumptions may be directly tested in terms of the operations themselves. Thus, having compared a with a' and a'' and concluded that they are approximately identical in length, one may concatenate a and a' and locate a body b of (virtually) the same length as ($a \circ a'$), thereby concluding that b = 2a. If one then had a third copy of a, namely a''', this would suggest that one could concatenate b and a''' and that this concatenation would yield (virtually) the same length as ($a \circ a' \circ a''$), since mathematically we know that if b = 2a, then b + a = 3a. If this particular operation did not yield (virtually) equal lengths, we would necessarily conclude that, for some reason, our "addition" in the physical sense does not correspond to addition in the mathematical sense and that therefore our measurement theory contains at least one faulty assumption. Thus we have a way of testing the measurement theory that involves only the measurement operations themselves, without having to introduce any additional variables as criteria for validation. This is an extremely important point.

Extensive measurement yields what we commonly call ratio scales, which involve an arbitrary unit of measurement (say, the length of body a) but which have a well-defined or nonarbitrary zero point. With ratio scales we are permitted a scale transformation of the form $X' = dX$, with $d > 0$, but not a so-called "affine transformation" of the form $X' = c + dX$, which modifies the zero point.

Unfortunately, the ideal of extensive measurement is difficult to achieve except in a very few instances. What does this imply about fundamental measurement in the social sciences? Can legitimate ratio scales be achieved by operational procedures that do not involve concatenations and that cannot be validated in terms of consistency checks such as are possible with weights on a balance or bars placed end-to-end? Krantz et al. (1971) devote considerable attention to this question, claiming that what are referred to as "difference measurement" and "conjoint measurement" can yield results that approximate those produced by concatenation operations possible in physics. But their arguments are both technical and highly abstract and, to the writer, not entirely convincing. Unlike the psychologist attempting to infer internal states from behavioral response patterns, however, the sociologist is often able to make use of counting operations on which to base various measures of group properties. To these we now turn.

Does Counting Provide Extensive Measurement?

It has long been recognized that the counting operation merely requires that there be well-defined, discrete units of analysis that can be classified unambiguously. Thus, for each such unit, say, the individual person, it is sufficient to have "measurement" at the nominal level, meaning only that such individuals can be sorted into equivalence classes such that, for any two individuals, one can decide whether or not they are members of the same class. When we *aggregate* these individuals, however, we may obtain scores for the aggregate that involve a definite unit of measurement, namely the individuals being counted. Does this provide a legitimate ratio scale, and is not this type of operation just as appropriate as concatenation in justifying the use of mathematical operations requiring such a unit and a nonarbitrary zero point?

Certainly we may compare two aggregates, let us say two countries or cities, with respect to such things as population size, percentage of males over age 65, numbers of housing units, or average size of household. Clearly, also, there is no ambiguity in claiming that one city is twice the size of another or that one country has twice the rate of unemployment as another, provided only that there is agreement upon the operations yielding the classifications of employed versus unemployed workers. This is true since, in effect, all individuals are treated as equivalent and therefore interchangeable. We can even imagine these individuals as being *transferred* from the one category to the other, as for example through a migratory movement between cities. Thus we may add 50,000 persons to one population and subtract 30,000 from a second and 20,000 from a third through the operation of getting individuals to migrate from the second and third populations to the first. Similarly, one may count and redistribute dollars, automobiles, houses, weapons, or form derived measures by taking ratios of such quantities. As a result, one may speak meaningfully of per capita income as a ratio scale, just as one can compute unemployment rates or the average number of household residents per room.

When one counts behavioral acts, there is often greater hesitation in assuming that such acts are interchangeable or that they can be physically "added" in any way that remotely resembles a concatenation operation. Here one encounters the difficult problem of determining the boundaries of a "unit act." Where behaviors shade imperceptibly into one another, or whenever they may be classified in more than one way, we encounter a "boundary problem" that does not arise whenever persons or distinct objects are being enumerated. More importantly, perhaps, we recognize that most such behaviors probably should receive differential weights depending upon their seriousness, intensity, duration, location within a sequence, or meanings to the actors concerned.

Lurking behind our discomfort with such counting procedures as justifying ratio-scale measures is one very important problem. It is often difficult to specify precisely the assumed relationship between theoretical construct and operational measure. Sometimes this is left entirely implicit. For example, one encounters discussions of "metropolitan dominance" which gets measured in terms of combinations of size and proximity variables, with the notion of "dominance" remaining undefined. But if such dominance has the connotation of "control" or "power over," it then requires a major intellectual leap to a measure that relies on sizes or spatial distances between cities. Similarly, if GNP per capita is intended to measure "prosperity," "industrialization," or some other construct, the assumptions necessary to link GNP per capita, as an operational definition, to "industrialization," as a theoretical construct, need to be made explicit. Or if suicide rates are taken as an indicator of "anomie," defined as a state of "normlessness" or breakdown of "social control," one is left with an uncomfortable feeling that ratio-level measurement has been obtained at the expense of directness of measurement.

Coleman (1964) has made the point that measurement by enumeration does not permit a direct validation of the measurement procedure in the same way that is possible when we may concatenate a number of different weight combinations so as to provide crosschecks on the operational procedures. I am not entirely convinced by this argument, as it is just as possible to move persons or objects about and count them in various ways as crosschecks. The problem seems to be elsewhere. Very often we resort to counting operations out of desperation, when we can find no other more direct way to measure the phenomenon in question. Instead of looking directly at norms and trying to assess departures from "normlessness," we posit a rather long string of consequences in terms of behavioral acts that may be counted. Or if we are interested in "economic insecurity," we look to one of its presumed causes, unemployment rates. Since we cannot measure "metropolitan dominance" we look at population sizes and spatial distances. Or we attempt to infer an individual's state of mind by the number of times he or she behaves in a certain way.

In all of these instances, it does not appear to be the counting operation per se that is creating the difficulty. Put another way, if the theoretical concepts were defined differently so as to be closer to the operational level, as for example in terms of relating sizes of cities rather than dominance, this issue of level of measurement and the inadequacies of counting operations would not loom so important. This suggests that our primary concern should be focused on the slippage between concept and operationalization, although it may be tempting to displace this concern onto the question of the proper level of measurement that can be presumed.

This lack of clarity concerning the basic theoretical concepts of interest may be one of the reasons for the dispute concerning the use of "ratio variables" in sociological research.[1] There are a number of strictly statistical issues relating to how ratios of two variables behave in relation to their two components. For instance, if one relates the size of a group to the proportion of its members playing a particular role, then the size variable will appear both as a numerator (divided by unity) of the first variable and a denominator of the second, thus leading one to expect a negative association between the two variables. Long (1980) has shown, however, that in spite of the common-sense appeal of such an argument, the actual direction of association will depend upon both exponents and intercepts in a rather complex fashion, and that there is no more reason to expect a negative association than a positive one.

Long makes the important point, however, that ratio variables may be very sensitive to measurement errors, so that although there is no necessary connection between the sign of an empirical relationship between two ratio variables and the positioning of their components (whether in the numerator or denominator), even slight underenumerations of, say, a population size may be sufficient to reverse the empirically determined signs of these relationships. Her results, for example, call into question the conclusions reached in a number of studies of crime deterrence. Some such studies have found that high crime rates are associated with low ratios of convictions to offenses, a set of results consistent with the argument that punishment deters crime. But in this instance, number of crimes appears as the numerator of one variable (crimes divided by population base) and as the denominator of the other variable (convictions divided by number of crimes). If, say, the number of crimes is underreported—as we know is the case—this biased measurement alone may be sufficient to produce a substantial negative relationship between the measured ratio variables, thereby possibly leading to erroneous conclusions.

Statistical and measurement-error issues are important, but they should not be confused with the question of how one goes about linking ratio variables, such as these, with the theoretical constructs they are intended to measure. If the theoretical concept is not clearly defined, we may expect continuing confusing debates concerning the legitimacy of ratio variables. It appears that many ratio variables are constructed at the macro level as substitutes for subjective (or objective) probabilities at the individual level. The deterrence theory approach to crime, for instance, is apparently based on the assumption that individuals have subjective probabilities of being caught and punished, and that these are in part based upon objective ratios of one kind or another—perhaps the proportion of crimes that are actually reported, or the proportion that result in a conviction. The ratio of convictions to actual (or reported) crimes may then be taken as a cause indicator of these subjective probabilities, with little thought being given to the other factors that may contribute to a distortion of such subjective probabilities.

Similarly, age-, sex-, or race-specific death or disease rates may be taken as measures of objective probabilities of risk for individuals assumed to be homogeneous with respect to these risks. Other ratio variables may be taken as indicators of efficiency, as for example the ratio of supervisors to production personnel. In all such instances, although the zero point of the operationally defined variables may be clear-cut, it does not follow that this will coincide with the zero point of the corresponding conceptual variable (e.g., zero subjective probability or zero efficiency).

The general point illustrated by these examples is that in addition to questions relating to the properties of one's research operations, and in particular whether concatenation or counting operations can be employed to justify the use of addition and multiplication as mathematical operations, there will often be the more problematic issue of whether or not the conceptual variables can be defined in such a way that zero points and measurement units "make sense." If not, then there will almost certainly be disputes concerning the legitimacy of statistical or mathematical analyses that presuppose that they do. We suspect that the concern one gives these matters will depend on where one falls along the continuum of "theorist" versus "empiricist." Those who adhere closely to operationalist stances will tend to dismiss these questions as strictly technical ones, whereas those who are more theoretically inclined will continue to feel uncomfortable about them. Unless this discomfort is translated into substantial efforts to clarify our theoretical concepts, however, there may be no greater meeting of minds than we seem to have at present.

DIMENSIONALITY, INFORMATION, AND ERROR

Those social scientists who have contributed most to the scaling literature have been very much concerned with this linkage question, and therefore it is desirable to pay attention to some of the important ideas that have come from this extensive body of literature. We shall not, however, go into the details of any of the specific techniques that have evolved over the past forty years or so. The issues with which we shall be concerned in this brief section are as follows: (1) the desirability of using data collection techniques that yield redundant information capable of testing for departures from scale properties and assumptions; (2) a concern for parsimony, in the sense of using a minimal number of dimensions to account for associations among measured indicators; (3) the need to state assumptions explicitly and to provide a mathematical model representing these assumptions; and (4) the desirability of paying careful attention to the criteria necessary to establish unidimensionality and metric properties.

One very important issue that has been raised in the scaling literature involves the desirability of obtaining redundant data that permit one to assess the degree to which any given scaling device fails to work. The reader is undoubtedly familiar with the basic ideas of Guttman scaling and the fact that Guttman defined unidimensionality in a very strict sense, such that the perfect scale has a cumulative property through which each individual's response pattern can be reproduced exactly if one knows that person's total score. That is, the items have the property that if we know that a respondent has endorsed a particular item, we will also know that all less extreme items will also have been endorsed. Put another way, if we know that someone has endorsed five items, we know that this person will have endorsed exactly the same items as someone who has endorsed four items, plus one more. There is thus no one who can be said to be higher than someone else in some respects but not in others. Clearly, this very restrictive definition of a perfect scale permits many nonscale responses or "errors." In other words, the instrument does not guarantee that a scale will be found. In fact, if there are more than five or six items, or more than two response categories per item, it will be difficult to find items that produce a nearly perfect unidimensional scale.

Coombs (1953) points out that it is highly desirable to use data collection techniques that yield a considerable amount of redundant information capable of enabling one to assess the reasonableness of one's assumptions. One should not "force" an ordinal scale on the data, as would be the case, for example, if judges were asked simply to rank five or six alternatives. Errors should be permitted, although Coombs points out that the social scientist faces a basic dilemma in deciding what to call "error." Put differently, he asks: "Do we know what we want, or do we want to know?" If we are willing to *assume* unidimensionality in the Guttman sense, then departures from the perfect scale pattern constitute "errors." But would we want to confront one of our respondents who has answered, say, a set of questions tapping social distance (which usually "scales") and tell that respondent that he or she has made an "error" in being willing to admit a member of a given minority to one's neighborhood, while not being willing to admit that person into one's occupation? Or should we admit the possibility that, for this person at least, the items do not order themselves in the expected fashion?

Consider the properties of three data collection methods: (1) getting judges to rank-order seven items; (2) asking them to examine all possible pairs, ordering the two items in each pair; or (3) giving them all the triads and having them rank items within each triad. The first procedure automatically yields a transitive ordering unless, of course, the judges refuse to cooperate. The second permits intransitivities to occur, since one may rank A higher than B, B higher than C, but C higher than A. Thus the second method of pair-comparisons provides a test for transitivity, although at the expense of extra work. Finally, the method of triads permits not only intransitivity but also inconsistency. For example, the pair (A,B) will appear in separate triads with C,D,E,F, and G and may not always be ordered in the same way in each triad comparison. This is completely aside from the question of transitivity among A,B, and C.

The method of triads permits the investigator to test for a greater number of departures from the ideal of transitivity, although at the cost of even greater inconvenience to the respondent. If the investigator is willing to assume consistency but not transitivity, then the method of pair comparisons is to be preferred to the method of triads, and if *both* transitivity and consistency can be assumed, then respondents can be given the simpler task of providing an outright ranking, thus forcing them to produce an ordinal scale. It is Coombs's clear preference to use techniques that permit the data to speak for themselves. That is, they should permit errors or deviations to occur, rather than our assuming them away.

A somewhat more complex argument illustrates the same point in connection with "parallelogram analysis" (see Coombs, 1964, ch. 4). Suppose a respondent is given seven items and then asked to pick the k of these that come closest to his or her own position. Suppose also that the items fall along a single dimension according to the ordering: A < B < C < D < E < F < G. Suppose we also assume that all individuals react to this same underlying dimension, but that each has a differing "ideal position" along this scale. Consider an individual whose ideal point is somewhere between the positions of items B and C on the dimension, but closer to B than to C. If this individual is asked to pick one item, he or she is assumed to select item B. But suppose the instructions are to pick two items? Will the items B and C be selected? Not necessarily, since possibly item A may be very close to B and actually closer to the respondent's ideal position than is item C, which may be far removed from B. But we may assume that this respondent will select either the (A,B) or the (B,C) pairs, rather than, say, the (A,D) or (B,D) pairs. In other words, only a small proportion of the total number of possible pair combinations will be selected, and if there are too many "deviant" pairs, the unidimensionality assumption will be called into question. Similarly, individuals asked to select three of seven items can be expected to choose only from among consecutive triplets. All other response patterns for the "pick two" and "pick three" situations can be represented in parallelogram form as follows:

Response Type	Pick 2 of 7: A	B	C	D	E	F	G
1	X	X					
2		X	X				
3			X	X			
4				X	X		
5					X	X	
6						X	X

Response Type	Pick 3 of 7: A	B	C	D	E	F	G
1	X	X	X				
2		X	X	X			
3			X	X	X		
4				X	X	X	
5					X	X	X

Coombs (1964) notes certain properties of these procedures that depend on the values of k and n, where n refers to the number of (ordered) items and k the number of items that are to be selected. First, if k = 1, it will be impossible to infer an ordering among the items, except by doing so in a priori fashion. But for k > 1, we will be in a position to infer the ordering among items on the basis of the response pattern. Second, the number of categories into which respondents can be separated will equal n – k + 1 and therefore will decrease as k increases. In our "pick 2 out of 7" case, we can see that there will be six "possible" ideal response patterns, whereas if respondents are asked to pick 3 out of 7, there will be only five such patterns.

Third, as k → n/2, the procedure becomes increasingly vulnerable to "errors," in that a coefficient of reproducibility will have a lower expected value under the null hypothesis of random patterns. Procedures that are highly vulnerable, in this sense, are desirable as *scaling criteria* in that, if these criteria are actually satisfied, one has considerable faith that the items in fact fall along a single continuum. But as scaling *methods* they may be less satisfactory, precisely because they are so stringent or intolerant of error patterns.

Finally, as k increases and becomes greater than (n + 1)/2, we encounter situations in which we are unable to distinguish the ordering among the middle items. For instance, if k = 5 and n = 7, there are only three "ideal" response patterns, assuming the specified ordering. A respondent may omit either of the extreme pairs (A, B) or (F, G), or if he or she falls close to the center, the extreme opposites A and G may be omitted. But items C, D, and E will always be selected among the five, making it impossible to tell the ordering among them.

These examples illustrate the essential point that different sets of instructions yield very different kinds of information, a point that is perhaps obvious. What is less obvious, however, is that these procedures also differ with respect to vulnerability to "error," and that therefore the redundant information they provide can enable the researcher to make adequate tests for dimensionality. Comparison of the "pick 2 of 7" with the "pick 3 of 7" instructions also illustrates tradeoffs that often exist, in this instance, between the desirability of obtaining finer distinctions (more categories) versus that of obtaining more redundant information useful for testing. One's choice in this connection in part involves an implicit answer to Coombs's question: "Do we know what we want, or do we want to know?" If we are willing to *assume* unidimensionality, then we may dispense with redundant information and thereby gain more knowledge (in this case about finer gradations along the continuum).

Had the respondents been given a more complex task and then asked to *rank* all of the items, we would be able to use Coombs's (1964) unfolding technique. This approach permits one to assess the relative sizes of the distances between items, thereby providing a close approximation to an ordered-metric scale in which distances can be ranked. We shall not elaborate on this procedure here, as it suffices to say that data collected in this manner permit one to order the midpoints between items in such a fashion that most of the segments between items can be ordered. For instance if A, B, C, and D are spaced as follows:

A   B   C   D

the fact that the midpoint between A and D falls to the left of the BC midpoint implies that the distance between A and B must be greater than that between C and D. With a larger number of items, similar statements can be made about a sufficient number of the distances so that a (nearly) ordered-metric scale can be achieved. The procedure is highly vulnerable to "error," however, since once more there will be many opportunities for respondents to deviate from the response patterns expected under the unidimensionality assumption. Thus, it turns out that the unfolding technique has been much more useful as a scaling criterion—or as an ideal model for assessing unidimensionality—than as a practical scaling device.

Turning finally to situations in which multidimensionality is anticipated, we find that all of the important methodological techniques useful in assessing dimensionality invoke the objective of arriving at as parsimonious a set of assumptions as is reasonably consistent with one's data. In using these procedures, one is always concerned with the tradeoff between simplicity, on the one hand, and goodness of fit on the other. In the case of latent structure analysis, the attempt is made to find the smallest number of latent classes capable of "explaining" a response pattern in the sense that all *within-class* correlations among items will be approximately zero (Lazarsfeld and Henry, 1968). In factor analysis, one extracts factors until the residual correlations among items are approximately zero, which is then interpreted to mean that the remaining causes of the responses are idiosyncratic to each item. And in nonmetric multidimensional scaling, or smallest-space analysis, the attempt is made to locate the smallest number of dimensions needed to represent proximities or similarities among items (Shepard et al., 1972).

The problem of assessing "error" is complicated in the case of multidimensional analyses because of the well-known fact that if sufficient complexity is permitted, it becomes possible to "account for" any given set of empirical results. Therefore, the reasonableness of any given result must be judged in terms of parsimony and interpretability, concepts that are wide open to judgmental disagreements. For instance, in latent structure analysis, it is known that if the number of items and allowable responses is fixed, it becomes possible to account for any response pattern, provided that a sufficient number of latent classes is postulated. Similarly, if the number of factors in a factor analysis begins to approach the number of measured indices, then all of the intercorrelations among these items can be "explained," in the statistical sense of that term.

A similar phenomenon occurs in the case of smallest-space analysis, in which the aim is to represent similarities s_{ij} between all pairs of objects (e.g., occupations or nations engaged in trade relationships) in terms of distances d_{ij} between them such that there is a close fit between the distances d_{ij} and the similarities s_{ij}. The criterion here is that the distances ought to be representable in a k-dimensional space in such a fashion that the more similar any two objects are to each other, the closer their distance ought to be. In only one or two dimensions can this not be done perfectly, so that there will always be a departure from the ideal, or a "strain" function that needs to be minimized. But as the number of dimensions is allowed to increase, this strain can be reduced close to zero.

"Failure" in each of these instances occurs whenever a reasonably simple structure cannot be achieved. Thus, if one must use eight factors to account for the intercorrelations among twelve measured variables, or if it requires four or five dimensions to represent the similarities among nine or ten occupations, the investigator will be inclined to admit failure to achieve a parsimonious solution. But there may also be a failure of another variety, namely an inability to *interpret* the underlying dimensions or latent classes in such a manner that others will accept this interpretation as plausible. As an aid to the interpretive process, additional assumptions may need to be invoked. For instance, in deciding on a rotational scheme in factor analysis, one will need to invoke a judgment as to the suitability of a criterion such as that of "simple structure," namely the idea that each of the unmeasured factors should load or correlate with a distinct set of measured variables, but have nearly zero correlations with others.

As is well known, there is no single or unique set of factors yielded by a factor analysis solution, nor do any of the multidimensional scaling techniques (such as smallest-space analysis) provide a unique set of axes or a single interpretational scheme. As might be expected under these circumstances, therefore, interpretations of any single set of empirical results will be wide open to challenge. What is especially important in the present context is that it will be difficult to pin down a criterion of "error." This is in contrast with an approach such as Guttman scaling or Coombs's unfolding technique, that imposes criteria based on a unidimensionality assumption, or one such as confirmatory factor analysis, that requires an advance specification of at least some of the parameter values and that may then be evaluated in terms of a well-defined goodness-of-fit criterion.

Perhaps the crucial point to make about all of these scaling procedures, however, is that their technical properties are well understood. Tradeoffs and dilemmas have been specified, so that researchers can select among them knowing both their advantages and disadvantages. This is because their assumptions and mathematical properties have been carefully examined, perhaps the primary reason that we seem to have advanced much farther in our understanding of the linkage between operational procedures and mathematical representations than we have in pinning down the relationships between theoretical constructs and these same operations. Our lag, then, is in this more theoretical area relating to conceptualizations.

Perhaps because the scaling literature has been heavily influenced by psychologists, who seem much more willing than sociologists to make strong (and unrealistic) assumptions about the generalizability of their findings, issues relating to comparability do not appear to have been given such systematic attention. There is, in fact, a surprising lack of discussion of problems likely to be encountered whenever homogeneity assumptions cannot realistically be made. Whenever measurement must be highly indirect, or an auxiliary measurement theory reasonably complex, the kinds of issues raised in the present chapter will be compounded by those that will be discussed in the next one.

Obviously, if we are to keep our sanity, compromises of one kind or another will have to be made. But unless these issues are thoroughly aired and specified as clearly as possible, we run the risk that investigators will devote their primary attention to those deficiencies that are best understood, neglecting others that are potentially of even greater importance. Let us return, then, to questions relating to generalizability and comparability, keeping in mind the desirability of linking them with important issues that have been raised in the scaling literature.

NOTE

1. See especially Akers and Campbell (1970); Freeman and Kronenfeld (1973); Fuguitt and Lieberson (1974); Kasarda and Nolan (1979); Long (1980); MacMillan and Daft (1979); and Schuessler (1973, 1974).

Chapter 3

The Comparability Of Measures

Since, in a very fundamental sense, the process of measurement involves an effort to construct operations that make comparisons of diverse objects possible, the claim that two or more measures are "noncomparable" across several actors or situations is indeed a devastating one. Very often, however, such a claim is couched in vague terms, so that the precise ways in which noncomparability occurs are unspecified. For instance, one commonly hears the assertion that a given behavior or stimulus takes on different "meanings" in two cultures, or even that "meanings" are noncomparable across several actors in very similar settings. Since noncomparability of measurements is obviously of central concern in any scientific enterprise, it is essential that efforts be made to pin down the specific ways in which measures may be noncomparable, so that we may move beyond such vague assertions.

Let us briefly consider two possible intents behind the noncomparability claim that we shall not pursue further. The first is that noncomparability is being invoked, rather automatically, to bolster the argument that scientific generalizations are virtually impossible. In effect, the stance being taken is the extreme form of an ideographic thesis that asserts that no two objects or situations can be compared because each is unique. Pushed to the extreme, this position would seem to cut off all possibility of linguistic communication. For instance, the descriptive statement, "In 1365 King Egelbert ruthlessly suppressed the peasant uprising" contains the words "king," "peasant," and "suppressed," all of which are assumed to have meanings to one's readers. This obviously presupposes a degree of comparability across persons who are called "kings," as well as those classed as "peasants." Clearly, the noncomparability argument can never be taken completely seriously if used as a blanket condemnation of efforts to generalize. The burden needs to be placed on those who would make this assertion to specify, rather clearly, the nature of the ways in which noncomparability is being claimed.

A second meaning to the term, however, is very likely to be confused with the one that we shall examine in some detail. Our own concern will be with noncomparability of *measures*, whereas it is often correctly asserted that two or more situations are noncomparable because of *uncontrolled variables.* Thus it may be claimed that a generalization based on small-group experiments cannot be carried over to a larger group because of the noncomparability of the settings or differences in group size. A generalization stated about American race relations may not hold for South Africa because the two situations are "noncomparable." Here, too, there is a tendency among some authors to utilize such blanket assertions, vaguely stated, to argue against the possibility of scientific generalizations. Each situation studied is in some crucial ways unique, thereby making comparisons difficult. But the emphasis here is not on the noncomparability of *measurement,* but rather on a number of uncontrolled variables. Once more, our position would be that the burden rests on the person making such an assertion to identify and try to measure the specific variables that take on different values in the supposedly noncomparable settings. Otherwise, the claim is inherently untestable. In a sense it is an obvious one, since no two objects are ever identical on all possible variables that might be identified. But it is useful only insofar as it leads to additional insights as to what these variables might be.

This "noncomparability of situations" argument, while not specifically focusing on measurement noncomparability, is not so readily distinguished from the measurement noncomparability thesis as one might think. This is because of the indirectness of most measurement, which requires auxiliary theories concerning the operation of other variables besides those being measured. Sometimes these auxiliary theories will become highly complex and may need to contain a number of variables that differ in values across settings. In particular, one's auxiliary theory may be very simple in one kind of setting but much more complex in another, so much so that the measurement operations may have to shift rather drastically between the two settings. If so, the "noncomparability of settings" argument may merge with that of the "noncomparability of measurement." Thus it would be a mistake to see the two issues as totally distinct, although without an explicit theoretical formulation it is often difficult to tell exactly what is being claimed.

The kind of noncomparability issue with which we shall be concerned in the remainder of this chapter can be conceptualized as one in which measurement is indirect and where the auxiliary measurement theories needed to connect theoretical constructs to their indicators may differ from one setting or individual to the next. In such instances, which are quite numerous, if it is possible to make these auxiliary theories explicit, it may then become possible to obtain greater comparability by controlling for certain of these variables or by performing a mathematical transformation of some kind. By way of a very simple illustration, if we know that two groups differ in size, and if this is the only variable that affects comparability, we may construct measures so as to standardize for size by working in terms of percentages or relative frequencies. Seldom, of course, will our problems be this straightforward.

Given that measurement requires an auxiliary theory linking constructs to indicators, whenever two settings differ with respect to the levels of any of these variables, we may anticipate problems of comparability that ideally require careful theoretical formulation to resolve. Consider the problem of inferring the mass of a body on the surface of the earth and comparing this mass with that of a body on the surface of the moon. If one uses a spring scale yielding a pointer reading that depends both on the "true mass" of the body and on the gravitational force near the earth's (or moon's) surface, then our readings in the two locations will be "noncomparable." The same body weighed in the two locations will lead one to infer different masses, using exactly the same operations, *unless* a correction is made for the different gravitational constants g near the surfaces of the two bodies. The auxiliary theories linking true mass to pointer reading are different in the two locations, or (if one prefers) a generalized version of the auxiliary theory would contain a variable g that is not necessarily a constant. If one knows the value of g, as well as the formula linking mass to gravitational attraction, one may then make a mathematical transformation to produce comparability in the two settings, and the puzzle is solved.

The implication is that, basically, there is no effective way to handle the comparability issue without an explicit auxiliary measurement theory that can be used to pin down the precise nature of potential noncomparability of measures across settings, time periods, or individuals. Obviously such auxiliary theories cannot be as precise as those used for indirect measurement in physics, but to the degree that such theories are incorrect or incomplete, the comparability issue will always lurk in the background. Since such auxiliary measurement theories are also likely to contain some variables that are of theoretical interest in their own right (in one's substantive theory), it is often the case that theoretical and measurement problems are confounded. For instance, respondents' SES or other background factors may affect their responses so as to produce measurement-error biases, but these same variables may also be causes or effects of the variables one is attempting to measure. The more complex the measurement theory, or the more indirect the measurement, the more likely this intertwining of substantive and measurement-error theories.

Whenever measurement operations depend in some essential way on the *simplicity* of the setting, this confounding of auxiliary and substantive theories is especially problematic (Wilken and Blalock, 1981). In physics, the fundamental measurement of nonderived concepts such as time, distance, mass, temperature, and electrical charge either does not vary from one setting to the next, or—as in the case of the earth-moon example—mathematical transformations are made to correct for noncomparability. But where such transformations cannot be made because of an inadequate theory, or where *incorrect* transformations are made, it will be impossible to tell whether differences found are due to measurement artifacts, true substantive differences, or both. In short, we are in trouble whenever the auxiliary measurement theory is poorly or incorrectly specified. The more complex this theory must be, and the more diverse the settings, the greater the likelihood of our confounding the two types of theories.

In view of all this, it is no wonder that the extreme operationalist position is appealing to many social scientists, or that investigators are content to stop short of theoretical formulations by simply reporting factual information and leaving it to others to wrestle with problems of noncomparability. As a result, they may simply report voting turnout percentages in different countries without concerning themselves with the "meaning" of voting behavior as a political act. Or they may report income distributions, adjusting for currency differences, without concerning themselves with other factors that affect living costs or important differences in the service structures of the several countries or regions. Similarly, they may record answers to identically worded questions or items that have been carefully translated from one language to another without concerning themselves about such matters as the salience or centrality of the issues, differential response biases, or other factors that affect comparability. In effect, the comparability issue may be sidestepped either by claiming that it is irrelevant whenever operations are virtually identical or by lowering the level of abstraction, making no pretense that the operations are intended to tap a more general construct.

Przeworski and Teune (1970: 119-121) make the important distinction between what they call "common" indicators, that are operationally very similar from one setting to the next, and "identical" indicators, that stand in exactly the same relationship to the true values from setting to setting. They suggest that common indicators may indeed also be identical, and that one would ordinarily expect common indicators to stand a better chance of being identical than noncommon indicators. Thus, if one asks a set of six questions in setting A, and then in setting B uses two questions that are exactly the same as those used in setting A, along with four others, it seems reasonable to assume that the two common indicators are more likely to be identical than the remaining four that are not common between the settings. But this all depends on the nature of linkages between the indicators and the variables they are intended to measure. It is a good common-sense observation, perhaps, but without an explicit theory it can remain no more than this. Przeworski and Teune are careful to point out that a research obsession with obtaining common indicators, as for example by extremely careful attention to the wording of interview or questionnaire items, in no sense guarantees that these items will also be identical ones. We might add that it also may give the investigator a false sense of security in the belief that the use of nearly identical items enables one to sidestep the comparability issue.

Much depends here, of course, on the level of abstraction or degree of generality involved. For instance, if the same question wording is used in surveys conducted periodically over several decades, this may provide valuable information as to trends in responses to that particular item, but possibly misleading information as to trends in some underlying variable it is intended to tap. Suppose, for instance, that white respondents are asked the question: "How strongly do you believe that the presence of blacks in your neighborhood will lower property values?" If trends are noted in responses over several decades, one may conclude that this particular belief about the relationship between minority presence and property values is being modified. It does not necessarily follow that anti-black prejudice is also being reduced, however, if there are simultaneous changes in the degree to which this particular belief is fashionable or "respectable" as a rationale for expressing anti-minority sentiments. In short, if the *relationship* between the item and construct is also changing in an unknown way, we shall not be able to separate this fact from any real changes that are occurring in the underlying attitude.

One major source of confusion in assessing comparability is the fact that, for some purposes, variables may be important in their own right, whereas, for others, they may merely serve as indicators of other variables. Some behaviors, for example, are of considerable significance theoretically and practically, whereas others are used primarily to help one infer postulated internal states. Contrast voting behavior or job performance, on the one hand, with a student's or an applicant's performance on a single test designed to measure extent of knowledge or "potential." Depending on the level of abstraction or generality required by one's theory, one may wish to consider a given behavior as merely an "instance" of a more general behavior type, or as a "direct" measure of the behavior of interest. For instance, one investigator may be interested in "political participation," one indicator of which is voting behavior, whereas a second may be interested in comparing the actual voting behaviors across several settings, without reference to other forms of political participation.

Therefore, in assessing comparability, one must always ask, "comparable with respect to what?" If the variable in question is being used as an effect indicator, say of some ability, value, or attitude, then one must ask whether or not the causal theories connecting the indicator to the construct or "true value" are the same across the settings or time periods being compared. Or perhaps the indicator variable is a cause of the unmeasured variable of interest, as for example when an experimenter introduces certain manipulations and infers that these manipulations have affected the variable of interest, say, the anxiety or motivational levels of subjects in experimental and control groups. Perhaps these same manipulations in a different cultural setting will have different consequences for these motivational states, implying noncomparability with respect to the consequences of the measured indicators.

In order to assess comparability, then, we need to construct causal models for each setting and then ask whether or not we expect these models to be identical, except possibly for parameter values that appear in the structural equations used to represent the respective models. If the models are expected to differ across settings, perhaps a more general formulation can be developed so that each setting can be represented as a special case. For instance, in setting A the first and second indicators may be affected by a common disturbing influence that does not arise in settings B and C. But perhaps in C one indicator of variable X may be linked to an indicator of Y, whereas this is not the case in settings A and B. If so, we might construct a more general model appropriate to all three settings, expecting, however, that certain of the coefficients will take on approximately zero values in one setting but nonzero values in another.

If the causal models connecting measured and unmeasured variables then turn out to be sufficiently complex, it may be unwise to refer to some of the measured variables as "indicators" of unmeasured ones, since the same measured variable may be an indicator of several unmeasured ones, and some of the indicator variables may even be directly linked to each other. Instead, it may be preferable to distinguish between measured and unmeasured variables by some visual device, such as using squares to represent the measured variables and circles for the unmeasured variables, as illustrated in Figure 3.1. One can then determine whether or not the system is identified, so that each of the coefficients can be estimated. If not, it will be necessary either to simplify the model by omitting arrows—thus

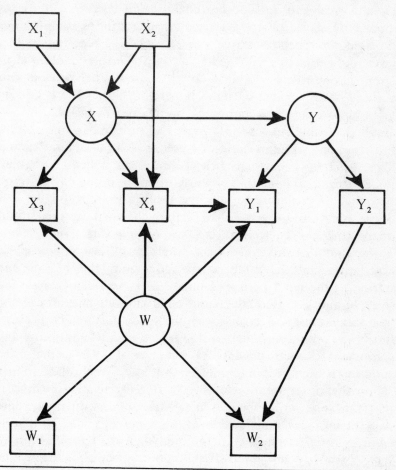

Figure 3.1

making the measurement theory somewhat less realistic—or to collect additional information so that the ratio of measured to unmeasured variables is increased. To the extent that these decisions can be made *before* the data have been collected, one may at least have a choice between these two alternative strategies. Once the data have been collected, however, the second alternative will be foreclosed.

Before concluding this introductory section and turning to a more formal and detailed consideration of specific differences among auxiliary theories, let us consider briefly some of the possible interpretations one may give to the assertion that a given indicator has a different "meaning" in one context than another. Suppose one is dealing with common behaviors in two cultural settings. One extreme possibility is that the behaviors have almost opposite meanings in the two settings. For example, belching may be interpreted as rudeness in one culture but as a sign of appreciation or politeness in another. Presumably, belching behavior is being used as an indicator of some underlying sentiment that is nearly opposite in the two settings. In effect, if one were to take the behavioral indicator X_1 as a linear function $X_1 = a + bX$ of the sentiment X, this would imply that the coefficient b takes on a positive sign in one setting and a negative one in the other. Much less extreme is the possibility that the value of the slope may differ from one setting to the next, perhaps being close to zero in one and very steep in another. Here, the equation linking the indicator to the true value would differ in a very particular fashion. Or perhaps the slopes would be equal but the intercepts different, implying a constant bias independent of the level of X. Or perhaps the equation is nonlinear in one setting but linear in another.

Another interpretation of the "different meanings" thesis is that the behavior concerned has different consequences in the two settings. An individual's vote may actually affect the outcome of an election in one country, whereas in another it may serve primarily an expressive function, indicating degree of support for the ruling party in a one-party system, or perhaps merely as a device for the actor to protect himself or herself from detection as a subversive. Still another possibility is that behaviors may be much more easily interpreted in one setting than another. In one, nearly all actors may agree on its meaning, whereas the situation may be much more ambiguous in another. Put somewhat differently, the auxiliary measurement theory may be much simpler in one setting than another, so that ease of interpretation is itself a variable. Presumably, the simpler the setting (e.g., a laboratory experiment), the more faith one has in the auxiliary theory and the less ambiguous the measures used.

Finally, two settings may differ in such a way that stochastic terms in auxiliary theories may not be identical. If $X_1 = a + bX + e$, where e represents a stochastic measurement error term, perhaps the variance in e differs from one setting to another. Or perhaps the error term is correlated with a different set of variables in the two settings. Noncomparability of measurement can involve all of these possibilities, as well as more subtle ones that we shall have to consider below. In short, "noncomparability" is basically a residual category of ways in which exact comparability does *not* hold. As a blanket term it is therefore of little value, except as a generalized warning to the effect that the equivalence of measures can never be taken for granted, even where identical research operations have been used.

It becomes obvious that with any degree of complexity we are likely to encounter many situations in which there will be a considerable number of unknowns. In causal models that contain a mixture of measured and unmeasured variables, the greater the complexity of the theory linking these variables—as measured by the number of arrows representing coefficients with unspecified values—the higher the ratio of measured to unmeasured variables must be for the system to be identified. That is, in many complex situations there will be too many unknowns relative to the number of pieces of empirical information, and the situation will become hopeless from the standpoint of estimation. This implies the necessity of constructing *multiple indicator* measurement-error models and of collecting data in such a way that a high percentage of variables are measured by more than one indicator. Those that are not will ordinarily have to be measured with very small error or else treated as totally unmeasured variables. Implied also is the important point that one's measurement-error theory needs to be thought through very carefully *before* data have been collected. Whenever possible, variables expected to be sources of bias also need to be anticipated and measured as directly as possible.

Also, insofar as possible, one needs to anticipate in advance of data collection the kinds of noncomparability problems that may arise whenever the findings of one's research are being compared with those in another setting or at a later point in time. As we shall see, it is extremely important to attempt to find at least some indicators that are as nearly equivalent as possible across settings, even where these may not be the best single indicators in any particular setting. Conceivably, one may need to use several different sets of (nearly) identical indicators. For instance, indicator X_1 may be assumed identical between settings A and B, whereas X_2 may have this property between settings B and C or perhaps for setting B at two different points in time. Anticipating noncomparability problems in very different settings or time periods will obviously be extremely difficult.

For this reason it is crucial that social scientists develop the norm of making measurement-error assumptions as *explicit* as possible. If an investigator studying situation A has succeeded in making such assumptions explicit, then someone trying to replicate the study in situation B will be in a much better position to state just where the assumptions about the settings may differ. He or she may then be able to collect a sufficient number of additional indicators to make an adequate comparison.

Some Definitions

Before proceeding with more specific discussions of particular noncomparable measurement situations, we need to state more clearly what some of our underlying models, terminology, and key definitions will be. Perhaps the most fundamental point that is sometimes overlooked in discussions of measurement-error models in statistical analyses is that whenever one writes down a mathematical or statistical equation linking indicators with theoretical variables, there must be some *substantive* rationale undergirding such an equation. Very commonly the connection is a causal one, which means that it can never be completely justified without resort to ontological assumptions and that, at best, it can only be subjected to indirect empirical tests. I would hope that this point has been made sufficiently often that the rationale can be accepted without prolonged dispute. Often the causal linkage between unmeasured and measured variables is one in which an unmeasured variable, say X, is assumed to cause an indicator X_i, say, a response. But numerous other variables may also belong in the equation, and there will also be occasions in which the indicator variable may affect the unmeasured one, as well as the likelihood that it may do so conditionally or in combination with other variables. Thus, the causal model for the auxiliary measurement theory may be complex.

Let us refer to different situations, time periods, or individuals on which the measures are taken as A, B, C, and so forth. For the most part, we shall confine our attention to two such settings A and B, with the extension of the argument to other settings being straightforward, at least in principle. We shall use the letters U, V, W, X, Y, and Z to refer to unmeasured variables, assuming that these represent "true values" of such variables. Obviously, the notion of true value will itself be extremely problematic for many variables, especially in those instances where no metric is readily imaginable or where the variable has not been carefully defined theoretically. To simplify the argument, however, we shall assume these true values to exist. Indicators of these true values will be represented by the corresponding letter, with attached numerical subscripts. Thus, X_1 will represent the first indicator of X, Y_3 the third indicator of Y, and so forth.

$$\text{Let } X_{iA} = f_{iA}(U, V, \ldots, X, Y, Z, e_{iA}) \text{ and}$$
$$X_{iB} = f_{iB}(U, V, \ldots, X, Y, Z, e_{iB})$$

where f_{iA} and f_{iB} are any general (and possibly different) functions of not only X, the true value of the variable being measured, but also a number of other variables U, V . . . Y, Z in either the substantive theoretical system or the auxiliary measurement theory. The terms e_{iA} and e_{iB} represent stochastic measurement-error terms, which may also differ between A and B. They may have the same or different variances in A and B, as well as different covariances with X or the other variables in the system.

We shall refer to X_{iA} and X_{iB} as being *identical* if and only if the two functional equations f_{iA} and f_{iB} are identical in all respects (i.e., both functional form and parameter values) *and* if both stochastic measurement-error terms are totally absent (i.e., identically zero). We shall refer to the two indicators as being *equivalent* if and only if the two functional equations are identical and if the stochastic terms in A and B have equal variances and the same covariance matrix with all other disturbance terms and other variables that appear in f_{iA} and f_{iB}.

This distinction between the identity and the equivalence of two measures in A and B is basically that the latter (less restrictive) correspondence permits stochastic measurement-error terms, provided that they have the same statistical properties across settings. Borrowing a term used in the educational psychology literature, if X_{iA} and X_{iB} differ only with respect to the measurement-error *variances*, and hence reliability coefficients, we may refer to them as being *tau equivalent* measures (Lord and Novick, 1968, p. 47). In the educational testing literature, of course, the notions of equivalence and tau equivalence usually refer to two different measures applied to the same subjects or settings rather than indicators utilized across settings or time periods, but the statistical arguments made in that body of literature carry over to different settings as well.

Since we shall ordinarily be concerned with more than one indicator of each variable, we must allow for the possibility that some indicators will be identical or equivalent across settings, whereas others will not. If $f_{iA} = f_{iB}$ for all indicators X_i of X, we shall refer to the *set* of such indicators as being *completely* identical or equivalent, as the case may be. If the two functions are identical or equivalent for only some indicators, we shall refer to this particular subset for which $f_{iA} = f_{iB}$ as constituting the *reference* indicators for situations A and B. Obviously, we may have a different set of reference indicators for the pair of situations (A, B) than for the pair (A, C) or (B, C).

In the special case where a given indicator serves as a reference indicator across all situations or settings being compared, we shall refer to such an indicator as being a *general* reference indicator, with the understanding that the notion of "generality" must always be relative to the totality of the situations being compared. Our aim, of course, is to obtain as many general reference indicators as possible. It may turn out, however, that such general reference indicators are inferior to other indicators that have greater reliability or are less subject to measurement-error biases in specific settings. The mere fact that an indicator can serve as a reference indicator across several settings does not mean that its other qualities are superior to those of other indicators.

Finally, as we have already implied, it is sometimes possible to apply mathematical transformations g_i to make indicators identical or equivalent across settings. We noted this in the case of the different gravitational constants at the surfaces of the earth and moon. Similarly, one may measure temperature with a thermometer or thermostat by using the coefficients of expansion of mercury or copper, obtaining (nearly) identical measures by taking these coefficients into consideration. Here we may distinguish among several possibilities, namely,

(i) $f_{iA} = g(f_{iB})$, where g is the same for all indicators X_i
(ii) $f_{iA} = g_i(f_{iB})$, where g_i differs for each X_i
and (iii) $f_{iA} = g_i(f_{iB})$, for a restricted subset of X_i

As an example of the first of these possibilities, each indicator in situation A might be made comparable to the corresponding indicator in B by dividing each set of scores by the size of each group. In the second case, a different transformation would have to be applied to each indicator, but as long as the exact transformation were specified this would create no special difficulties. In the third, more common possibility, only some of the indicators could be transformed mathematically, whereas the remainder could not. Finally, of course, there is the remaining possibility that none of the indicators used in one setting can be transformed to yield identical or equivalent indicators in the second setting. It is this last kind of situation that creates the greatest conceptual and practical difficulties in comparative research.

Obviously, it will be only rarely that one can specify the functions f_i or g_i exactly, but reasonable approximations can be tried out, their implications noted, and certain empirical predictions noted and tested. For instance, in the case of tau equivalent or equivalent indicators, one expects that the *patterns* of correlations across settings will be highly similar. For equivalent indicators, the numerical values of certain coefficients may even be identical except for sampling errors. If reference indicators can be located, and if the patterns of associations among these reference indicators are highly similar, then one may combine these reference indicators with other indicators that are themselves noncomparable to obtain additional insights. But if no indicators are comparable, and if no transformations can be made, the situation may become completely intractable with respect to one's ability to generalize across such situations. If so, it will at least be to our advantage to know this fact before attempting the impossible or before needlessly investing our time in data collection.

The Scope, Inclusiveness, and Indirectness of Measures

Problems of comparability are closely bound with the question of just how general a theoretical concept is intended to be. We may distinguish two very different meanings of the notion of "generalizability." The first, which we shall refer to as the *scope* of the measure, refers to the diversity of the populations and settings to which it is to be applied. Can it be applied only to a specified type of person, to a much broader class, or to all human actors? Can it be applied in all settings or merely a restricted subset of settings, as defined in some fashion? As a general rule, we anticipate that the broader the scope of the concept, the more complex will be the measurement-error theory needed to relate the theoretical variable to its indicators.

For instance, if the single indicator X_1 is related to the true X by the simple equation $X_1 = a + bX$ in a given setting, as we move to other settings we do not expect that the "constants" a and b will remain the same in the new setting. If so, then these parameters are really variables, so that a more complex equation $X_1 = U + VX$ might have to be used, where the variable U has replaced a, and V has replaced b. We might then need a set of additional variables to explain the values of U and V in different settings. Or if there is a particular source of nonrandom measurement error in setting A, we might expect to find a different source, or perhaps several such sources, in setting B. A much more complex auxiliary measurement theory would then be needed to cover all of these situations, in much the same fashion that simple laws of motion have to be made more complex when a body is falling through a medium that produces friction that retards the velocity.

There is also a second meaning to the notion of generalizability that we shall refer to as the conceptual *inclusiveness* of the variable. One concept may refer to a range of phenomena β that are contained in a larger set α (i.e., $\beta \subset \alpha$). For instance, α may refer to "power," whereas β may refer to a special type of power called "authority." A third phenomenon γ may refer to a still smaller subset, "religious authority." Or perhaps α refers to measures of differentiation, β to hierarchical differentiation or inequality, and γ to a specific type of inequality, say income inequality (Blau, 1977). Ordinarily, as we attach adjectival qualifiers to a concept (e.g., "religious" or "income"), we decrease the inclusiveness of the concept, though not necessarily the scope of its applicability in terms of the actors or settings to which it can be applied. Thus, scope and conceptual inclusiveness are distinct aspects of what we usually think of as the generalizability of the concept or variable. Presumably, the narrower the inclusiveness of the concept, the more restrictions we place upon the kinds of indicators that may be used to measure it, and this also includes the number of *common* indicators as well. But the greater the inclusiveness and scope, the less likely that those indicators that are common to a diversity of actors and settings will also be *identical* or *equivalent* indicators across the full range of applicability of the concept.

As scientists, we hope to increase both the scope and inclusiveness of our most important concepts, but as implied, we must also expect to pay a price in terms of the complexity of our measurement-error theories and the reduced likelihood that we can find very many indicators that will be not only common (i.e., operationally nearly identical), but also equivalent. The basic reason for this is that as the complexities of our measurement theories increase—for example, as we begin to allow for multiple causes of measurement error that vary across settings—it becomes less and less plausible to assume that operationally identical procedures will yield nearly equivalent measures. *The more indirect the measurement operations, the more difficult it becomes to achieve generalizability and equivalence simultaneously.*

There is a kind of tradeoff of dilemma faced by the social scientist, in which as we gain generalizability we lose equivalence, or as we gain equivalence we must sacrifice generalizability. Likewise, as I have argued elsewhere (Blalock, 1979a), if we wish to gain generalizability while not sacrificing precision in our predictions, we shall need to increase the complexity of our measurement-error theories. These tradeoffs or dilemmas are especially disturbing, scientifically, the more indirect the measurement.

The degree of indirectness of a measurement procedure is also a deceptively simple idea. As a first approximation, we might think of the degree of indirectness as a function of the number of causal arrows needed to connect X to an indicator X_i in a causal chain. If $X = X_i$, there being no such arrows, we might refer to the measurement as "direct." If $X \rightarrow X_i$, the indirect procedure would be relatively more direct than if another unmeasured variable W were needed, as in the chain X

→ W → X_i, and so forth. But as soon as we begin to add further complications to the model in the form of sources of measurement error that themselves are possibly linked to the true value X, the degree of indirectness is perhaps much less important than the *complexity* of the measurement-error model, as indicated by the number of causal arrows, nonlinearities, or other peculiarities. As a general rule, we would expect that as the scope and inclusiveness of our variables increases, so will the complexity of any general measurement-error model needed to "cover" the full range of this scope or inclusiveness. Thus we will pay a considerable price for the advantage of generality, and this price will be relatively greatest for variables that are only indirectly measured, even in the simplest of situations.

The most obvious instances of indirect measurement are those that arise whenever we are attempting to infer a postulated internal state, such as an attitude or a utility, on the basis of behaviors of various kinds. The more complex the behavior, in the sense that it is likely to satisfy several goals at once or be differentially motivated from one setting to the next, the more complex our measurement-error theory will have to be, even where the concept is defined in such a way that it is not very inclusive. As we then extend its inclusiveness, holding constant its scope, we may expect to get into difficulty very quickly. Difficulty in this sense refers to the need for a very complex measurement theory that will likely contain a large number of unknowns as well as questionable assumptions.

This difficulty is likely to occur not only in connection with efforts to infer internal states, but also with respect to many forms of *behaviors* that have been defined theoretically in terms of either internal states or supposed consequences of these behaviors (Blalock, 1979b). For behaviors that have been defined in such a way that inclusiveness is very narrow, it is often possible to utilize manifest characteristics of these behaviors that permit very direct measurement. For instance, one may define "hitting" behavior as involving the movement of the arm and hand or fist toward an object, with a certain minimum velocity, and the actual making of contact. (We may then *infer* that the hitting has been painful to or has injured the other party.) We may similarly define shooting behavior, kicking behavior, and so forth. Contrast these highly specific behaviors with the concept of "aggression," which is generally defined to be much more inclusive.

In order to provide a sufficiently inclusive definition that covers a wide range of manifestly different behaviors, it is very convenient to invoke either a common intent (such as the goal of injuring the other party) or a common effect (such as that of actually injuring the party). In either of these cases it becomes necessary to construct a causal theory, either in terms of the motive or the consequence of the behavior. For subtle forms of aggression, such a theory may become highly complex, especially where the aggressive behavior serves other purposes as well and where it is also advantageous to avoid punishment or retaliation. The essential point is that even with behaviors, as we extend the inclusiveness of the theoretical definition, we will very often find it necessary to invoke much more complicated measurement-error theories, many assumptions of which may be untestable.

THE USE OF COMMON INDICATORS IN
MULTIPLE-INDICATOR ANALYSES

The multiple-indicator approach to data analysis, about which there is now a considerable body of technical literature, involves a very general strategy that permits one to use combinations of common indicators and those that are unique to specific settings.[1] One of the major advantages of this approach is that it requires one to specify the assumed causal connections between indicators and unmeasured variables, including those that may be producing nonrandom measurement errors of various types. But, like all other data analysis approaches, it is also vulnerable to abuse by those who may be tempted to use it too routinely, without first looking very carefully at the assumptions it requires. In particular, there may be a temptation to rely too heavily on common indicators, merely because they are common, and to assume that they are not only common but also equivalent or identical indicators as well.

If there are a sufficient number of common indicators across settings or studies, this will assist the analyst who wishes to splice together the results of several studies. But before jumping into one's statistical analysis, one must first take a very careful look at the nature of one's common indicators and their relationships with the unique indicators, asking a series of questions. Why is it that only some of the indicators are common ones? Is it reasonable to suppose that their commonness has resulted from certain peculiarities that need to be taken into consideration in the analysis? Perhaps it is mere coincidence that two or more investigators have used the same indicators, as for example nearly identical question wording. Perhaps there has been a deliberate effort to replicate a study by using very similar items, where feasible. If so, however, one must then ask why it is that not all items used are common. What is it the common indicators share that the others do not, and what possible biases would result if one used only the common indicators in the analysis?

Obviously, there will be many different kinds of possibilities that cannot be anticipated in a general discussion such as this. Several rather obvious ones can be noted, however. Perhaps there are some very general items that are roughly comparable from one setting to the next, along with much more specific ones that are easily dated or that are only relevant in a local setting. For example, if one is trying to measure prejudice toward a given minority, say blacks, it may be advantageous to ask white respondents a set of very general questions, such as those tapping one's willingness to associate with blacks at work or in one's social club. But there may be a set of highly topical issues, such as a pending piece of legislation, a controversy over school busing, or a particular political candidate, that may be much more salient to respondents at that particular time and place, and thus much less likely to elicit platitudes as responses. These latter questions would no doubt have to be revised in a replication study, with doubts being raised as to their comparability across settings. Nevertheless, in each specific setting it may be advisable to combine sets of "immediately relevant" items along with much more general ones. In designing a set of items that might be used in a replication study at some later point in time, however, it may be extremely difficult to anticipate just which items will retain their generality. Will mandatory school busing still be a topic at issue ten years from now? How about abortion? Defense spending? Or capital punishment?

If one were to select out only the common indicators across several settings, the question that would need to be asked is whether they should also be treated as equivalent or identical indicators of a theoretical construct such as political conservatism, anti-minority prejudice, or alienation from work. Recalling our earlier distinction between common, equivalent, and identical indicators, the answer to this question depends upon the equations used to link these indicators to the unmeasured variables, and whether the coefficients in these equations can be assumed to be constant across settings.

Most likely, an assumption of equivalence cannot be directly tested without supplementary information provided by the behaviors of *other* indicators that themselves must be assumed to behave in specified ways (see the Appendix for illustrations). Suffice it to say that an explicitly formulated measurement-error theory will be necessary to assess such questions. Most certainly, one should not jump to the conclusion that common indicators can automatically be assumed equivalent or identical. Yet this will be the naive investigator's greatest temptation.

Another reason that we may expect to find common indicators, as well as unique ones, is that there may be an extensive diffusion of traits across contexts. Suppose, for example, that country B borrows country A's constitution, while superimposing its own unique political structure on this formal document. In both societies we may then find common offices or titles, supposedly similar judicial systems and election procedures, and even manifestly similar political acts on the part of the average citizen. But say the act of voting may have different "meanings" in the two systems, being a mere ritual exercise in the one society but not in the other. Members of legislative bodies in the two societies may also behave formally in much the same ways, but with very different consequences. Or one religion may have borrowed a set of rituals from another, with the meanings of the acts and beliefs being quite different in the two religious settings. Occupational titles may look very much the same in two different bureaucratic organizations, whereas the actual roles attached to these titles may be substantially different. Or, if one looks at the "same" setting across time, behavioral acts that were very important at one point in time may continue to exist as survivals, without having the same symbolic meaning or purpose that they previously had. In all these instances, one would need a clear definition of the theoretical construct or variable being measured before one could assess whether or not these common indicators should be considered equivalent (or identical) as well.

In other instances one may simply be given lists of items, some of which are not common across settings. For instance, lists of occupational titles may contain some occupations that are unique to one or two settings. Some organizations may have offices, departments, or roles that are not comparable to those of the others, even though the titles used may be roughly equivalent. Some countries have both a president and a prime minister, whereas others may have a king and a prime minister, or perhaps just a president. The role of priest may vary from religion to religion.

Whenever one is confronted with slightly different lists that contain both common and unique elements, one must ask whether some of these lists are accidentally incomplete and mere samples of more complete lists, or whether the differences reflect real differences in the settings themselves. If aggregating decisions must be made involving the clustering of occupations, one will then be faced with the problem of deciding whether common indicators can be treated in the identical way in each setting. For instance, should all Protestant denominations be lumped together in all settings, or merely in some of them? If one leaves out the unique occupations or denominations, what kinds of biases may this produce? To help answer such questions, it will be helpful to ask why it is that all items are not unique and what peculiar characteristics items must have in order for them to be common across settings.

Reference Indicators in Multiple-Indicator Models

Suppose we are given a multiple-indicator model, such as that of Figure 3.2, in which certain indicators may be subject to sources of nonrandom error, as for example W in Figure 3.2. Since the true values of the unmeasured variables X, Y, and Z are unknown, and will therefore be insensitive to an arbitrary linear transformation, we may select one of the measured indicators for each unmeasured variable to supply its metric. For instance, we may set the slopes or "loadings" linking X_1 and X, Y_2 and Y, and Z_3 and Z each equal to unity. If this were done across several settings or subsamples, it is then quite likely that the loadings for the remaining indicators will differ across these settings. The indicators selected to provide metrics for the unmeasured variables have been referred to as "reference indicators" in the multiple-indicator literature (Wiley, 1973; Schoenberg, 1972).[2]

Having selected a set of reference indicators, it then becomes possible to study differences in variances across settings or samples. This would not be possible, however, if each unmeasured variable were expressed in standardized form (within each setting), having a zero mean and unit standard deviation.[3] This use of reference indicators provides an obvious advantage in assessing comparability whenever differences in variability can be expected across such settings or subsamples. But one must also be careful to select, as reference indicators, measured variables that are very simply related to the underlying constructs. For instance, in Figure 3.2 we would not want to use X_3, Y_1, or Z_1 as reference indicators because of their presumed biases due to their common cause, W. Of course, if we were willing to assume exactly the same parameter values linking W to each of these indicators across settings, or if we were willing

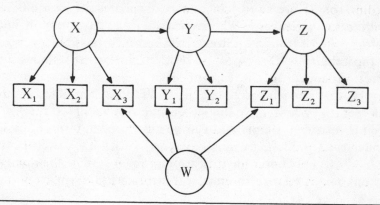

Figure 3.2

to assume that W has been perfectly measured in each setting, we could introduce the proper adjustments in each of these reference indicators. But we would ordinarily not wish to make such strong assumptions regarding the operation of biasing variables such as W.

A more subtle but nevertheless important assumption about reference indicators is that the parameters in the equations linking these variables to their respective constructs are identical across settings. In particular, we would want to assume equal slopes across settings and, if we were also interested in comparing means across settings, we would also want to assume a knowledge of the intercept values as well. Ordinarily, this implies that we need to select, as reference indicators, not only *common* indicators, but *equivalent* ones as well. The operationally inclined investigator might not be interested in assessing the reasonableness of this assumption, taking common indicators as reference indicators primarily on the basis of their convenience in terms of availability.

Path-analytic procedures that work with standardized variables in effect "force" comparability on one's measures, regardless of empirical differences that may exist with respect to variances. As noted elsewhere (Blalock, 1976), a similar phenomenon occurs whenever categorized variables (including ordinal ones) are used, since slope estimates are confounded with error variances.[4] Whenever two or more common indicators can be found, however, it becomes possible to assess comparability with respect to both (unmeasured) slopes and error variances. In the case of strictly random measurement-errors that are uncorrelated with all other variables in the theoretical system, including other indicator variables, the situation is relatively simple and can be illustrated in terms of easily understood models. In more complex situations, however, one is likely to encounter identification problems, since the number of unknowns relative to empirical information is apt to be too large.

Consider simple effect indicators X_i related to the true X by equations of the form $X_i = a_i + b_i X + e_i$. Making the assumption that the stochastic measurement error terms e_i are uncorrelated with true X values, this implies that the variances of the measured indicators will be functions of three terms, σ^2_x, b_i^2, and and $\sigma^2_{e_i}$ according to the formula

$$\sigma^2_{x_i} = b_i^2 \, \sigma^2_x + \sigma^2_{e_i}$$

Although we will have sample estimates of the variances for the *measured* X_i, we will not be able to estimate any of the three quantities on the right-hand side without further assumptions. If we are trying to compare results of two different settings A and B, the mere fact that the variances of indicators are equal does not mean that we may safely assume that the corresponding slopes (or error variances) are equal. Our suspicion is that many investigators will make the implicit assumption that slopes and error variances are identical across settings, but obviously this assumption will not always be justified. The essential point is that *some* assumptions will be needed to make these or other cross-setting comparisons.

The obvious first step in making comparisons using the multiple-indicator approach is to construct separate models for each setting, noting the existence of common and/or equivalent indicators by common symbols or visual devices such as squares, rectangles, circles, or ovals drawn about such indicators. Let us suppose that the model of Figure 3.2 applies to setting A, whereas in B we have available only the indicators X_1, X_3, Y_2, Z_1, and Z_3 plus some additional indicators unique to that setting. We would then be able to use the common indicators X_1, Y_2, and Z_3 as reference indicators, provided we were also willing to assume something definite about their respective slopes or loadings in the two settings. If the equivalence of all three reference indicators were assumed, one could then carry out separate multiple-indicator analyses in each setting, using all of the available information about unique indicators as well.

Such an equivalence assumption would permit one to assume comparability in the metrics of the three unmeasured variables X, Y, and Z. If one were also willing to assume multivariate normality in the true values and also all error terms, plus assuming that the models were correctly specified, the (unstandardized) parameter estimates linking the true values could then be computed and compared across settings. Perhaps the slope linking X to Y is steeper in setting A than in B. Had standardized path coefficients been used, however, one could not infer this fact without making additional assumptions about the variances in the true values in the two settings.

This comparison procedure obviously depends rather heavily upon some rather strong assumptions about the indicator variables, as well as the correct specification of the measurement-error models across settings. Maximum-likelihood methods, such as Jöreskog's covariance structures procedure programmed as LISREL, are known to provide minimum-variance estimates and hence maximum efficiency as compared with other ad hoc estimation procedures (Hauser and Goldberger, 1971; Jöreskog, 1973). But if the models contain specification errors—as will practically always be the case with realistic measurement-error models—these procedures also have the major disadvantage of spreading errors throughout the entire system. That is, if a model is misspecified in one of its parts, say in terms of the indicators of Z, the biases produced will ordinarily not be confined to this single portion of the model but will be distributed in such a fashion that it will be extremely difficult to locate the faulty assumptions without investigating separate submodels.

For this reason, both Costner and Schoenberg (1973) and Burt (1976) suggest supplementing the customary test criteria for the full model with procedures that in effect break the larger model down into component parts. Burt, in particular, points out that the theoretical specification of an unmeasured variable will depend on the measured variables that have been used in the analysis. In the case of Figure 3.2, for instance, one might "measure" (and interpret) X by using only the three effect indicators X_1, X_2, and X_3. In contrast, one might use the entire model or perhaps the submodel that omits Z and its indicators. Any specification errors involving Y or Z would not affect the measurement of X or its interpretation in the first instance, but could introduce serious biases if the full model were used.

Costner and Schoenberg provide illustrations showing that an inspection of the residuals obtained by comparing the actual correlation matrix of indicators with a predicted matrix will often lead one astray. Furthermore, "corrections" in the models suggested by patterns among these residuals will have the unfortunate effect of producing an excellent fit between the theory and one's data, even where these corrections do not correspond to the true model that produced the data. In short, one can very easily be led astray by ad hoc modifications designed to patch up an incorrectly specified overall model. Costner and Schoenberg, along with Burt, therefore suggest that one not only compute coefficients based on the entire model, but also on various submodels as well.

While we cannot go into these suggested procedures in detail, a similar principle holds in instances where we wish to make comparisons across settings and where possibly different overall models and indicator sets are used for different settings. In addition to computations based on each of the separate full models (using all indicators), we would suggest that one also "purge" each setting's model of all indicators that are not common ones. Obviously, if there are more than two settings this could be done pairwise. For instance, one could use only the common indicators to compare settings A and B. If setting C contained some indicators in common with A, but a different subset in common with B, one could conduct three separate comparisons of A with B, A with C, and B with C, in each instance using the maximum number of common indicators. Further illustrative validating procedures are briefly discussed in the Appendix.

NONCOMPARABILITY WITH RESPECT TO SLOPES AND INTERCEPTS

Perhaps one of the most common implicit arguments behind the claim that two situations are noncomparable with respect to a particular measurement procedure is the notion that the linkages between theoretical construct and indicator are characterized by different slopes or intercepts. We shall briefly consider two kinds of examples, both of which appear to be rather common, in which noncomparability with respect to slopes is especially likely to arise. In the first case, the true relationship between the construct or theoretical variable and the indicator is nonlinear, and settings A and B are such that the preponderance of cases in A fall in a different region of the curve than do most of the cases in B. In the second case, which we believe to be a very common one, the functional relationship between the true value X and an indicator X_i cannot accurately be approximated by a simple linear equation $X_i = a_i + b_i X$, where b_i is a constant. Instead, b_i is itself a *variable* W_i, so that a more adequate representation of the equation would be $X_i = a_i + kW_iX$, where W_i may possibly represent a different conceptual variable for each indicator being used.

Nonlinear Relationships Between
Theoretical Variables and Indicators

To illustrate the nonlinear situation, suppose the theoretical variable represents a utility value attached to an outcome of some type, say, receiving a given dollar income. Such utilities are likely to be subject to satiation, so that the functional form of the relationship between the utility X and the income X_1 might be of the form indicated in Figure 3.3. Suppose that the theory predicts that a subjective state—here, the utility—affects some behavior Y. Perhaps X represents satisfaction with one's income and Y represents behavior toward one's children, job performance, or voting behavior. Lacking a satisfactory measure of the subjective state X, one may attempt to measure this through the cause indicator X_1—here, income. If X and Y are linearly related, the model then clearly implies that income X_1 and behavior Y will not be linearly related, but instead will be related by an increasing function with a decreasing slope, as for example a logarithmic function, a segment of a parabola, or a power function with exponent between zero and one.

Now, if a setting A is such that the bulk of the cases fall toward the left portion of the curve, whereas for B they fall closer to the upper extreme, then the slope linking Y to X_1 will be steeper in A than in B. Obviously, if we had a direct measure of X and an explicit theory to this effect, this prediction could be tested rather simply. Unfortunately, however, if X is unmeasured we could not distinguish this particular model from one that involved a linear relationship between X_1 and X but a nonlinear one between X and Y. This would require multiple indicators of X, as well as explicit theoretical predictions regarding the forms of the relationships of each X_i with X. For instance, if it were assumed that the relationship between X_2 and X is linear, one could then choose between the two alternatives. Or perhaps one could locate a third indicator, X_3, expected to be related to X in still a different fashion, say, via a threshold mechanism implying an increasingly accelerating positive slope.

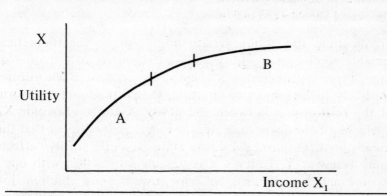

Figure 3.3

Possibilities of these types are often overlooked in path-analysis and factor-analysis models which impose linearity on the functional relationships between constructs and indicators. Therefore, anyone using these techniques not only needs to think through the presumed causal structure of the model, but also needs to ask whether or not (within the range of variation being studied) a strictly linear equation form is really justified. If not, and if the sample can be subdivided on variables expected to yield subsamples falling at positions similar to those of A and B in Figure 3.3, crude tests of the theory become possible.

It should also be kept in mind, as already noted, that the "blind" use of a program such as Jöreskog and Sörbom's (1978) LISREL will tend to spread errors due to such misspecifications through the causal system. Neglected nonlinearities in one part of the system may therefore not be easily detected without the aid of careful conceptualization. Where substantial nonlinearities in connection with specific kinds of indicators are expected, it therefore becomes crucial to augment such a set of indicators with others that are not expected to produce such nonlinearities, and it also becomes crucial to examine the possibility of nonlinearities in a localized part of the overall model before entering one's indicators into a larger equation system.

We suspect that there may be a relatively large number of so-called "background variables" that produce nonlinear relationships with unmeasured internal states. Consider formal education, as measured by years of schooling. There may be a satiation phenomenon in connection with certain kinds of "knowledge" variables, such as information about foreign affairs or birth-control techniques. Also "education" is used for some purposes as a surrogate for one's credentials, so that the true functional relationship between years of schooling and one's "qualifications" may be approximated by a step function. There may be a substantial increment between completing 11 and 12 years of schooling, but virtually none between completing 10 and 11 years.

Often, especially in survey research, "years of education" is simply inserted into one's data analysis without careful attention to just what one means by "education" or the conceptual variable being tapped. The same may also apply to other "experience" variables that have been measured simply by time of exposure, either to TV watching, Sunday school, or work experience. For some of these variables, the credentializing factor may be of overriding significance, whereas for others a satiation phenomenon may be of greater importance. If the mechanisms that involve the unmeasured internal states are not specified, and if the research is conducted in an atheoretical fashion, it may not even occur to the investigator to check for nonlinearities or differences in slopes across subsamples.

Multiplicative Models

The literature on multiple indicators, as noted, virtually ignores the possibility that certain other variables in one's model (as exemplified by W in the discussion that follows) may *multiply* with either an indicator variable or the true value of X, possibly with variable exponents. In the discussion that follows, we shall assume the exponent of a multiplicative term to be unity, thereby simplifying the argument to preclude the possibility that the exponent of W in setting A may differ from the exponent in B. Consider two types of examples that have been discussed in somewhat greater detail elsewhere (Blalock, 1975, and Namboodiri et al., 1975).

First, suppose that some stimulus or cause indicator variable X_1 has a differential impact on two kinds of actors, or in the settings A and B. For instance, suppose X_1 is the presence of a certain percentage of minority members, but that the theoretical variable X of interest is the threat posed by the minority. In setting A, a rather small increase in minority percentage may cause a substantial increase in threat, perhaps because of a very tight labor market situation. In B, in contrast, the sensitivity of the majority to the minority may be nowhere near as great, so that the slope W connecting X and X_1 is much less steep. Or A and B may represent two kinds of actors, say, A those who are in closest contact with the minority and B those who are rather remote. As another example, perhaps X_1 represents the percentage of the local labor force that is unemployed, whereas the conceptual variable is "fear of unemployment." The slope connecting X and X_1 may again vary by setting or type of actor.

As a totally different kind of model, consider an effect indicator X_1 representing a measured frequency that is some fraction of the true frequency X. Perhaps X represents the true but unmeasured crime rate, whereas X_1 represents reported crimes or number of crimes for which the guilty party has been apprehended or convicted. If so, we may represent X_1 as the true X multiplied by a factor W representing this proportion. Obviously, the value of W may vary from one setting to the next, or by type of crime or by characteristics of persons apprehended or convicted. For example, W may be much smaller for white-collar crimes than for crimes of violence or property offenses.

In all of these examples, we recognize that W may be causally related to other variables that appear in the theoretical system, including the true value of X or of variables that may depend upon X or be its immediate cause. Hence, if one were to write down the misleading equation $X_1 = a_1 + b_1 X$, in the case of an effect indicator (exemplified by the crime measurement example), one would expect the coefficient b_1, which is really W in disguise, to vary from one setting to the next. Of course, if the true value of X were known, this possibility could be investigated directly, either through covariance analysis or by inserting interaction terms into a dummy-variable analysis, with the dummy variables representing the different contexts or subpopulations. But we are assuming, of course, that the true X is unknown.

Once more, if one has multiple indicators available, and if one can reasonably assume that only *some* of the indicators are subject to this difficulty, then one may use the remaining indicators as reference indicators in order to infer what is going on and, perhaps, to infer the nature of the variable W that is behind this difference in slope coefficients. But even where such additional indicators are available, it will also be advantageous to theorize about such Ws that multiply with either X or the X_i and to obtain reasonably direct measures of these Ws where possible. For instance, one might attempt to ask respondents about the perceived threat of the minority or unemployment to themselves, their neighbors or work associates, or to "people like yourself." Or it may be wise to conduct careful methodological studies comparing crime victim reports, self-reported criminal acts, and conviction rates for different kinds of crimes and offenders in order to develop reasonably specific measurement-error theories concerning the adequacy of different indicators of crime rates, so as to assess the variability of slope coefficients.

One would also want to theorize and collect data about the other variables that may affect W or the variability among such slopes. Throwing the X_i into computer programs that impose linear additive assumptions may again prove misleading to the extent that differences among slope coefficients are simply averaged out over nonhomogeneous subpopulations. This temptation is perhaps less serious when one has several distinct empirical studies that are being compared, or perhaps two different time points, but even in these latter instances an explicit theory that attempts to predict and account for differences in slopes should be helpful. More generally, whenever one writes down an equation system with supposedly constant coefficients, one should always develop the habit of asking of each coefficient: Is this slope really a constant? If not, then what variables are likely to affect its behavior and how are these variables linked to the other variables in my causal system?

Differences in Means or Intercepts

Measures may also be noncomparable in very simple ways, such as involving constant or systematic biases that produce mean or intercept differences. For instance, it is often claimed that standardized examinations penalize blacks and other minorities whose scores tend to be lower than those of whites. If, for example, X represents "true ability" (assuming this could be conceptualized theoretically), and if X_i represent a series of different tests, all of which involve performances of various types, then perhaps for whites $X_i = a_i + b_iX + e_i$, whereas for blacks the comparable equations are $X_i = a_i' + b_iX + e_i'$, where the slope coefficients are identical for both races, and where the disturbance terms have expected values of zero for both groups. Let us suppose, however, that intercept values tend to be higher for whites, giving them higher measured scores for identical true X values. Within each racial group, the X_i scores might prove equally effective in predicting to some criterion Y, but comparisons across groups would be misleading unless an appropriate correction could be made for the intercepts. Likewise, assuming an identical distribution of true X values for both groups, the mean performance scores X_i would also differ, leading to the impression that whites have higher abilities on the average.

How could such a bias ever be uncovered? One approach would be to construct alternative tests that, on the face of it, use items that do not depend on "culture-bound" socialization practices that favor the one group over the other. But if such tests were then constructed, and if these showed smaller racial differences or even a reversal of intercept values, one could likewise claim that this second set of tests is also biased, this

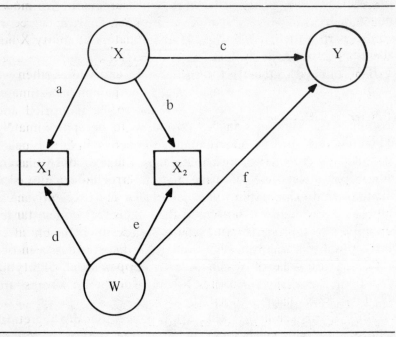

Figure 3.4

time in favor of blacks. Without an extremely clear notion of what one means by the true value, as well as a procedure for establishing a meaningful zero point that is comparable for both groups, there may be no possible way of resolving the matter unless one is willing to *assume,* a priori, that the true means for the two groups are identical. This has, in effect, been the implicit assumption behind many legal and moralistic claims that any tests that produce unequal means are ipso facto biased or discriminatory.

Scientifically, a more satisfactory kind of resolution would be to theorize about other variables that may affect the mean or intercept differences, to measure these as directly as possible, and to introduce them as control variables in one's regression equations. Perhaps degree of confidence, practice with similar tests, or specialized knowledge (e.g., vocabulary) accounts for the racial differential. We must then allow for the possibility that these very same variables may also account for performance differences on some criterion variable, as for example job performance scores. For instance, the measurement-error model might be as depicted in Figure 3.4, in which W (say, degree of confidence) affects not only the two indicators of ability X but also the performance level Y.

If W operates similarly for both blacks and whites, then we would expect to obtain roughly the same parameter estimates for both groups, assuming the model to be identified and assuming the variances in X, Y, and W to be approximately equal in both groups. In effect, the objective in this type of approach is to specify more completely the sources of bias by developing a more realistic measurement-error model. But even if all such sources of bias were identified and explicitly measured, we might never be able to detect this fact. For instance, should one stop looking for possible sources of bias only after approximate equality in average measured scores has been obtained? Such a criterion obviously presupposes the validity of the theoretical assumption that the true group means are identical.

Still another possibility is that the conceptual or theoretical variable is multidimensional and that the indicators X_i are tapping only a subset of these dimensions. For instance, they may be tapping that form of intelligence that calls for symbolic reasoning, or perhaps the ability to respond rapidly to a series of discrete or unrelated questions, rather than to follow through in a sustained fashion on a more complex problem. The only way to begin to answer this kind of objection, of course, is to postulate distinct types of intelligence and then to design batteries of tests that are extremely different in terms of task demands. The multitrait-multimethod approach of Campbell and Fiske (1959) is admirably suited to this particular strategy.

In sum, whenever one discovers intercept or mean differences across groups or settings, it seems wise to search for explanatory variables that may affect these values. If these variables are then brought into the analysis explicitly, and if the intercept or mean differences disappear, this *may* mean that the sources of measurement biases have been uncovered. But one must also face up to the possibility that no biases existed in the first place, and that the "true scores" actually differ across such groups. Sometimes, as in the case of racial or ethnic differences, we may be very reluctant to accept this latter interpretation, but as social scientists, we must also be equally careful to search for sources of possible biases even where *no* differences are initially found. One suspects that whenever means or intercepts are approximately equal across groups, social scientists are more likely to be inclined to accept the "no bias" thesis, just as they are often tempted to assume that when there is close agreement among observers or judges (i.e., high reliability) this is also an indication of negligible measurement error (i.e., validity as well as reliability).

NONCOMPARABILITY WITH RESPECT TO COMPLEXITY OF SETTINGS

One rather common implied meaning of noncomparability is the notion that two situations cannot easily be compared because one is far more complex than the other. If one were permitted to throw out all comparisons in which some settings were slightly more complex in some way than the others, this would indeed represent a very serious obstacle to scientific generalization. Presumably, one handles many kinds of complexities by introducing control variables. If variables cannot literally be held constant in a given setting, then hypothetical controls may be introduced through some sort of statistical adjustment, i.e., a paper-and-pencil manipulation of numerical scores after they have been recorded through the measurement operation. For instance, one may adjust incomes to control for workers' experience, education, sex, or race. But something much more profound may be intended by the assertion that complexities per se create problems of noncomparability.

The issue arises, for instance, whenever it is claimed that laboratory experiments are "artificial" and therefore noncomparable with presumably more complex, "real-world" natural settings. Insofar as such a claim is stated in a highly general, vague way to discredit experimental research, it need not be taken seriously. But to the extent that there is the valid argument that the measurements used in laboratory situations depend in some essential way upon the simplicity of the setting, one needs to look very seriously at the issue of generalizability (Wilken and Blalock, 1981). For instance, if the measurement of a body's length or its mass had to require very different operations outside the laboratory than within it, and if there were no precise theories that permitted transformations between the two sets of measurements, then the physicist would indeed be in for difficulty. Similarly, if utilities are estimated in laboratory settings by forcing subjects to make extremely simple choices, or if aggression is measured in terms of the frequency of button pushing, there will inevitably be comparability issues that arise whenever these same measurement procedures cannot be used in more complex situations. This is acknowledged in the literature on so-called "external validity," but is often not faced squarely enough by those who rely heavily on evidence based on extremely simple experimental settings.

What we need is considerably more thought devoted to the problem of identifying specific ways in which differences in complexity may affect measurement comparability, quite apart from the question of the sheer number of uncontrolled variables that may need to be brought into one's substantive theories. In the present section we shall focus on only two such issues: (1) the implications of differential complexity for indirect measurement, where one or more effect indicators are being used to infer an unmeasured variable that is only one among several possible causes; and (2) some implications when complexity affects aggregation decisions regarding alternative behaviors. In both instances we shall again see the need for explicit measurement theories, especially for those situations that are sufficiently complicated to require rather complex causal models.

Differential Complexity and Effect Indicators: The Measurement of Discrimination

In instances where effect indicators are being used, it is often convenient to assume that, apart from minor random disturbances, the only cause of the effect indicator is the theoretical variable of interest to the investigator. Although we shall illustrate this particular problem with the example of inequality measures as indicators of discrimination, it is well to point out the generality of the problem with a totally different kind of illustration, namely, the use of behavioral acts as indicators of postulated internal states. Many behaviors are defined theoretically in terms of some motivational state (Blalock, 1979b). For instance, aggression may be defined as behavior oriented toward injuring some other party, avoidance as behavior intended to reduce contact, competition as behavior oriented toward achieving goals subject to constraints of scarcity, controlling behavior as being oriented toward getting others to do something one wants them to do, altruism as involving the intent to help others without benefitting the self, and so forth. But, especially in complex situations, we often find that a single behavior serves several purposes at once. Aggression may be instrumental in limiting competition, altruism may help one achieve status, and movement to the suburbs may simultaneously reduce contact with a minority and lower one's taxes.

Thus the indicator X_i may be affected not only by the variable X that it is intended to measure, but by other variables such as V and Z. Furthermore, these other variables may themselves be linked with X, so that it is by no means clear that X_i is always an appropriate indicator of X. The reasonableness of the indicator, or any set of indicators, may vary from situation to situation. Consider the four situations A, B, C, and D as represented in the models of Figure 3.5.

Although each of these situations could also be illustrated with reference to behaviors as indicators of internal states, let us consider the example of inequality measures of racial or ethnic discrimination. In setting A, suppose it is reasonable to assume that the *only* cause of inequality X_1, apart from idiosyncratic factors, is employer discrimination X. If so, we could very easily infer discrimination, provided that we collected a sufficient number of cases to eliminate the effects of sampling errors from

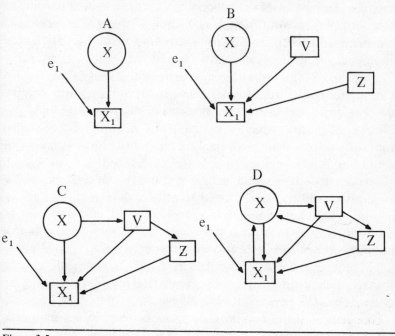

Figure 3.5

serious consideration. In situation B, however, most social scientists would agree that it would be advisable to obtain a "purified" or corrected measure of discrimination by controlling for V and Z, assuming that each of these variables could be perfectly measured. Perhaps V represents the educational inequality between white and black applicants and Z their experience differential. In setting B, then, we would adjust statistically for V and Z, perhaps by regressing X_1 on V and Z and then using the residuals to infer discrimination X (see Blalock and Wilken, 1979).

Suppose, however, that employer discrimination X (at earlier time periods) has directly affected the educational differentials V between whites and blacks, which has in turn affected applicants' opportunities to obtain prior work experience. This is the situation depicted in model C. In the still more complex situation D, past levels of inequality X_1 may have fed back to affect employer discrimination X, and perhaps it is also true that prior work experiences of whites and blacks have affected employer discrimination. How would we want to measure discrimination X in either of these latter situations?

A number of clarifications would be needed, as for example the distinction between current levels of discrimination and the earlier ones that may have affected V and Z. In D we would also want to distinguish between current and earlier levels of inequality since we are allowing for a feedback of earlier inequality to subsequent discrimination. Obviously, such distinctions would imply the need to collect data at several points in time. The major point, however, is that our measurement of discrimination will depend upon the model we use, and if this model becomes too complex we encounter the very real possibility that it will be underidentified. If so, we will be confronted with a difficult choice, with the temptation being to pretend that the complexities can be assumed away.

Likewise, if the necessary data to measure variables such as V and Z are unavailable, it may be tempting to pass the whole matter off with the disclaimer that, "of course, we would have liked to control for education and prior experience but were unable to do so." In short, we may hope that readers may not pay careful attention to the implicit assumptions. Or we may substitute imperfect indicators of V and Z, thereby ignoring the still more complex models in which V and Z have to be measured with errors that may be nonrandom. For instance, if we use "years of formal education" as our measure of "education," but if quality of education is lower for blacks than whites (as is often claimed), then our "control" for education in reality introduces an additional source of bias. Such a bias *might* possibly cancel with biases in the opposite direction, but perhaps it may amplify them. Without an adequate measurement-error theory, there will be no way of even predicting the directions of such biases, to say nothing of their magnitudes.

What are our options? One possibility is to confine our attention to situations such as A or B, saying nothing about more complex possibilities. This would be intellectually honest, but in doing so we run the risk of our study being "replicated" naively in settings such as C or D, without the investigator thinking through the implications of these more complex models. This is a very real danger whenever one takes too literally the advice to replicate using operationally identical common measures or to construct numerical indicators by using identical formulas or statistical procedures.

At the very least, we would recommend that even in simple settings such as A and B, the investigator state his or her assumptions explicitly, noting that in the particular setting studied some very simple assumptions seemed justified empirically. We also suggest that the investigator think through the implications of the measurement procedure for somewhat more complex situations, discussing how it would have to be modified in these situations. This second kind of cautionary note, if it were to become common practice, would not only alert other investigators to possible complications; it would also sensitize the original investigator to the need for studying these more complex situations and paying attention to the problem of generalizability in instances where measurement procedures would have to be modified. Clearly, no one can possibly anticipate all of the complexities that will occur in other settings, but attempts to examine realistic alternatives would be a step in the right direction.

Noncomparability With Respect to Alternative Behaviors

Regardless of whether or not behaviors are defined in terms of some motive or other internal state (e.g., aggression as behavior intended to injure someone), we recognize that there are often many alternative forms of the "same" behavior, or perhaps alternative means to the same objective. Furthermore, settings may differ with respect to the number of such alternatives that are available, practical, or legitimated. For instance, one may select among a number of occupations, all of which provide economic security or status. There are many forms of deviance or criminal behaviors. Political or other arenas for participation often permit several alternatives. Diverse recreational or religious alternatives may be available, with the number of specific forms of these alternatives being determined by a diversity of cultural or structural variables.

If we wish to obtain measures of such behaviors that are comparable across settings, we will be faced with a number of problems, including (1) that of arriving at reasonably complete lists of such behaviors, and therefore of deciding criteria for inclusion and exclusion that are comparable across settings; (2) deciding how to aggregate or to score these behaviors, when more than one are possible in each setting, implying a prior need to decide whether they combine additively, multiplicatively, or in some other fashion; and (3) deciding whether or not other variables in each setting need to be controlled, as discussed previously. If one were to use simplistic operational criteria, such as blindly insisting that only common behaviors be utilized, it is very likely that the measures used would be much more reasonable in one setting than in another. We suspect that, once again, measurement may be much more adequate in very simple settings than in complex ones.

Suppose, for instance, that in setting A there are four alternative forms of behavior (say, four forms of political participation or four occupations from which to choose). In setting B there may be nine alternatives, three of which are virtually identical to those in setting A. It would obviously be foolish to select only the three alternative behaviors common to both settings unless it were reasonable, theoretically, to redefine the conceptual variable more narrowly so as to include only these three alternatives as measures of the variable of interest. As the number of settings is increased, however, one would likely find that this particular strategy would become self-defeating, since it would require a lower level of abstraction, as well as increasing the likelihood of making highly misleading inferences across such settings. For example, if voting behavior became the only common indicator of political participation across seven nations, but if the importance of the vote in influencing election results varied considerably across these settings, the notion of "political participation" would seem to lose its meaning as a generic concept if it were made synonymous with voting. Similarly, if widely different forms of aggression were permitted across settings, with only a few forms found in common, then the limitation of measures of aggression to these few common forms would produce biased results in some of these settings.

If we assume, then, that proper measurement would require a reasonably complete listing of possible alternative forms within each setting, and that the lists in each setting will not be identical, how can we proceed once the lists have been constructed? Obviously, a reasonably clear theoretical definition of the variable of interest will be needed unless strictly ad hoc procedures are used. Let us consider several examples before proceeding.

Suppose we are trying to construct a "seriousness of delinquency" scale appropriate to several different societies. We obtain reasonably complete lists of types of delinquency in each society. Let us assume that we even have data available that tell us, for samples of individuals, how often they have engaged in each form of delinquency. Suppose that setting A contains many fewer types of delinquency than setting B, and that we wish to allow for the possibility that one form of delinquency may substitute for another in some sense. How would we obtain comparable scores in the two settings?

As a second example, suppose we are concerned with several different ways of gaining status within a community, but also with temporal or resource constraints on most actors. For instance, one way to gain status may be to become a successful surgeon. Another may be to operate a small business and to win high office in the local Chamber of Commerce. A third may be to use one's accumulated wealth to throw expensive parties and join important social organizations. A fourth may be to run for political office. Conceivably, an actor may attempt combinations of these means, but rarely will it be possible to use all of them. Furthermore, the nature of the constraints may vary from one setting to another. In a very large community it may be impossible to follow more than a single path, and furthermore it may be much less necessary to do so than in a second setting.

As our final example, let us consider political participation as an illustration of the more general class of participation measures that involve the notion that one may play a number of different roles, either simultaneously or sequentially. One may vote, give money, volunteer for services to political parties, write letters, join protest organizations, or seek offices of one kind or another. Suppose we wish to construct a single measure representing degree of political participation where the weights assigned to these several activities may not be constant from one setting to the next, or where there may be several distinct dimensions of participation that require different weighting schemes. For instance, one dimension may refer to the sheer amount of activity or energy invested, regardless of the impact it may have on some outcome, such as an election. A second dimension, however, may refer to the importance of the contribution, regardless of how much time or energy was involved.

In all of these examples, as soon as one is confronted with the several lists of alternative behaviors, one is also likely to recognize a need for clarifying the theoretical construct before proceeding. In the delinquency example, one might wish to distinguish seriousness from frequency of acts, just as one could distinguish among several dimensions of community status in our second illustration. Any weighting scheme or rule for aggregating the behaviors into a composite score will need to involve a set of *criteria* that depend upon these conceptualization efforts. In all three of our examples, for instance, it may be advisable to separate a sheer "quantity of behavior" dimension (e.g., number of deviant acts or duration of participation) from some "importance" or "intensity" or "seriousness" dimension.

The former type of dimension can presumably be scored much more easily than the second by simply counting the number of acts or recording their duration. Of course, in order to do so it becomes necessary to have a virtually complete and non-over-lapping list of behavioral alternatives in each setting.

An importance, seriousness, or intensity dimension, however, requires much more careful conceptualization. In particular, it will be necessary to decide whether to weigh the items on the basis of *subjective* assessments by relevant judges or to use some outcome criterion on which the several behaviors might be regressed in order to obtain the proper weights. Two important points can be made about these measurement processes. First, the "comparability" assessment across settings should involve the similarity of the *processes* of obtaining the weights rather than the identity of the weights themselves. Using identical weights across settings requires either an implicit or an explicit theory to the effect that the variables that affect these weights take on similar values in all such settings. Few social scientists would want to accept such an assumption without empirical evidence. Second, the criteria for obtaining these weights need to be tied very closely to the theoretical definition of the concept being measured. In principle, the theoretical definition should clearly imply the nature of such criteria.

If the theoretical criterion involves some kinds of subjective judgment of seriousness, status, or importance, then the pro-cesses used in each setting will require one to use some sample of appropriate actors to provide the weights. For instance, the seriousness of different types of delinquent acts might be judged by a random sample of adults, by persons in positions of authority, or perhaps by actual victims of these acts. There might or might not be close agreement among these diverse kinds of judges, in which case one might want to build the degree of consensus on weights into the theory as a separate variable.

If an "objective" criterion were used to derive the weights, such a criterion would also have to be comparable across settings, if indeed this were possible to achieve. Or there might be multiple criteria, with different sets of weights obtained for each. If so, the similarity of weights across such criteria might also vary by setting, with weight similarity perhaps being an additional variable that would need to be considered in one's theory. For instance, if the contributions of diverse behaviors to several different outcome variables could be assessed, it is entirely possible that one set of behaviors would require large weights for one type of outcome but lesser weights for another. If so, actors might experience role stresses or "inconsistent" performance ratings that might not occur in different settings. Thus, if there are multiple objective criteria or differential subjective assessments of the several behaviors, but if only a single criterion is used in one's measures, comparisons across settings may be misleading.

If distinct behaviors are being aggregated, as for example when different types of delinquent acts are weighted and summed, one must also be careful that the aggregating function is appropriate. Most commonly, as we have implied, such aggregate scores are obtained through an adding process, implying that alternative behaviors are interchangeable when appropriately weighted. That is, a given amount of money contributed to a political campaign counts the same as a fixed number of hours committed to "doorbelling" or telephoning voters. Or so many units of occupational prestige can be exchanged for a particular position within an important organization, or perhaps a given income. As a first approximation, such additive aggregation operations may indeed be reasonable, but several other simple alternatives should also be considered.

One possibility is that the separate behaviors combine multiplicatively, implying that someone who uses a diversity of behaviors will obtain a considerably higher score than someone who concentrates heavily on a single behavior. In effect, bonus points are given to the "all around" performer in contrast to the specialist. In the extreme case, if there are k different behaviors, it might be necessary to engage in all of these forms in order to receive a high score. Each behavior may, however, receive a different weight, as represented in the multiplicative equation

$$Y = kX_1^{\alpha_1} X_2^{\alpha_2} \ldots X_k^{\alpha_k}$$

where Y represents the total score, the X_i represent levels of behaviors of each type, and the exponents α_i represent weights. In this very simple type of equation, a score of zero on any behavioral dimension would yield a total score of zero unless the weight for this dimension were taken to be zero. In different settings we would expect different weights for each dimension, and if a certain form of behavior were irrelevant in a particular setting we could take care of this possibility by setting the corresponding alpha equal to zero. This illustrates the point that comparability does not require identical weights across all settings, provided that the weights have been obtained by comparable operations, such as deriving them from judges' estimates.

A second kind of possibility—perhaps a very realistic one for many kinds of alternative behaviors—is that there is a diminishing returns phenomenon in operation through which a high score on one dimension is sufficient to obtain a high overall score, regardless of one's scores on the other behavioral dimensions. This nonlinear model is not the same as one that permits the substitution of one form for another, but instead is one that may give the highest scores to the specialist. Again, allowing for unequal weights among behavioral dimensions and standardizing every variable so that its upper limit is 1.0, such a situation could be represented by the equation (or weighting scheme)

$$1 - Y = (1 - X_1)^{\alpha_1} (1 - X_2)^{\alpha_2} \ldots (1 - X_k)^{\alpha_k}$$
$$Y = 1 - (1 - X_1)^{\alpha_1} (1 - X_2)^{\alpha_2} \ldots (1 - X_k)^{\alpha_k} \quad \text{or}$$

For instance, if someone performed close to the maximum level on X_1, then the term $(1 - X_1)$ would be very close to zero, and unless α_1 were also very close to zero, the entire product term would be close to zero, making Y very close to unity, its upper limit.

It is even possible that the functional form of the aggregating function could differ from one setting to the next, being additive in setting A and multiplicative in B. One would hope, however, that a suitable general function could be constructed allowing for parameter values that vary from setting to setting. Presumably, one would want to conduct a series of pilot methodological studies in each setting to determine what kind of function to use, and whether or not to expect widely divergent weights. For instance, if weights were being determined by judges, as seems appropriate in both the seriousness of delinquency and status illustrations, the judges could be presented with a set of criteria, singly and in combination, and asked how serious (or prestigeful) the act or set of acts would be. Magnitude estimation techniques might be used, for example, by setting a standard act (say, stealing a TV set worth $200) equal to a given score (say, 10) and then asking judges to provide scores for other single acts (skipping school or committing rape) or act combinations (such as stealing the TV *and* committing the rape). One could then assess whether combinations of acts are more appropriately scored in an additive, multiplicative, or other fashion. Once more, it is essential that the *process* of obtaining the weights be sufficiently explicit so that it can be applied in diverse settings.

A CAUTION ON BIASES

In concluding this chapter, it is important to emphasize that intellectual blinders or ideological biases may cause one to omit important complications from one's measurement-error model. In the case of effect-indicator models, as illustrated in the discrimination-inequality example, the temptation may be to rule out alternative causes of the effect indicator that one would prefer to ignore. For instance, if the behavior of the minority itself affects inequality levels, it may be convenient to leave this variable out of one's analysis by pretending that, for example, whites and blacks have been perfectly matched on all relevant variables so that inequality scores may be equated with employer discrimination. Such a potential bias may have different consequences across settings, however. It may be a very reasonable assumption in setting A, but not in B. Therefore, one cannot automatically assume that where such biases exist, they will have equal implications for measurement in all settings. Likewise, if for any reason one were to leave out certain kinds of delinquent behaviors (say, marijuana use) from one's aggregate measure, this may have a differential impact from one setting or type of individual to the next. For this reason, it is again important to emphasize the necessity of explicit theoretical formulations that lay open to public inspection exactly what assumptions are being made in each measurement decision.

NOTES

1. For nontechnical discussions of the multiple-indicator approach, see Costner (1969) and Namboodiri et al. (1975). More technical discussions can be found in Goldberger and Duncan (1973), Hauser and Goldberger (1971) and Jöreskog (1970).

2. Note that our own usage of the term "reference indicator" is somewhat more restrictive than that implied by Schoenberg or Wiley.

3. Kim and Ferree (1981) point out that *some* variables are appropriately standardized prior to one's analysis. Following Hargens (1976), they note that standardization may be justified whenever comparisons are made according to criteria that are unique to each setting. For example, prestige ratings may be compared by locating individuals in relation to means and standard deviations unique to each group.

4. This point will be discussed in greater detail in Chapter 4.

CHAPTER 4

CATEGORICAL VARIABLES, CONCEPTUALIZATION, AND COMPARABILITY

The current chapter is concerned with a number of conceptualization problems involving the use of categorical variables. A major thesis throughout the chapter—and one that will recur in the remaining chapters as well—is that one of the most important roadblocks to successful conceptualization in the social sciences has been our tendency to rest content with descriptions and data analyses that do not grapple with the assessment of dimensionality but instead rely very heavily on categorical data and discussions of named categories that are multidimensional in nature.

There are undoubtedly many reasons why sociology and political science appear to have followed this path to a much greater extent than psychology and economics, although all of the social sciences share the tendency to varying degrees. In part, the phenomenon may be seen as a function of the "maturity" of a discipline, if one accepts the thesis that sciences pass through stages of development that can be examined roughly in terms of the degree to which the science relies very heavily on historical, descriptive, classificatory accounts in contrast with the much more deductive efforts that involve what Northrop (1947) referred to as "concepts by postulation."

Given the great emphasis on the interpretation of historical events and the description of current phenomena of (passing) applied interest which constitute the bulk of the sociological literature, it is no wonder that categorical data and classificatory schemes have been so popular among sociologists. It will be our thesis, however, that unless dimensionality issues are seriously addressed, and unless our aspiration levels for measurement accuracy are considerably raised, it will remain virtually impossible to make progress in assessing comparability or in developing and testing theories of a reasonably general level. The sections that follow examine this assertion from several different perspectives.

NONCOMPARABILITY DUE TO MULTIDIMENSIONALITY OF CONCRETE SITUATIONS

Analyses using nominal scales and categorical data have always been popular in sociology, political science, and certain kinds of social psychological research. Yet nominal scales present formidable problems of theoretical interpretation once one moves beyond simple dichotomies. One of the reasons for this fact is that more often than not, the use of such nominal categories and associated data-analysis techniques encourages conceptual laziness and undue attention to concrete "named" groupings, such as regions of a country, types of industries, religious denominations, occupational categories, or specific political issues or even named candidates. Comparability questions are then almost impossible to handle, except on a very intuitive basis or with reference to some overly simplistic "proxy" variable, such as community size or geographic proximity. In most such instances, it is even difficult to know how to begin to get a conceptual or theoretical handle on the problem.

Consider a number of examples of comparability problems stemming from the use of named categories. In attitudinal research or studies of community power structure, the focus of attention is often on specific concrete "issues," such as the Equal Rights Amendment, mandatory school busing, abortion, urban renewal, health insurance, the construction of a major bridge, or the election of a specific candidate for office. Such issues are often very convenient to study because people have real opinions about them, political forces take sides, and various actors engage in specific actions that may be compared with their expressed attitudes. Sponsoring agencies are interested in public opinion regarding these concrete issues rather than more general dimensions they are presumed to tap. Also, at the time of the study they often seem to be extremely important and much more general in their implications than they are perceived to be in retrospect a decade or so later, or by observers who are reasonably far removed from the scene. Furthermore, in some respects they are indeed similar to other issues that have been of importance elsewhere. Because they are "hot topics," it always seems advisable to study them quickly while they are still relevant. Given budgetary limitations, however, the survey research team or participant observers focus their primary attention on these particular issues. The result is a research report that is rich in specific details but that involves a very low level of abstraction. When another somewhat comparable situation is later studied, there is no good way to compare the two results, since the issues have changed.

As a second example, consider the number of ad hoc groupings of organizations, social clubs, work assignments, and environmental settings that enter into our theories as exogenous or background factors somehow or another related to experience variables. We recognize that Methodists brought up in rural North Carolina are in some ways similar to Methodists raised in a medium-sized city in Ohio, but we are not quite sure how or why, and so we enter "Methodist" as a dummy variable into a regression equation and hope that something will come out of it. Or we expect that "professionals" will have relatively similar role experiences, regardless of specific occupation, and we even hope that this will be true across national boundaries. We lump the Kiwanis and Rotary Clubs together as "civic associations," in contrast with religious or business groupings. And we assume that Congregationalists, Southern Baptists, and Quakers are sufficiently similar to be lumped together as Protestants, whose voting behaviors may then be compared with those of Catholics and Jews. If we compare the results of a study with those of a replication conducted, say, a decade later, we cross our fingers and hope that the results are comparable as long as the labels for these categories have not changed.

Whenever group properties are being compared, it is often necessary to chop these groups up into smaller subunits in order to obtain heterogeneity measures, such as indicators of inequality or segregation. Thus, cities are subdivided into census tracts, political wards, school districts, or blocks. States are divided into counties of very unequal sizes and shapes. Nations are divided into states, provinces, cantons, or other political districts. Complex organizations are subdivided into departments, divisions, branches, or whatever. The social scientist must take these subunits—and the criteria used to create them—as given in spite of the fact that all sorts of historical or ad hoc factors may have been responsible, initially, for the subdivisions.

It will be possible to obtain simple measures of group size, with which the subunits can be compared. But in other respects, issues of comparability will be very much in doubt. It will often be convenient to sidestep the issue, either by not mentioning it at all or by expressing a concern to the reader and then ignoring the fact in one's actual data analysis. A more conservative approach, empirically, is to analyze the different data sets completely separately, leaving it to the reader to make comparability inferences if he or she wishes. Thus one may write separate chapters on each of five different countries, communities, or religious denominations without ever attempting to integrate or compare the findings.

In all of these kinds of situations, the basic problem arises because of the multidimensionality of the nominal variable. Any reasonably complex political issues, for example, will involve at least three or four distinct dimensions, which means that if a metric were available it would have to be described or located in terms of a k dimensional vector. A second issue might differ substantially from the first along, say, three of these

dimensions but be extremely close to it along a fourth. Someone who is primarily interested in this fourth dimension—say,
an ardent feminist to whom women's issues are much more
salient than any others—may classify the two issues together as
being highly similar, whereas someone else might perceive them
as being very different. A smallest-space analysis used to assess
similarities along a number of such dimensions might help to
resolve this kind of problem, provided that the number of
distinct dimensions were not too large. But such dimensional
assessments are rarely made for many of our most important
nominal variables, and in fact cannot be made unless the number of categories is reasonably large relative to the number of
dimensions that underlie the categorization scheme.

The only plausible way to come to grips with comparability
issues in connection with nominal-scale variables such as these
would appear to require some sort of dimensionality assessment, no matter how crude it may be initially. In order to make
any grouping decisions, as for example to combine issue areas,
religious denominations, or communities, it is obviously necessary to make similarity judgments that are either explicit or
implicit or else based on some ad hoc criterion such as geographic proximity or popular labels. Where the number of initial
categories is relatively small, the issue may be sidestepped by
treating each category as distinct, but obviously this will
become unmanageable once the number of categories reaches
forty or fifty, at which point some grouping or scoring criterion
will inevitably be invoked.

The danger of imposing one or two dimensions on the nominal groupings is that whatever labels we attach to the continua
that are created, they are likely to be confounded with other
closely correlated dimensions that may in fact suggest very
different theoretical interpretations. Thus, religious denominations may be ordered with respect to fundamentalism, which
may turn out to be closely associated with rankings they might
have received had they been rated by prestige, or an ordering of
occupations by prestige may be very similar to an ordering by
power or average educational level. Counties ordered along a

rural-urban continuum may be very similarly ordered according to political liberalism or cosmopolitanism, and so forth. If one then refers to these variables as religious fundamentalism, occupational prestige, or urban-rural background, the interpretations given to the results may be quite different from those that referred to religious prestige, occupational power, or community cosmopolitanism. We shall discuss this problem of the confounding of unmeasured dimensions in greater detail in Chapter 6.

The analyst dealing with a complex, multidimensional setting or contextual variable is faced with a basic dilemma. It may be treated as a nominal scale, as for example in analysis of covariance or dummy-variable analysis. This will result in greater "explained variance" (assuming the categories are not collapsed) than if the categories are scored in some fashion and these scores entered into the equation system. The latter scores, implying some stronger set of assumptions regarding dimensionality, will be more easily interpretable. Such interpretations, however, may be misleading to the extent that one ignores other dimensions or variables highly correlated with the ones that have been selected. For example, one may think in terms of "occupations" as unordered categories, or of "occupational prestige." The latter orientation implies a theory of how the "occupations" operate to affect the dependent variable, say, political liberalism. This theory may be more implicit than explicit until other investigators attempt to order or score the categories in a slightly different fashion and provide competing explanations for the phenomenon in question. Such is beginning to occur in the case of the "status attainment" literature (Horan, 1978; Wright, 1978; and Udy, 1980), but there can be very long intervals during which a given ordering criterion completely dominates the empirical literature.

Therefore, the move toward ordering or scoring categorical variables is subject to risks. It is difficult to imagine how the comparability question can ever be resolved, however, until efforts are made to try out alternative dimensions and to investigate their empirical interrelationships. This suggests the strategy of scoring or ordering the categories, say, religious denominations, in several different ways, and seeing whether or not there are substantial differences in one's empirical results. This requires that the number of categories is reasonably large before grouping them, implying the advisability of working initially with fine-grained categories of occupations, religious denominations, or territorial units, and combining these into smaller numbers of categories only after careful empirical investigations.

A more atheoretical or exploratory approach can also be used as a form of sensitivity analysis to assess the degree to which different categorization schemes really make a difference in one's analysis. For instance, if the counties in one state are much smaller and more numerous than in another state, one can pretend that they are roughly the same size by combining adjacent counties in the former state and redoing the analysis. Or one can gradually reduce the fine-grained nature of a detailed occupational categorization scheme to see whether this has any important impact on other coefficients when "occupation" is controlled. This kind of approach is in fact being used increasingly in connection with the occupation variable, but it does not seem to have been utilized at all systematically in many other fields, as for example in the study of religious denominations, the "contextual effects" literature, or in cross-cultural analyses of political systems.

INTERPRETING CATEGORICAL DATA

Let us make what appears to be a reasonable philosophical assumption about the scientific enterprise, namely that any "laws" that we may discover are partly a function of our own conceptualization and measurement processes. Just as it would be meaningless to ask about a law interrelating pressure, volume, and temperature of gases without having first defined these three concepts, it is also nonsensical to ask whether or not the relationship between, say, domestic violence and industrialization is linear unless both of these latter concepts have been given operational meaning.

If all of the variables appearing in a theoretical formulation have been precisely defined such that ratio-scale measurement has been attained, one may then make a restricted set of permissible transformations that allow one to state the law in mathematically equivalent forms. For example, in the very simple case of a linear equation $Y = a + bX$, if one prefers to express X in terms of pennies rather than dollars, one knows exactly how the slope coefficient must be modified so as to express exactly the same law in terms of the new X units. Likewise, if one were to subtract 10 from each Y value, one could adjust the intercept coefficient accordingly. Or if one wanted to redefine X as, say, log Z, or as $W + 3W^2$, the same law could be rewritten as $Y = a + b \log Z$, or as $Y = a + b (W + 3W^2)$, in which case Y would no longer be a linear function of either Z or W.

With strictly ordinal data we are much less restricted in terms of the numbers of possible transformations, but this also means that our deductive apparatus will be much less powerful. Furthermore, certain kinds of questions no longer make sense, and, although we may ask whether the relationship between two ordinal variables is monotonic, it is meaningless to inquire about linearity or any other specific form of a monotonic relationship, such as a logarithmic one. When our measurement slips to the level of ordinality, we also lose the ability to answer what would otherwise be meaningful questions about the laws we would wish to establish. This is why we are eager to push up the level of measurement, if not to that of an interval scale, then at least to that of an ordered metric in which distances between points along a continuum can themselves be ordered. For instance, with ordered-metric variables it becomes possible to make crude tests for threshold or satiation types of non-linearity. I have argued elsewhere (Blalock, 1974) that some variables that are often treated as ordinal—variables such as relative power or prestige—may in fact be measured at this ordered-metric level and thus weak tests made of hypotheses relating to different monotonic forms of nonlinearity.

What happens when we have only categorical variables for which no ordering is implied? Clearly, as we all recognize, our results will depend on the categorization scheme—such things as how many categories we use, our choice of cutpoints, the number of ties, our marginal distributions, and measurement errors in assigning individuals to categories. But can we say much more than this? In what sense can we say that one categorization scheme is "transformed" into another? When we collapse categories creating a smaller dimensional table from a larger one, what theoretical or methodological principles, if any, can we invoke? And if categorization decisions are treated as arbitrary or a matter of convenience, how can we assess comparability across different settings, or, for that matter, across different categorization schemes? If one obtains more or less the same results when categorization schemes vary, this provides a degree of reassurance. But what if one does not? What can one say, other than noting that the results differ and then attempting an ad hoc explanation for this difference? And if different schemes are used, is there anything analogous to a mathematical transformation that can enable one to decide whether or not the "laws" also differ?

It is my distinct impression, based on readings of numerous articles in the sociological literature but not a detailed content analysis of them, that whenever investigators rely on categorical data, questions such as these are seldom asked. Authors will note that certain decisions about categorization have been made, that these have had to be somewhat arbitrary and based on data-availability considerations, and that (perhaps) several alternative categorization schemes have been tried. But once the analysis begins, investigators often treat marginal distributions as given and fail to ask what the implications might have been had the X or Y marginals differed. Nor do they ask questions concerning constraints upon these marginals imposed either by the investigator or by "reality." Such constraining factors are not built into the theoretical model or equation system, except sometimes as control variables. The most sophisticated literature on this subject within sociology stems from the analysis of mobility tables, where efforts are sometimes made to separate out "structural mobility" (evidenced by different marginal totals for, say, sons and fathers) from what might be termed net or "true" mobility (Pullum, 1975). Even this literature, however, pays surprisingly little attention to the question of how the *investigator's* choice of categories or cutpoints may also constrain these marginals.

Many categorical schemes used by social scientists are, of course, imposed upon us by others who have collected our data, or by the labels that are commonly used to pigeon-hole individuals, organizations, or territorially based units. Thus, it is relatively easy to categorize respondents according to their religious denominations, whereas the distinction between "fundamentalists" and "nonfundamentalists" is much less clear-cut. Likewise, sociologists can be distinguished from political scientists according to the field in which they received their doctorates, or the department in which they are employed, whereas it is much more difficult to categorize different kinds of sociologists. Persons who reside in the same politically defined territory can rather easily be distinguished from those who live in a different one, whereas their "subcultures" or "contexts" cannot.

Given the obvious need to cut corners with respect to data collection, data analysis, and theoretical interpretations, it is no wonder that categorical data analyses are highly popular. It is also no surprise, however, that issues of comparability and generalizability are sidestepped or discussed in highly concrete terms, as for example a discussion of specific occupations in a very delimited number of nations. In short, the level of abstraction tends to remain low and discussions of measurement error are confined to matters relating to classification errors and ambiguities in classifying cases close to category boundaries.

Human behaviors are practically always highly constrained, so that actors can seldom locate themselves close to their ideal points. Thus one may have to select among five specific jobs or three places of residence or perhaps a dozen potential spouses. Whenever multidimensional criteria are involved, as for example five or six characteristics of occupations, the actor must then select a single concrete option, or perhaps combine at most two or three. The investigator recording only a few such choices for each subject or respondent is therefore basically in a position of having far too little information concerning the actual preferences of these actors, or what the distribution of choices would have been had there been a large number of replications and a different set of concrete options. As a result, it is usually most convenient to lump these constrained alternatives together according to a categorical scheme and then to *classify* (rather than score) the individual into one of a small number of categories.

But how are these categories selected, how are somewhat different behaviors or characteristics lumped together, and what labels get attached to these categories? Here we clearly need a series of ethnomethodological studies designed to examine the everyday behaviors of social scientists or others who make these decisions. As Udy (1980) has suggested, the tendency of sociologists to classify occupations along a prestige dimension may well have been due, initially, to the convenience of the Edwards scheme and its early adoption and use by the Census Bureau. The various and highly diverse set of Protestant denominations are, we presume, often grouped together because of the historical accident that they all had somewhat similar common roots, although presumably these communalities will be much less relevant for some theoretical purposes than for others. And some of our "ethnic groups" are now classed together because of a policy decision made in Washington to lump them together for affirmative action purposes. One often finds it difficult to obtain data that would permit a disaggregation of the diverse category of persons classified as "Asian American" or as "Hispanic." Therefore, "ethnicity" is usually treated as a categorical variable in data analyses, although the investigator might prefer otherwise.

Even where the disaggregated data are available, however, there is a strong tendency to combine categories in conventional ways—perhaps to achieve "face comparability"—without thinking through the implications of this categorization process for theoretical analyses in which continuous variables would ideally play an important role. Thus, if ethnic groups vary in terms of status, differential opportunities, or the possession of specific kinds of resources, one may be unable to uncover this information on the basis of a classification scheme that has obscured such differences among, say, "Asian Americans" or "Hispanics." The same applies, of course, to all kinds of occupations that have been lumped together under the title of "Professional."

It will obviously be impossible to discuss questions such as these by referring to more than a few types of specific variables or classification schemes. Instead, we shall focus on a series of methodological points that seem to apply to a variety of these more specific variables. The primary aim is to encourage the reader to ask these and similar questions of his or her favorite categorical variable, whether this be a background factor, a current contextual variable, a choice behavior, or a characteristic of a macro unit.

COLLAPSING DECISIONS AND MARGINAL DISTRIBUTIONS

Decisions about one's categorization scheme usually involve a peculiar mixture of at least four ingredients: (1) practical data availability considerations; (2) already existent labels or categories; (3) some notion of similarity, which may be multidimensional; and (4) expected or actual marginal distributions. Having already commented, very briefly, about the first two of these factors, let us concentrate in this section on the remaining two, though recognizing that our fundamental difficulty in coming to grips with how one treats such data consists of the high degree of likelihood that these four factors will contribute to the categorization process *in an unknown way,* so that the exact rationale for the final scheme will usually be difficult for even the investigator to specify. Yet, as we shall argue, one's interpretation of a given set of data may very well depend upon the assumptions made about this categorization process. At least this will be true to the extent that one attempts to go beyond the immediate data at hand in an effort to supply a theoretical interpretation in terms of another set of variables that have not been directly measured by the classification scheme.

To simplify our problem, it will be convenient to assume that the researcher begins with a very fine-grained set of categories, as for example a detailed set of several thousand occupational categories or a complete listing of all religious denominations and sects. In other words, we shall assume that these categories have already been named and that the individuals within them are completely homogeneous with respect to whatever latent variables we may have in mind. We may then ask, "By what process are these categories *combined* into a much smaller number, let us say 15 or 20?" In this way we assume away the problem of data availability. Let us also assume, probably unrealistically, that the investigator ignores the existence of any popular labels or readily available classification schemes and that respondents—if they have been asked to classify themselves—are likewise uninfluenced by these schemes.

Even under these idealized conditions, we would anticipate that the resultant classification will be an unknown combination of two kinds of considerations, namely some (multidimensional) similarity judgments and either an expected or an actual frequency distribution. It is this constraining of marginal distributions in poorly understood ways that, we shall argue, presents formidable problems of interpretation. Before elaborating on this point, let us contrast it with one in which the investigator is dealing with a relatively simple ratio scale, such as age. Assuming that ages will not be grouped, one simply takes the distribution of ages as given and does not modify any of them according to whether or not they are empirically rare or numerous. As a result, the variance of age is completely determined by one's data and the metric (e.g., years) that has been used.

Where we are dealing with two such interval or ratio scales and, say, a linear relationship of the form $Y = a + bX + e$, where we make the usual assumptions about the disturbance term e required for ordinary least squares, we then know that we may express the variance in the dependent variable Y as a function of three quantities σ_x^2, σ_e^2 and b, as follows:

$$\sigma_y^2 = b^2 \sigma_x^2 + \sigma_e^2$$

since, by assumption, X and e are uncorrelated. If we were to categorize both X and Y, we would expect that the Y marginals would be a function of the X marginals. But for such categorized data, would we have any way of explaining these Y marginals, causally, in terms of the variance in the disturbance term and a slope coefficient? These latter quantities would, of course, be unknowns and would be confounded together and expressable only as conditional probabilities (Blalock, 1976). Thus, for categorized variables we have only three quantities: row and column marginals and cell frequencies which can be transformed into estimates of conditional probabilities. We have lost the fourfold distinction among dispersions in X and Y, the variance in a disturbance term, and a separate slope coefficient that is determined by an empirical process, as well as our choice of units of measurement. Clearly, something has been sacrificed in the process of categorization.

Although neither sociologists nor political scientists are accustomed to paying much attention to the estimation of slope coefficients, this confounding of two totally different quantities in categorical analyses has profound implications for the maturation of the discipline. Especially as one attempts to increase the scope of one's generalizations, it becomes essential to examine slope differences across settings, for reasons already discussed. But it is also decreasingly likely that variances in error terms will remain equal across very diverse settings. Therefore, it becomes absolutely essential to separate out these two very different sources of variation in one's dependent variable.

Put differently, conditional probabilities—the building blocks of categorical analyses—are functions of error variances in variables that have been totally neglected by one's theory. This is not a very happy circumstance to be in unless one is in a position to make some rather strong assumptions about these omitted variables. It is often difficult enough to justify *covariance* assumptions about these disturbance terms. The added assumption that their variances are equal across settings will be virtually impossible to justify on theoretical grounds. Yet without such an assumption, even with ordinal data one cannot interpret slope analogues—such as Somers's d_{yx}—as yielding comparable estimates of true slopes (Blalock, 1976).

If we assume that Y is causally dependent on X plus a number of unknown variables whose effects are summed in the disturbance term e, then it seems reasonable to think in terms of Y marginals that are produced by the following idealized process. We first decide upon the categories for both X and Y. If there were implicit interval scales underlying both X and Y, this would amount to deciding upon the sizes of the intervals defining the class boundaries of the categories of both X and Y. The X marginals could then either be considered random variables or might be fixed by design, for example, by selecting a stratified sample in which the number of cases in each X category has been predetermined. We then think in terms of conditional probabilities p_{ij} representing the probability of being in the ith row (representing the ith category of Y), given that one is in the jth column (or the jth category of X). The Y marginals would then be determined from the X marginals and these conditional probabilities by summing across each row. The entire table could be displayed as follows:

	X categories					
	X_1	X_2	X_3	$\ldots$	X_c	
Y_1	$p_{11}\ N_{.1}$	$p_{12}\ N_{.2}$	$p_{13}\ N_{.3}$	$\ldots$	$p_{1c}\ N_{.c}$	$N_{1.}$
Y_2	$p_{21}\ N_{.1}$	$p_{22}\ N_{.2}$	$p_{23}\ N_{.3}$	$\ldots$	$p_{2c}\ N_{.c}$	$N_{2.}$
Y_3	$p_{31}\ N_{.1}$	$p_{32}\ N_{.2}$	$p_{33}\ N_{.3}$	$\ldots$	$p_{3c}\ N_{.c}$	$N_{3.}$
$\vdots$	$\vdots$	$\vdots$	$\vdots$		$\vdots$	$\vdots$
Y_r	$p_{r1}\ N_{.1}$	$p_{r2}\ N_{.2}$	$p_{r3}\ N_{.33}$		$p_{rc}\ N_{.c}$	$N_{r.}$
	$N_{.1}$	$N_{.2}$	$N_{.3}$	$\ldots$	$N_{.c}$	$N_{..}$

(Y categories label on left side)

Thus we would obtain the first Y marginal by summing, getting

$$N_{1.} = \Sigma_j\ P_{1j}N_{.j}$$

and so forth for the remaining Y marginals. These Y marginals would be "constrained" only in the sense that they were determined from the X marginals and the conditional probabilities. One would not know these Y marginals, however, unless the X marginals were given.

Categorical analyses that take cell frequencies as functions of marginal totals, plus a term representing the relationship between X and Y, seem to involve a peculiar kind of inversion of what we are taking, here, to be the causal processes at work.[1] We are taking the Y marginals to be *dependent*, rather than given, just as in the case of the linear model we take the variance in Y as a function of the variance in X, the variance in the disturbance term, and the slope coefficient (squared). The only difference is that we have replaced the latter two terms by the conditional probabilities of being in a particular Y category, given X. Notice that we are taking the categorization scheme as predetermined, just as we assume that the units on X and Y have been determined prior to obtaining the distributions of either X or Y.

Regardless of the rationale for taking cell frequencies as functions of *both* marginals—a rationale that we believe needs further justification—it seems clear that if the investigator bases the categorization scheme for Y on some predetermined criterion regarding marginal totals (e.g., forcing a split at the median or quartiles), something peculiar is taking place that does not have a direct counterpart in the regression model. Returning to our example of the decision process through which, say, occupations are categorized, it is clear that any such decision must inevitably constrain one's marginals in a way that ungrouped ages are not constrained. This is true because one must end up with a finite number of categories, no matter how many. In practice, one will also want to group the occupations in such a way that there will not be too few cases in each of the categories. Whether this is done completely ex post facto or on the basis of prior information, this implies that the resulting empirical frequencies will be partly a function of a choice of cutpoints not determined by theoretical considerations alone.

Unfortunately, it will usually be impossible to assess the *degree* to which such a constraint is operative. As we have noted, the marginals will be partly a function of "reality" and partly a function of decisions that have been based on a knowledge of this reality! Sometimes, of course, marginals will be determined by the investigator's choice of cutpoints, as for example when a distribution of scores is divided into quantiles. To the extent that this has been the explicit intent of the investigator, we therefore know in advance what the distribution of marginals will be. Thus, the analogue of either σ_x^2 or σ_y^2 will have been totally constrained. But if the investigator "eyeballs" an empirical frequency distribution and collapses categories to get a "sufficient" number of cases in each row or column, it will be next to impossible to assess the degree to which these marginals have been constrained. How would we compare several data sets for which different investigators have used similar, but rather vague, classification procedures?

Quite aside from this matter of combining categories according to expected or actual marginal totals is the question of *which* categories are sufficiently similar to be combined. Judgments of this sort obviously depend upon either some explicit procedure (such as cluster or smallest-space analysis) for assessing similarity or, more likely, a subjective assessment based on an implicit weighting of latent dimensions. For instance, why are psychologists and sociologists lumped together? Why doctors and dentists? Electricians and plumbers? Or nurses and teachers or farm managers and farm laborers? If the rationale for classification is explicitly based on a single dimension, then of course the categories may be ranked along this dimension and the level of measurement considered at least ordinal.

Presumably, it is because of the *multidimensionality* implicit behind the classification scheme that one is unwilling to treat the categories in ordinal fashion. But if so, how does one justify the classification scheme in the first place? By what criteria were the subcategories combined? How was "similarity" assessed, if not by applying implicit or explicit weights to a set of underlying dimensions? In other words, if one takes the categories as given in the first place, one may not be too unhappy about treating the categories as unordered. But if one treats them as problematic, it is difficult to reach any conclusion other than that the picture is theoretically confusing. In the face of this, it is no wonder that from the standpoint of a strictly statistical analysis, it is most convenient to leave the categorization process unexamined. But will this not have implications for one's interpretations of the data, and in terms of one's ability to assess problems of generalizability and comparability? Indeed it will.

The problem we are concerned with here can also be seen as one of aggregation, where the aggregating or grouping criterion has not been made explicit. As will be stressed in Chapter 7, if the criterion for aggregation is not simply related to the variables that appear in one's theory, it will be almost impossible to get a clear understanding of what the implications of aggregation will be (Hannan, 1971; Irwin and Lichtman, 1976). We may anticipate that aggregation of categories will produce the same kind of confounding as occurs when individuals are grouped according to spatial criteria that are complexly related to unmeasured causes of whatever dependent variable is being examined (Blalock, 1979b). At least in these latter instances the grouping criterion—spatial proximity—is known, though difficult to interpret theoretically.

Efforts to make the categorization process explicit appear to be necessary as a first step, though certainly not a sufficient one. Therefore, we recommend self-conscious attempts to state these criteria as carefully as possible, even where they are initially poorly understood. Doing so may also make it somewhat easier to answer the question, "Are categorization schemes comparable across different settings, even in instances where the same categories have been used?" Needless to say, this task will be a difficult one and should probably first be attempted with a relatively small number of our most frequently used categorical variables.

CONSTRAINTS IMPOSED BY SOCIAL DEFINITIONS AND DATA COLLECTORS

The social scientist is rarely in the ideal position of having available a large number of categories to be collapsed in a diversity of ways. In the first place, there will be constraints imposed in terms of the ways in which actors are categorized socially. That is, certain categories will be defined as "real" by the actors themselves, so that attitudes and behaviors will be influenced by these social definitions. Sociologists are sufficiently socialized to the importance of these social definitions so that we would hardly be tempted to impose our own arbitrary classifications on the data if these were not compatible with those that have been socially defined as real. Second, even where there is no ambiguity as to the "reality" of one's classification scheme, it is often the case that the data analyst will be constrained by the way the data have been collected: the way items have been worded, the forced choices made available to the respondent, or the set of category codes used to delineate background information.

In the case of the first type of constraint, we may admit that whenever category boundaries have been clearly defined socially, they should certainly be used in the empirical and theoretical analysis, though perhaps alongside other, more analytical classificatory schemes. This is especially true whenever these social definitions are considered to influence behaviors. For instance, if "blacks" are defined as a discrete category in the United States but not in Brazil, or if distinctions are made among orthodox, conservative, and reformed Jews in one setting but not in another, these facts will probably be relevant in helping to explain other differences between the respective settings. This suggests incorporating into one's data analysis and theory variables that tap the *degree* to which boundaries are more or less clear or relevant to the phenomena being explained. One problem, however, may be that different actors within the same setting may be using somewhat different social definitions. Some may distinguish among, say, orthodox and reformed Jews, whereas others may not.

Ideally, then, in instances where we expect social definitions involving labels or categories to be important, our theories need to take account of these definitions in some fashion. Usually, however, it will be difficult to collect the detailed information needed to make these assessments with any degree of accuracy. If so, then as part of either the substantive theory or one's auxiliary measurement theory, we would need to address at least the following two questions:

(1) To what degree are category boundaries clearly defined by the relevant actors, and do these social definitions coincide with those we are using?; and

(2) If these social definitions are relevant to the phenomenon in question, exactly how are we assuming them to operate, and how would we insert them into our explanatory models?

If we have attempted to make our assumptions reasonably explicit, it will then be at least somewhat easier for others to assess comparability across settings. To the extent that social definitions are ad hoc, involve multidimensional criteria that seem unique to a given setting, or in other ways do not coincide with a more "rational" set of classificatory criteria, the theorist will be confronted with a series of dilemmas similar to those faced by social scientists who attempt to construct "social typologies" based on combinations of incompatible criteria (McKinney, 1966). As a general rule of thumb, in trying to come to grips with how one can formulate general theories that utilize both types of criteria (social definitions and more rationally based ones), it seems wisest to attempt our most general theoretical formulations in terms of conceptualizations that are as unidimensional as possible, while bringing in more complex social categorization schemes by adding distinct variables pertaining to such matters as the clarity of class boundaries, the extent to which actors are in agreement about these boundaries, how behaviors are affected by them, and so forth.

The second type of constraint that is often faced by one who is doing a secondary analysis of data already collected—or by one who is financially constrained to asking only a very few questions on a given topic—is that of being given only a very small number of categories to begin with. Suppose a respondent has been asked to check one of five categories to indicate his or her religious denomination, occupation, or preference among several political options or candidates. In effect, the analyst will be confronted with a situation involving missing information, whereas ideally it would have been preferable to collect redundant data to assess consistency and dimensionality, as well as to fill in intermediate points or permit a wider variety of responses.

The expensive nature of survey research, when coupled with our very limited (and diminishing) financial resources, has unfortunately placed social scientists in a position such that this type of situation is a very common one. We are simply too poor to be able to afford the "luxury" of more detailed information, and we also recognize that respondents are apt to lack the patience or ability to provide it, anyway. Under these circumstances it is then tempting to make a covering statement to the effect that one wishes that the data had been more complete, and then to proceed as though this is all that can be done. Problems of comparability are then similarly dismissed as "beyond the limits of this study."

The only plausible resolution to this very real sort of impasse seems to be that of formulating theories that involve unidimensional variables rather than unordered categories, and then stating explicitly one's assumptions as to how the specific categories that have been used relate to these unmeasured variables. Where there is a single dimension that predominates (e.g., occupational prestige), it may then be plausible to treat the categories as ordered. Where there are only two dimensions (say, prestige and power) that are moderately intercorrelated, a partial ordering may be plausible, in which case certain category combinations may be collapsed and treated as "tied." Simple assertions to the effect that such and such a categorization scheme has been treated as ordinal, or that several categories were combined because of small numbers or their similarity to one another make it almost impossible to assess comparability. Nor can they be justified on the grounds that, without collapsing, one's data analysis or presentation would become too complex. Complications brought about by a failure to theorize or to state one's assumptions can hardly serve as an adequate justification for making arbitrary decisions needed to satisfy statistical requirements. Simplifications need to be made on theoretical rather than statistical or pragmatic grounds.

The remaining section of this chapter illustrates the kind of conceptualization process that might be followed. Further examples are given in Blalock and Wilken (1979).

PREDICTING CHOICE BEHAVIORS: AN ILLUSTRATION

Choice behaviors are often so highly constrained that if one were to examine these behaviors without benefit of other information, it would be difficult to order these choices in a meaningful way or in fact to predict such choices theoretically. If individuals were afforded a wide variety of choices, say among occupations that could be rated according to a number of distinct dimensions, then we can imagine them locating themselves close to their ideal points with respect to each of these dimensions. That is, they would select precisely those occupations that afforded just the right amounts of job security, independence, prestige, income, working hours, recreational opportunities, compatible work associates, and so forth. If we knew their utilities for each of these objectives, along with their subjective probabilities of obtaining them through each job, we might then be able to predict their choices reasonably well. Furthermore, if individuals could continually move among occupations without cost, we can imagine them gradually sifting themselves among these occupations according to their preference patterns, either through a maximizing strategy or a satisficing one.

Obviously, this sort of choice situation does not exist in the real world. Often we know only the first choice of each individual or, worse still, the occupation that he or she ended up in as a result not only of the individual's preference ordering, but also that of the employer's as well. Furthermore, each actor will have a unique set of resources so that the realistic choices available to one actor will not correspond exactly with those available to another. Resultant outcomes of choices will be *jointly* affected by the decisions of other actors as well. Lacking the information necessary to dimensionalize these choices, the only way out may seem to be that of treating them as unordered. One may ask, however, whether it would then be possible to *predict* these choices in any theoretical fashion. Of course, we may always use a person's previous choice pattern to predict a future one, or we may construct a matrix containing characteristics and choice patterns among other similar actors, but this type of atheoretical approach begs the question of how one can then explain these choices. Furthermore, it is difficult to see how one can ever assess comparability or generalizability except in the restricted sense of seeing whether or not the matrices constructed for one setting look similar to those for another.

Let us illustrate by trying to relate two categorical variables: religious denomination and occupation, assuming that the categories for each attribute have been agreed upon in advance but that there are a sufficient number of categories so that a reasonably parsimonious summarizing procedure is desirable. Suppose, for example, that we have eight religious denominations and eleven occupational categories. One could always make a series of descriptive statements of the form, "Methodists tend to become dentists and lawyers, whereas Episcopalians and Jews tend to become doctors and scientists." In a trivial sense, such descriptive statements enable one to attach a conditional probability statement to any given individual, such as, "If Herbert Brown is a Methodist, he is more likely than Samuel Clubb, an Episcopalian, to become a lawyer." Or one could compare occupational distributions in two different countries to find out whether or not the same religious denominations tended to be over- or underrepresented in specific occupations. But how would these results be accounted for theoretically?

Admitting that both religious denomination and occupation cannot be uniquely ordered without, at the same time, committing oneself on a very simple set of theoretical assumptions, what strategy can we employ in terms of conceptualizing an additional set of variables useful in providing such a theoretical explanation? If one is willing to assume that important behavioral choices are guided by such things as goals, values, or utilities attached to these goals, and expectations or subjective probabilities that these goals will be achieved more readily through one course of action than another, this suggests positing a series of intervening variables, each of which is reasonably unidimensional. In the case of occupational choices made by persons socialized in different religious denominations, we would want to try to identify as many relevant goals, utilities, and expectations that might be expected to vary among persons in different religious denominations and occupations. For simplicity, let us confine ourselves to two such dimensions, X_1 and X_2. Suppose that X_1 represents the quality of one's work habits, conscientiousness, or some such dimension, and X_2 represents the value the individual attaches to providing services (of specified kinds) for others. We assume that occupations will differ with respect to demandingness of work and also the average level of this type of service they provide. Religious denominations also may differ in terms of the values they place on developing good work habits and on entering occupations oriented toward serving others.

Suppose the investigator lacks information as to specific X_1 and X_2 scores of the individuals being studied, but nevertheless would like to make some predictive statements concerning the relationship between religious denomination and occupational choice. If the average levels of X_1 and X_2 were available for each religious denomination, we could then insert a predicted value for each individual according to his or her denomination. Ordinarily, we would not expect these predicted X_i values to be too highly correlated, which is to say that the religious denominations would not be ranked in the same order on both dimensions. Of course, if the correlation between the predicted X_1 and X_2 scores were perfect, this would imply that the denominations would have been scored on the two dimensions such that a linear transformation would suffice to yield the one set of scores from the other. If so, the two variables would be totally confounded and either one of them would be sufficient to yield the same predictive information as that provided by a multiple regression equation involving both variables. This same kind of consideration can obviously be generalized to any number of intervening X_i.

One way to conceptualize the process is to think in terms of denominations and occupations ordered in a number of distinct ways. If denominations are ordered according to average scores on X_1, this ordinal variable may then be related to occupation, as ordered in some other way, or perhaps according to a very similar conceptual variable. Thus, it may be that denominations can be ordered in terms of the degree to which they emphasize the importance of a lifetime of service to others. Occupations could be ordered according to a slightly different conceptual variable, namely the degree of opportunity they provide for their members to help others. The prediction then becomes that there will be a positive monotonic relationship between denominations ordered according to the first criterion, and occupations according to the second.

One difficulty with this approach is that since both denominations and occupations can be ordered in a number of different ways, and since the relationship between a background variable (such as religious denomination) and occupational choice is likely to be complex and multidimensional, proceeding in a bivariate fashion such as this is unlikely to yield very definitive results. An alternative is to posit a series of intervening variables and to formulate one's theoretical argument primarily in terms of these variables, rather than denomination or occupation per se. In effect, one's denomination will be taken as a cause indicator of certain experience variables which are scored according to denomination. A Methodist may receive a very low score on one dimension, an intermediate one on another, and a high score on two others. Similarly, occupations may be scored on several work-related dimensions. The theoretical argument would then be stated in terms of experience variables related to occupational preference or choice dimensions, such as the position of the selected occupation on any given continuum.

When one compares across settings, the theoretically defined variables would remain the same, but the scoring system might very well have to be modified. Perhaps the occupations would be rated differently along the income dimension, the amount of job security they afford, or opportunities for service. Or a given religious denomination may be more fundamentalist in orientation in one society or community than in another. Therefore, to apply this procedure systematically would require a series of intensive studies through which both denominations and occupations were scored along each of the relevant dimensions. Were such information available to survey researchers, it would then be possible to confine the data collection effort to a series of simple questions about religious preferences or occupation, with these categories then being scored on the basis of this more detailed information. The words "occupational" and "religious" may then be used as adjectival modifiers referring to specific dimensions, such as occupational prestige or religious fundamentalism. This is, of course, a generalization of the strategy that has been successfully used in scoring occupations according to the Duncan (1961) index of prestige.

In this way, the "same" nominal scale may be used to provide measures for several reasonably general theoretical variables. As we shall discuss in Chapter 6, however, dimensionalizing categorical variables in this fashion involves an attendant risk of confounding a number of unspecified variables with those that have been identified. We are faced with a dilemma similar to that posed by Coombs. Do we know what we want, or do we want to know? The higher our measurement aspirations, and the stronger the assumptions we impose, the greater the potential payoff, but also, the more likely that an interpretive error will be made.

LINKING GENERAL EXPERIENCE DIMENSIONS WITH BACKGROUND VARIABLES

We surmise that one of the primary reasons that empirical investigations have failed to provide cumulative evidence linking commonly used background variables to either attitudes, values, or other internal states, on the one hand, or to behaviors, on the other, is that there is little consensus on a list of reasonably general experience dimensions that may be related to both the background variables and behaviors in question. Ideally, what we seem to need is a reasonably short list of perhaps ten to twenty experience dimensions that are essentially content-free and therefore capable of being used across a wide variety of settings and as explanatory variables for a diversity of behaviors.

In addition to such a listing of experience dimensions, we would of course also need to take account of the salience or relevance of each background variable for that experience in a given setting. For instance, one's religious denomination may be irrelevant in setting A but not in setting B, and similarly for

one's race, sex, age, or occupation. Therefore, degree of relevance or importance would have to appear explicitly in some
way in each theory. In the case of an additive equation, for
example, relevance would presumably affect the appropriate
slope coefficient. Where a multiplicative function is more appropriate, relevance might enter into the corresponding exponent.

In our own very incomplete listing of possible experience
dimensions that follows, we shall ignore considerations of relevance, salience, or importance, merely noting that not all
dimensions will be equally relevant to all background variables
in all settings. Likewise, we shall not address the question of
how relevance or salience may change over time or vary across
individuals. Nor shall we distinguish between relevance as perceived by the actors concerned and "objective relevance" or
objective importance as measured in some other way.

*Respect and Status Awarded by Important Reference
Groups.* A common type of experience variable that we assume
is common across a wide variety of settings is the degree to
which the actor is awarded respect and status, however the
latter may be named or titled. We are basically referring to one's
ordinal position, in comparison with some set of others, along a
prestige continuum. Occasionally such statuses may involve a
specific metric, as for example a monetary prize or a numerical
score, but the more usual situation will simply involve a rough
ranking of some kind. Situations may differ, however, with
respect to the number of distinct ranks, the explicitness of the
criteria used in awarding status, the probability of an actor's
changing status over a given time interval, the overtness of the
competition for status, the rules by which such competition is
regulated, and so forth. Each of these latter factors may, of
course, serve as a separate dimension relating to this particular
type of experience variable, and exposure to a very competitive
system in which statuses are achieved and lost very rapidly may
have a differential impact on persons with diverse background
characteristics.

Consistency of Expectations Regarding Behaviors. Regardless
of the *content* of the specific expectations to which actors are

exposed in diverse settings, there are several distinct dimensions that refer to the consistency of these expectations. First, there may be several sets of actors who expect very different behaviors, so that it is virtually impossible for anyone to conform to all sets of expectations simultaneously. Second, whereas all actors may agree on their expectations, the simultaneous conformity to these expectations may be difficult or impossible, given whatever resources the actor has at his or her disposal. Third, expectations may change over time, either in a predictable and "consistent" manner or erratically and in a fashion over which the actor has little or no control. There are a host of sociological and psychological theories to the effect that inconsistent and unpredictable expectations produce strains in the individual and that, consequently, they affect behaviors. Some theories also link these inconsistent or incompatible expectations to background variables, or to the occupancy of peculiar combinations of positions. Thus, status-inconsistency theory typically posits ambiguities or role strains for occupants of statuses that are, in some sense, defined as "inconsistent" (Lenski, 1954; Jackson, 1962; Blalock, 1967). Similarly, the Gibbs and Martin (1964) theory of status integration and suicide posits that certain types of role combinations will be empirically rare because of peculiar combinations of expectations that make their joint occupancy stressful.

Homogeneity of Behaviors Among Persons with Common Group Membership. Sometimes members of a given group or category behave very similarly to one another, either because they are expected to do so or because they have very similar interests and experiences. In some societies, for example, there may be a very rigid division of labor by sex or age, so that someone who does not conform to the pattern in question clearly stands out. But for other kinds of behaviors, the group or category may be irrelevant to the behavior, with the usual result that individuals cannot be "typed" or their behaviors predicted on the basis of a knowledge of this characteristic. In our own society, for instance, persons of different religious denominations ordinarily do not have distinct occupations, nor do they dress dissimilarly. Yet men and women do have different occupations and dress patterns, though sex differences in both respects have been diminishing over recent years. Presumably, whenever highly important behaviors are closely related to group or category memberships, this will have important implications in terms of individual aspirations and expectations, the kinds of social controls that will be applied to those defined as deviant, and to behavioral expectations concerning a host of relatively minor behaviors not otherwise functionally linked to the important behaviors in question. Issues relating to degrees of freedom in selecting among alternative behaviors are obviously linked to homogeneity of the category in comparison with differences among categories.

Degree to Which "Escape Options" are Available. Another content-free dimension that seems closely related to the above dimension is the degree to which the actor finds it possible to escape from or avoid the experiences in question. One type of escape option that is not always available is that of changing group or category membership. Thus, if nearly all members of a religious denomination behave alike, and are regarded similarly by outsiders, one may sometimes change religious affiliation. But the costs of changes vary by degree, as well as being related to other group or category memberships one may have. For instance, a young child or dependent adult may find it impossible to escape. A member of a racial minority may never be able to change his or her identity, whereas a member of an ethnic group may sometimes do so more easily, especially if economic resources permit one to change communities or "buy" one's way into nonminority circles. Here, we are apt to get into matters of visibility, anonymity, and homogeneity of expectations, which is to say that the variables associated with this and other dimensions will be interrelated. The hope is, of course, that reasonably general theories can be stated and tested in such a way that our understanding of these interrelationships is furthered.

Degree to Which Actors Possess Important Resources. Although the nature or content of expectations placed on individuals will vary, each actor will be able to meet these expectations and receive status and respect in return to the degree to which he or she possesses those resources that are needed to perform satisfactorily. Whether these resources be obtained through inheritance, training, or any other means, and regardless of how others may account for their possession, any actors who do not possess them will obviously be handicapped as compared with those who do. Admittedly, however, actors' perceptions and explanations concerning resource possession and mobilization will interact with actual performance to affect such things as self-confidence, expectations and aspirations for the future, and perceptions of one's own level of competence relative to that of others. It will also affect one's interactions with others, including the degree to which others attempt to dislodge these resources from the actor or to denigrate either the resources or the ways in which they have been mobilized.

Degree to Which Socialization and Learning Experiences are Compatible With Demands. Since one important mechanism through which resources are acquired involves socialization, it is also important to assess the degree to which these experiences actually equip the individual to cope with later experiences, including expectations for performance. Have the necessary technical and interpersonal skills been learned and are they appropriately applied? We recognize here the possibility that many actors may have been well socialized to play certain roles but not others, and that the expectations currently facing those persons may involve a very different set of skills than those which have been learned. Basically, then, we are concerned not only with how well the "appropriate" skills have been learned, but also their compatibility with others that may, in effect, have to be unlearned or that are, at best, irrelevant to current demands.

Amount of Affective or Emotional Support Given the Actor. Regardless of the setting or issue being studied, there will be varying degrees of social and emotional support provided the actor by significant others in the environment. There will also be subjective reactions or interpretations of this support. Does the actor feel alone, alienated from others, and disapproved, or just the opposite? And when each actor's experiences have been aggregated over a number of specific settings, has that actor experienced an overall balance that involves a high or a low degree of such affective support? To what degree have there been a distinctive set of actors who have provided such support and, perhaps, another set who have interacted with the actor in almost the opposite fashion, resulting in the actor's perceiving the world as composed both of close friends and mortal enemies, as opposed to other actors whose behaviors vary more along a continuum of supportiveness?

Extent to Which Actor Has Endured Hardships, Conflict, Danger, or Threats. Again, almost regardless of the settings involved, we recognize that some actors have a much less threatening and harsh set of experiences than do others. Here we are concerned with such things as deprivations (absolute and relative), tension levels and overt conflict experienced, or the extent to which actors have been exposed to more or less continuous threats of such hardships or tension levels. Some age cohorts, for example, have been subjected to warfare or extreme economic hardships that other cohorts may have missed. We naturally expect that, when aggregated, such cumulative experiences will also impact on expectations, the degree to which the actor trusts others, and the nature of that actor's interactions, especially when placed in situations that are sufficiently similar to remind the actor of these earlier experiences.

Degree to Which Emphasis Has Been Placed on Achievement and Performance. As frequently noted in the literature on achieved versus ascribed characteristics, settings vary with respect to how status is awarded and behaviors evaluated. Where performance and achievement are considered far more important than ascribed characteristics, a different set of resources will be needed and actors will evaluate themselves in different terms from settings in which such performance is irrelevant. This will obviously affect the degree to which the actor believes that he or she has control over his or her destiny, and will interact with the degree to which the necessary resources are possessed or are thought to be obtainable.

The Permeability of Important Reference Groups. Groups vary in the extent to which memberships are accessible to actors of various types, and this implies that from the standpoint of any given actor there will be an array of groups, formal and informal, that are more or less accessible to that person. There will be both a perceived probability of access, as well as an "objective" one in terms of the characteristics of that individual. To the extent that a group constitutes an important referent for that actor, and yet is effectively closed to his or her admission, there will not only be an experienced frustration, but we may anticipate that expectancies and aspirations will also be affected. Where entry is expected to be difficult and rewarding, but not totally blocked, the promise of future entry may also serve as an important motivating force for achieving relevant skills or other attributes, as well as helping to shape that individual's conduct. Aggregating over a number of different reference groups of varying degrees of permeability (for a given actor), we expect that the experiences gained will also have important impacts on personality characteristics such as self-esteem, self-confidence, aspirations, and attitudes toward persons of both higher and lower status.

Degree to Which Total Experiences Lead to Consistent, Integrated Orientations. Some actors have a set of experiences that "add up" in a consistent direction, perhaps to give them either a very pessimistic or optimistic set of expectations or a very definite set of purposes or sense of direction. For others, the experiences represent a much more confusing or inconsistent picture of the way they may expect to be treated, what is important, or how they are expected to behave. Status-inconsistency theories, for example, often posit that individuals experiencing inconsistent status dimensions are sometimes treated in accord with the highest of their several statuses, and sometimes the lowest. Such persons may be subjected to strains as a result, or their interactions with others may be difficult to predict or otherwise be ambiguous. Or some actors may have been subjected to one very different set of expectations during one period of their lives, or with one set of actors, from that which they encounter at other time periods or with other actors. As a result, their self-image may be confused or their characteristic reactions highly ambivalent. In a sense, what we are referring to in connection with this dimension is the *degree* of consistency among experiences, regardless of their directions or contents, and so we are necessarily involved with some notion of aggregating these experiences and assessing how diverse or incompatible they may have been. In addition to this matter of degree of inconsistency or incompatibility is the question of the temporal sequencing of these experiences. Have they occurred in a more or less random order, or has there been a definite trend in one direction or another?

Degree to Which There Have Been Dramatic Changes in Experiences. For some actors, experiences more or less flow into each other without there being abrupt changes, so that it is extremely difficult to pinpoint specific sources of attitudes, perspectives, or other personality characteristics. For others, there may have been rather dramatic or drastic shifts: such things as the death of a parent or sibling, a sudden change in one's environment, an illness, a job loss or retirement, the birth of a child and a sudden loss of confidence, and so forth. The very abruptness of these changes, along with the need to develop a new set of skills or social relationships, may have had important consequences for the actors concerned, quite apart from the content or nature of these shifts. Like a number of the other dimensions we have discussed, such changes may have also affected one's expectations about the future, as well as one's ability to cope with this future or a new set of circumstances. They may have also affected the actor's orientation toward strangers or changes in the environment, as well as such attitudinal dimensions as ethnocentrism, authoritarianism, or tolerance for ambiguity.

General Comments

The above list of dimensions, or really clusters of dimensions, is not intended to be either mutually exclusive or exhaustive. The intent has been to specify a reasonably brief set of dimensions that are sufficiently broad to be relevant to a diversity of settings and behaviors of interest to social scientists, as well as being such that actors could be located along these dimensions, given sufficient information about their past experiences. But being rather general, each of these dimensions poses a host of measurement problems that suggest to us why it is that many investigators have found it much easier to bypass them in favor of simple lists of background factors that are at least capable of yielding classification schemes based on more directly observable characteristics.

It is our contention that if these and other experience dimensions could be more satisfactorily conceptualized and then measured, we would be on much more solid ground in linking the more readily observed background variables to behaviors in diverse settings. Furthermore, even without accurate measures of these experience variables, it should be possible to state a series of theoretical arguments that, together with some assumptions linking these dimensions to background variables, may lead to testable hypotheses that indirectly shed light on these theories. For instance, one can rather easily predict that blacks and whites in the United States will differ, on the average, along a number of these experience dimensions. Therefore, even without measures of the experience variables themselves, one may predict specific behavioral differences between blacks and whites on the average.

As previously noted, however, a problem will occur because of the large number of distinct experience dimensions and the confounding of these dimensions whenever the number of background categories is not large. Thus, if one is comparing only three or four ethnic groups, religious denominations, or types of home communities, one is very likely to find that these will be ranked in precisely the same order, according to average experience levels and along several dimensions, making it impossible to choose among several different explanatory systems. If blacks have simultaneously experienced situations in which they have had little access to necessary resources, where expectations were inconsistent, where important reference groups were closed to them, where they were consistently low-status members, and where they have experienced much greater hardships on the average than other actors, then it will be exceedingly difficult to decide which of these mechanisms, if any, is primarily responsible for their attitudes and behaviors. If, on the other hand, one can find *subsets* of blacks who have experienced one set of phenomena but not others, one stands a much better chance of unravelling the mechanisms involved. Or if one can work with, say, fifty or sixty different occupations, rather than five or six gross categories, it becomes much more possible to score these occupations on a diversity of dimensions according to average experiences of their members.

Therefore, if the direct measurement of these dimensions proves too difficult, but if one wishes to retain them in our theories in order to generate highly specific predictions linking background factors to behaviors (or attitudes), several things will be necessary. First, the number of background categories will have to be reasonably large. This in turn implies that each category will need to be reasonably homogeneous with respect to relevant experience dimensions, suggesting the need for internal distinctions or subcategories. Second, we shall need much better information about average levels of experiences for each of these categories, so that even though we may not have experience data at the individual level, we will be in a position to predict these experiences rather well from a knowledge of a combination of background characteristics. And third, we shall need some rather clear-cut theoretical predictions that relate these experience variables to reasonably general types of behaviors, rather than behaviors that are so highly specific that they pertain to only a very narrow range of settings that differ in unspecified ways from the settings in which the experiences were gained. In short, we shall need both good theories and an explicit set of auxiliary measurement theories linking experiences to both sets of measured variables.

NOTE

1. Prediction logic, as developed by Hildebrand et al. (1977), does not suffer this defect of utilizing measures that depend on the marginals of dependent variables and, furthermore, is more oriented toward a priori predictions based on theoretical arguments. For some reason, however, it does not appear to have been used by sociologists to anywhere near the extent of log-linear approaches.

CHAPTER 5

SOME IMPLICATIONS OF OMITTING
VARIABLES FROM
CAUSAL EXPLANATIONS

It goes without saying that any explanatory model of a complex reality must inevitably be oversimplified. In particular, it will always be necessary to omit many variables from a causal model, not only in order to preserve one's scientific sanity, but also because of the practical limits imposed by one's budget and ability to measure most of the variables that one would ideally like to include in the model. Typically, an investigator will find it necessary to justify such omissions either in terms of a lack of adequate knowledge or the inability to measure many such variables. But the convenience of the investigator, a lack of resources, and the inadequacies of existing theory—though all being very real and important—are not sufficient reasons for justifying such omissions on *scientific* grounds. That is, if such omissions could be shown to lead to serious biases or erroneous inferences, then no matter how poorly equipped the investigator might be, the scientific community could hardly justify the research enterprise unless it could be assured that such deficiencies might be corrected.

Given the obvious impossibility of ever achieving theoretical closure on a problem, this implies that it would be helpful to base such decisions on strictly methodological-theoretical grounds rather than pragmatic ones. If, for example, it could be shown that the omission of certain kinds of variables would not actually distort one's inferences, and that their inclusion would merely help one interpret one's conclusions rather than modifying them, then we would have a methodologically sound rationale for deciding that their inclusion would not be worth the added cost. The essential problem, of course, is that until they are included, we will never *know* whether or not our assumptions about their behavior are actually correct. But at least we may say that if one is willing to assume certain things about their behavior, then they may safely be ignored.

THE OMISSION OF INTERVENING VARIABLES

We apply this principle to many kinds of trivial cases. For example, we omit variables that are not expected to be related to any other variables in the system. In recursive models we do not include variables thought to be dependent on the variables in which we are interested. In the case of simple causal chains of the form $W \rightarrow X \rightarrow Y \rightarrow Z$ we know that (except for sampling errors) if we regressed Z on W, ignoring X and Y, we would get the same slope estimate b_{zw} as would have been obtained had we included X and Y and used the product $b_{zy} \, b_{yx} \, b_{xw}$.

This (justified) omission of intervening variables in recursive models is a great convenience, since it would manifestly be impossible to include all intervening links in causal sequences. But it does not follow that in the more general nonrecursive case we can also omit such variables, since it is well known that in these models we cannot legitimately study each equation in isolation from the others. Since there may be no single "dependent" variable, since many variables will be *both* dependent and independent, and since the simple notion of an "intervening variable" may also break down in such instances, it is by no means clear just what is and is not permissible in terms of omissions of variables from the model. Of course, this is quite apart from the question of which variables can easily be measured and which cannot, or just what resources the investigator has available.

The notion of an "intervening" variable has been used in several senses, but in the social psychological literature it has often been given the connotation of being an unmeasured internal state or postulated property that intervenes between situational factors or stimuli and the behaviors or responses of individuals. Because of the difficulties encountered in obtaining indirect measures of such internal states, these intervening variables have often been considered as constituting a kind of inscrutable "black box" that, under some circumstances, may safely be ignored. Similarly, macro-level sociologists may have available a number of indicators of situational factors such as unemployment rates, degree of urbanization, GNP per capita, or global characteristics such as type of political system, predominant religious beliefs, and so forth. They may also have available a number of indicators of responses in the form of rates of behavior—suicide and homicide rates, drug addiction rates, measures of discrimination, voting percentages, and the like. But they may completely lack any measures of attitudes, values, perceptions, or motivational levels. Can the latter safely be ignored on the macro level as well as the micro level? Under what circumstances? The fact that a given investigator may *have* to ignore them because of a lack of data does not mean that it is theoretically legitimate to do so.

The situation is very straightforward in the case of *linear* additive models and recursive systems. Where possible non-linearities are involved, there may be situations in which there are definite advantages to retaining the unmeasured intervening variables in one's theory. Another obvious possibility is that there may be interactions between, or nonadditive joint effects of, certain situational stimuli and particular kinds of internal states, so that the omission of the latter obscures differences among individuals by lumping them all together. We shall return to this kind of possibility later in the chapter, since it bears directly on the results we shall obtain in the intervening sections. We shall concentrate initially on complications that may be introduced in the case of nonrecursive models in which we wish to allow for possible feedback between the "dependent" variables and some of the "intervening" variables. Our illustration will be in terms of feedbacks between behaviors and internal states, but there are many other substantive problems for which the structures of the causal models are similar.

It is often assumed that behaviors may be affected by situational factors and motivational states or attitudes, but that the behaviors may be taken as dependent variables that do not influence either the stimuli or the internal states. Such models are of course far too simplistic—although most data *analyses* typically presuppose them to be true. We know that repeated behaviors bring about reactions that serve as stimuli for later acts and that persons' perceptions, attitudes, and even basic values may become modified as a result of these reactions. Therefore, many of our behaviors influence subsequent internal states unless they are never responded to or repeated.

If measurement occurs only once, or insufficiently often to enable one to infer these sequences, it may be impossible to say a whole lot about the relative magnitudes of the influences in the two directions. But we anticipate that in most normal situations, where the mutual interaction does not break down or change erratically, the feedback effect serves to stabilize both the behaviors and the internal states until a new stimulus produces a change. Notions such as "balance" and "strains toward consistency" clearly imply such processes, as does the labelling-theory approach to deviancy. The idea is that an individual's behavior generates a response that shapes his or her self-perceptions, which in turn affect later behaviors in such a manner as to stabilize both the behavior and the internal state. If in fact such feedback processes do occur, is it still legitimate to try to infer the effects of the situational factors on the behavior, while omitting the internal states from the model? Intuitively based arguments now seem much less appealing. Even if they were intuitively appealing to some of us, they would still need to be justified in terms of sound methodological principles.

It turns out that this kind of problem can be tackled by formulating the issues in terms of the differences between what econometricians refer to as "structural equations" and "reduced forms" of these equations (see Johnston, 1972; Christ, 1966; Duncan, 1975; or Namboodiri et al., 1975.) We shall see that the models without the intervening variables can be taken as reduced forms, whereas the full models (with these variables included) can be treated as the structural equations, with the realization that *no* model or set of equations can ever be really complete. We shall see that there *are* certain things that can be accomplished with the reduced forms, and that inferences based on these simplified models will not necessarily be misleading. But we also lose something by having to resort to these reduced forms, and after discussing a number of specific causal models, we shall return to a general discussion of the practical implications in terms of measurement and conceptualization.

A Simple Recursive Model

Let us begin with a recursive model of the type that has characterized much of the empirical work in social psychology, at least insofar as the latter has been concerned with the relationship between internal states and behavior at a single point in time. In Figure 5.1 we have two situational factors or stimuli, labelled as Z_i and represented as exogenous variables to which there is assumed to be no feedback. We may imagine that there are two situational factors, such as unemployment and discrimination rates, over which the individual has only negligible control. The two variables X_1 and X_2 are internal states, perhaps two attitudinal dimensions or levels of motivational arousal. The behavior is designated as X_3, the model implying that the exogenous variables directly affect the internal states, which in turn affect the behavior X_3. Obviously, this model is oversimplified in a number of respects, some of which will be dealt with in succeeding models. We use the common letter X for both the internal states and the behavior, since we shall later wish to allow for feedback among them, thereby treating them

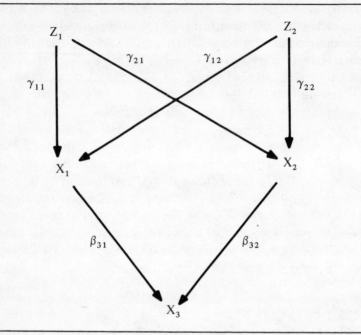

Figure 5.1

as a set of endogenous variables whose equations must be handled simultaneously. The Z_i are taken as unexplained, though they may be correlated for unknown reasons.

If all variables were perfectly measured, we could estimate the direct effects of each variable on the others by using ordinary least squares to estimate the (partial) regression coefficients. The total (direct and indirect) effects could then be assessed, either by using standardized path coefficients or by taking simple functions of the unstandardized coefficients. I shall operate with the latter, which are invariant across populations characterized by the same numerical values of the structural parameters. The standardized path coefficients are in addition functions of ratios of standard deviations peculiar to each population or time period.

There are three endogenous variables in the system. These are variables toward which at least one arrow is directed, and we may write an equation for each of these variables. I shall follow the practice, common in econometrics notation, of representing the causal parameters interrelating the X_i by β_{ij} and the direct (partial) influences of the Z_j on the X_i by γ_{ij}. The (linear) equations are as follows:

$$X_1 = \gamma_{11}Z_1 + \gamma_{12}Z_2 + \epsilon_1$$

$$X_2 = \gamma_{21}Z_1 + \gamma_{22}Z_2 + \epsilon_2$$

$$X_3 = \beta_{31}X_1 + \beta_{32}X_2 + \epsilon_3$$

where for convenience we have omitted the constant terms by taking deviations about means, where we assume that $E(\epsilon_i) = 0$, for all i, and where in the case of recursive systems it is possible (though perhaps unrealistic) to assume that none of the disturbance terms are correlated with the independent variables in their respective equations. These assumptions permit the use of ordinary least squares (OLS), which will give unbiased estimates of the β_{ij} and γ_{ij}.

Now let us suppose that X_1 and X_2 are either unknown or unmeasured. This means that we cannot estimate any of the β_{ij} or γ_{ij}, which are referred to as "structural parameters." This implies that we will be unable to sort out the component effects, but it does not necessarily follow that we cannot estimate the total impact of changes in either Z_1 or Z_2 on X_3, the behavior in question. We may put the issue specifically as follows. We first attempt to solve the equation for X_3 in terms of the two exogenous Z_i alone, without X_1 or X_2 appearing in this equation. Whenever we express a single endogenous variable as a function of the exogenous variables alone, we refer to this as a "reduced form" (Namboodiri et al., 1975, ch. 11.) It is a generalization of the notion of a "solution," where in this case the solution contains not only constants (e.g., $X_3 = 5$) but also the Z_i as well. This solution, if it is available, enables one to predict the levels of the Xs once the values of the Z_i are inserted. And, as we shall see, it enables us to assess the relative importance of the Z_i in terms of their effects on X_3. But perhaps such a reduced form does not exist, and perhaps it could not be estimated from the data.

Fortunately, it turns out that it is always possible to obtain the reduced form if we are given the structural parameters β_{ij} and γ_{ij}. And if we have (perfect) measures of Z_1, Z_2, and X_3 we may also estimate the reduced-form parameters (referred to as $\P_{ij}$) from the data. In terms of the above model it can easily be shown that, if we eliminate X_1 and X_2 from the equation for X_3, we get

$$X_3 = (\gamma_{11}\beta_{31} + \gamma_{21}\beta_{32})Z_1 + (\gamma_{12}\beta_{31} + \gamma_{22}\beta_{32})Z_2 + \eta_3$$

$$= \P_{31}Z_1 + \P_{32}Z_2 + \eta_3$$

If the disturbances ϵ_i in the structural equations are assumed to be independent of the exogenous Z_i, then since the disturbance term η_3 in the reduced-form equation is a function of these ϵ_i and the (constant) parameters, the disturbance term in the reduced form will also be independent of the Z_i, and OLS may be used to estimate the reduced-form parameters $\P_{ij}$.

In the more general case, where we admit the probability of reciprocal causation among the X_i, it will not always be possible to estimate the structural parameters β_{ij} and γ_{ij} from the estimates of the reduced-form parameters $\P_{ij}$, since there may be more of the former than the latter. When this is not possible, we say that at least some of the equations are underidentified. In the recursive case, however, we will be able to identify or estimate all of the structural parameters provided that (1) there are no *exact* linear relationships among the variables appearing in causally prior equations, and (2) all variables in the system are perfectly measured. The former situation is not of present concern to us, though we should note that if either the Z_i or the intervening variables X_1 and X_2 are too highly intercorrelated, we can anticipate that sampling errors of the parameter estimates may be unusually large. It is the second possibility that is of interest to us, since we are assuming that neither X_1 nor X_2 is being measured.

What this set of equations tells us is that if we were to bypass X_1 and X_2 altogether and estimate the reduced-form parameters $\P_{ij}$ using OLS, we would have inferred the same *total effects* of Z_1 and Z_2 as would have been the case had we been able to include X_1 and X_2. Furthermore, the equations make sense intuitively. The coefficient $(\gamma_{11}\beta_{31} + \gamma_{21}\beta_{32}) = \P_{31}$ represents the effects of Z_1 tracing through two paths. If we were to increase Z_1 by one unit, we would change X_1 by γ_{11} units, and this would mean a change of $\gamma_{11}\beta_{31}$ units in X_3 via the path though X_1. Similarly, a unit change in Z_1 would change X_2 by γ_{21} units and therefore change X_3 by $\gamma_{21}\beta_{32}$ units via the intervening variable X_2. If we were unable to measure X_1 and X_2 we would not be able to decompose the total effect of Z_1, and we would therefore have a less "rich" explanation, but we would not be misled. A similar argument applies, of course, to the effects of Z_2 on the behavior X_3.

The recursive model has become familiar to many sociologists, so that the above arguments may be intuitively obvious. They have been provided primarily as a basis for comparison for the nonrecursive case where the situation is by no means as obvious. In order to develop the latter type of model more fully, it is perhaps wise to begin with a very simplified case in which Z_1 affects only X_1, Z_2 affects only X_2, and the two intervening variables do not influence each other. We may then turn to some more complex situations to examine their implications.

Some Feedback Models

In all of the models to be discussed, we shall assume that there are some truly exogenous variables, to which there is no feedback from any of the X_i. In reality, there will undoubtedly be certain "situational factors" that are basically unaffected by the actors concerned, so that this assumption becomes entirely plausible. But there will be other situational factors which in fact may be modifiable by the actions of these persons. We shall

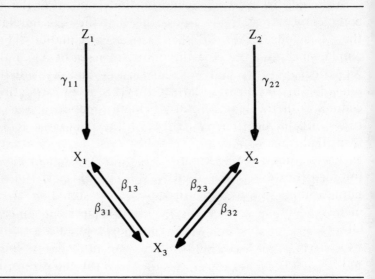

Figure 5.2

not include any of the latter variables in our very simple illustration, but merely note that the latter kinds of situational factors should be treated as endogenous X_i rather than exogenous Z_i.

We shall continue to assume that the "intervening variables" X_1 and X_2 represent internal states of individuals, though more generally they might also represent situational factors (say, reactions of siblings or parents) that might be subject to feedbacks from the behavior variable X_3. The reader may therefore think of X_1 and X_2 as two attitudes that influence behavior and that are in turn modified by earlier behaviors, or as situational factors that affect the actor and that are partially subject to his or her influence. We consider first the model of Figure 5.2, in which there is reciprocal causation only between X_3 and X_1 and between X_3 and X_2, but none between the two "intervening" variables themselves. Our equations become:

$$X_1 = \beta_{13}X_3 + \gamma_{11}Z_1 + \epsilon_1$$
$$X_2 = \beta_{23}X_3 + \gamma_{22}Z_2 + \epsilon_2$$
$$X_3 = \beta_{31}X_1 + \beta_{32}X_2 + \epsilon_3$$

Although the ϵ_i are assumed to be independent of the Z_i, it is completely unreasonable to assume that they are unrelated to the "independent" X_i in their respective equations. For example, since ϵ_1 represents the omitted causes of X_1, and since X_1 affects X_3, we fully expect that ϵ_1 and X_3 will be correlated. This invalidates the use of OLS as an estimating procedure, with the biases in OLS being a function of the magnitudes of the coefficients. Each of the equations is exactly identified, since $k - 1 = 2$ variables have been omitted from each equation and since the necessary and sufficient condition for identification is also met in each case (Fisher, 1966). This implies that alternative procedures for estimating the parameters might be used if all variables were perfectly measured. Of course, we shall again be concerned with the situation in which X_1 and X_2 are unmeasured (and probably unknown as well). Therefore, we shall be interested in the reduced-form equation for X_3 in terms of the (measured) exogenous variables. Eliminating X_1 and X_2 from the equation for X_3 we now get:

$$X_3 = \frac{\beta_{31}\gamma_{11}}{1 - \beta_{13}\beta_{31} - \beta_{23}\beta_{32}} Z_1 + \frac{\beta_{32}\gamma_{22}}{1 - \beta_{13}\beta_{31} - \beta_{23}\beta_{32}} Z_2 + \eta_3$$

and therefore if $\Delta = 1 - \beta_{13}\beta_{31} - \beta_{23}\beta_{32}$

then $\P_{31} = \dfrac{1}{\Delta}\beta_{31}\gamma_{11}$

and $\P_{32} = \dfrac{1}{\Delta}\beta_{32}\gamma_{22}$

Notice that the denominators in the expressions for the $\P_{ij}$ are equal, and we have designated them as Δ. It will turn out for more complex models that the comparable denominators will be the same, and we shall likewise refer to these denominators as Δ so as to remove some of the details from the algebraic representations. These Δs are the determinants of the matrix of the betas and never involve the gammas. We shall comment on their behaviors at appropriate points. For this particular model we note that if X_3 does not feed back to influence either X_1 or X_2, then $\beta_{13} = \beta_{23} = 0$ and $\Delta = 1$ for the recursive case. If so, we have the very simple result that $\P_{31} = \gamma_{11}\beta_{31}$ and $\P_{32} =$

$\gamma_{22}\beta_{32}$, as would be expected by common sense or by tracing the paths from Z_1 to X_3 via X_1 and from Z_2 to X_3 via X_2.

The crucial thing to note, however, is that since the coefficients of Z_1 and Z_2 have the same denominator, and since their numerators do not involve the feedback coefficients β_{13} and β_{23} we may estimate the *relative* total impacts of Z_1 and Z_2 even though we do not know anything about the exact magnitudes of these feedback terms. In other words, no matter what the actual value of Δ may be, we know that the (least-squares) estimators of $\P_{31}$ and $\P_{32}$ will be proportional to $\gamma_{11}\beta_{31}$ and $\gamma_{22}\beta_{32}$, respectively. This implies, for example, that if X_3 fed back to influence X_1 but not X_2, this would not in any way affect our estimates of the *relative* total effects of Z_1 and Z_2. We would, of course, have much more detailed knowledge if we had in fact measured X_1 and X_2 and could have estimated the separate structural parameters.

By omitting the intervening variables, we thus lose information about Δ. It can be shown that the necessary conditions for the stability of a dynamic model, of which this static version is a special case, imply that Δ cannot be zero (Baumol, 1970; Blalock, 1969). That is, if we have observed that the situation has stabilized after Z_1 and Z_2 have been shifted, we infer that the feedback processes at work among the X_i have worked themselves out and that each X_i has stabilized. If, however, we note that X_3 continues to increase (or decrease) indefinitely after the Z_i have been shifted to new fixed values, then (if we rule out the operation of other Z_i that are continually changing) we may infer that the feedback among the X_i has produced an unstable situation, in which case our static model will be inappropriate and we should not attempt to estimate the "total effects" of the Z_i using cross-sectional data.

The feedbacks from X_3 may be either negative or positive, or perhaps even negative to X_1 but positive to X_2. If both are negative, then the signs of β_{ij} and β_{ji} will be opposite. In effect, negative feedbacks will tend to dampen the total impacts of the Z_i by making Δ greater than unity. Thus, suppose Z_1 operates to increase X_1 and that, without feedback, this change in X_1 would also increase X_3. With negative feedback, this increase in

X_3 will then *decrease* X_1, this decrease in X_1 again decreasing X_3, which will then increase X_1 and then X_3, producing another decrease in X_1, and so forth. Of course, it is possible that these increases and decreases will have larger and larger amplitudes until there is an explosion, but the more usual situation will be one in which they reduce in magnitude until they are negligible. The point is that negative feedbacks will result in numerically smaller changes in X_3 (and also the intervening variables) than would have occurred without the feedback. This is reflected in the fact that $\triangle > 1$.

Similarly, if there is positive feedback, then an increase in X_3 results in an additional increase in X_1, which further increases X_3, and so forth. In this case, $\triangle$ will be less than unity (although generally positive, unless there is accelerating change), and the total impact of a unit change in either Z_1 or Z_2 will be greater than would have been the case had there been no such feedback. We note once more, however, the important fact that the *relative* impacts of Z_1 and Z_2, as measured by their ratio, are not affected by the relative sizes of the feedback coefficients β_{13} and β_{23}. Without measures of X_1 and X_2 we cannot assess these coefficients, or even their signs, but we have the knowledge that our inferences regarding the relative impact of changes in Z_1 and Z_2 will be correct.

We may now turn to the somewhat more general model of Figure 5.3, which allows for the possibility that either Z_i affects both X_1 and X_2, as well as for the mutual influence of X_1 and X_2 on each other. We may obtain a number of special cases by setting some of these coefficients equal to zero. It should be specifically noted, however, that we do *not* allow for feedback from any of the X_i to Z_1 or Z_2. This basic model can easily be generalized, without changing any of the principles involved, to handle additional Z_i and X_i. Our three structural equations now become:

$$X_1 = \beta_{12}X_2 + \beta_{13}X_3 + \gamma_{11}Z_1 + \gamma_{12}Z_2 + \epsilon_1$$

$$X_2 = \beta_{21}X_1 + \beta_{23}X_3 + \gamma_{21}Z_1 + \gamma_{22}Z_2 + \epsilon_2$$

$$X_3 = \beta_{31}X_1 + \beta_{32}X_2 + \epsilon_3$$

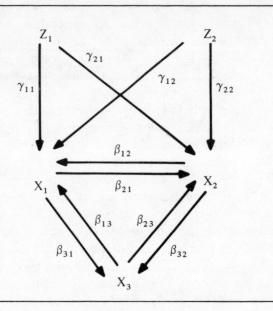

Figure 5.3

The equations for X_1 and X_2 are underidentified, since no variables have been left out of either equation. This implies that even with perfect measurement of all five variables, it would be *impossible* to estimate the separate causal parameters without modifying the system in some essential way, either by specifying lag periods or introducing additional variables. We again assume that X_1 and X_2 are unmeasured and want to obtain the reduced-form parameters $\P_{31}$ and $\P_{32}$, which can be estimated by OLS. The expressions for the $\P$ coefficients now become:

$$\P_{31} = \frac{1}{\Delta}[\gamma_{11}(\beta_{31} + \beta_{21}\beta_{32}) + \gamma_{21}(\beta_{32} + \beta_{12}\beta_{31})]$$

$$\text{and } \P_{32} = \frac{1}{\Delta}[\gamma_{12}(\beta_{31} + \beta_{21}\beta_{32}) + \gamma_{22}(\beta_{32} + \beta_{12}\beta_{31})]$$

$$\text{where } \Delta = 1 - \beta_{12}\beta_{21} - \beta_{13}\beta_{31} - \beta_{23}\beta_{32} - \beta_{12}\beta_{23}\beta_{31} - \beta_{13}\beta_{21}\beta_{32}$$

Once again, we see that the denominators of the coefficients for Z_1 and Z_2 are the same, that the feedbacks β_{13} and β_{23} from X_3 to X_1 and X_2 enter only into the denominator Δ, and that the numerators (within brackets) consist of the complex functions of the structural parameters that we would have obtained by tracing the effects of each Z_i forward to X_3. For example, there are now four compound paths from Z_1 to X_3. Two of these go through X_1 and two through X_2. One of those through X_1 goes directly to X_3, whereas the second goes indirectly to X_3 by way of X_2. Of the paths that go through X_2, one goes directly to X_3 and the other indirectly through X_1. A similar situation holds for the coefficients of Z_2.

In effect, the full model (if identified) would permit one to estimate all of these component parts, whereas the reduced-form coefficients $\P_{31}$ and $\P_{32}$ give us only the total impact of (unit) changes in the Z_i. In this particular underidentified model, measures of X_1 and X_2 would do us no good because of the fact that the separate coefficients could not be estimated anyway, without further a priori assumptions. Because of the additional feedbacks between X_1 and X_2, the expression for Δ has become more complex. The important point is that, regardless of the size of Δ, the relative impacts of Z_1 and Z_2 will not be affected. They will be the same as if there were no feedback from X_3 to either X_1 or X_2.

It is important to note that in this more complex model, as well as those that follow, the feedback or reciprocal causation between X_1 and X_2 *do* affect the relative magnitudes of $\P_{31}$ and $\P_{32}$. That is, if one were to alter the magnitudes of β_{21} and β_{12}, this would affect the relative values of the coefficients estimating the impacts of Z_1 and Z_2 on X_3. It is crucial to keep this fact in mind.

Let us consider the model of Figure 5.4, in which we allow for additional effects of Z_1 and Z_2 that do not go through the intervening variables X_1 and X_2, to which there is feedback from X_3. We can conceptualize these additional links to X_3 as being "direct," or we might postulate some additional intervening variables that have not been measured. When we add these two new paths to X_3, we do not affect the equations for X_1 or X_2 in any way. The new structural equation for X_3 becomes

$$X_3 = \beta_{31}X_1 + \beta_{32}X_2 + \gamma_{31}Z_1 + \gamma_{32}Z_2 + \epsilon_3$$

which is now underidentified since, as was true for the equations for X_1 and X_2, none of the coefficients have been set equal to zero by a priori assumption. Put in other terms, if we knew the values of all of the structural parameters in these equations, we could solve for the reduced-form parameters $\P_{ij}$. With our data, we may estimate the $\P_{ij}$ using OLS, *but we cannot travel the reverse route.* Given the estimates of the $\P_{ij}$ from the data, we cannot estimate the structural parameters, because there will be too many unknowns, some of which have to be given a priori values (usually zero) before the others can be estimated.

Therefore, it would have done us no good to have obtained the X_1 and X_2 measures. Our reduced-form equation for X_3 now becomes:

$$X_3 = \P_{31} Z_1 + \P_{32} Z_2 + \eta_3$$

$$\text{where } \P_{31} = \frac{1}{\Delta} \left[\gamma_{11} (\beta_{31} + \beta_{21}\beta_{32}) + \gamma_{21} (\beta_{32} + \beta_{12}\beta_{31}) + \gamma_{31} (1 - \beta_{12}\beta_{21}) \right]$$

$$\P_{32} = \frac{1}{\Delta} \left[\gamma_{12} (\beta_{31} + \beta_{21}\beta_{32}) + \gamma_{22} (\beta_{32} + \beta_{12}\beta_{31}) + \gamma_{32} (1 - \beta_{12}\beta_{21}) \right]$$

and, as before, $\Delta = 1 - \beta_{12}\beta_{21} - \beta_{13}\beta_{31} - \beta_{23}\beta_{32} - \beta_{12}\beta_{23}\beta_{31} - \beta_{13}\beta_{21}\beta_{32}$. The only differences between these results and those for the previous model consist of the added terms involving products of γ_{31} and γ_{32}, respectively, and $(1 - \beta_{12}\beta_{21})$.

Before commenting on these terms, let us consider the model of Figure 5.5, which it turns out will involve a similar kind of expression. Figure 5.5 differs from Figure 5.3 in that we have added a third exogenous variable Z_3 that does not act through either X_1 or X_2 and that has been represented as having a direct path to X_3. Thus, the models of Figures 5.4 and 5.5 have in common the feature that we have drawn in additional paths to X_3 that do not involve X_1 or X_2. Of course, there may be unknown feedback mechanisms involving additional intervening variables, but we assume that these can be neglected. Our question in connection with Figure 5.5 is whether the presence of feedbacks among X_1, X_2, and X_3 will in any way affect our inferences concerning the relative total impacts of the Z_i, when one of the latter does not involve the equation for X_1 or X_2. The new structural equation for X_3 becomes

$$X_3 = \beta_{31}X_1 + \beta_{32}X_2 + \gamma_{33}Z_3 + \epsilon_3$$

Since we now have three exogenous Z_i, the reduced-form equation for X_3 has three $\P_{ij}$ to be estimated. The expressions for these $\P_{ij}$ in terms of the (unknown) structural parameters are:

$$\P_{31} = \frac{1}{\Delta} \left[\gamma_{11} (\beta_{31} + \beta_{21}\beta_{32}) + \gamma_{21} (\beta_{32} + \beta_{12}\beta_{31}) \right]$$

$$\P_{32} = \frac{1}{\Delta} \left[\gamma_{12} (\beta_{31} + \beta_{21}\beta_{32}) + \gamma_{22} (\beta_{32} + \beta_{12}\beta_{31}) \right]$$

$$\P_{33} = \frac{1}{\Delta} \gamma_{33} (1 - \beta_{12}\beta_{21})$$

where Δ, which is based only on the beta coefficients, remains as before. We see that the first two $\P_{ij}$ are exactly the same as those for the model of Figure 5.3 and that the third consists of the single γ_{33} multiplied by the same factor $(1 - \beta_{12}\beta_{21})$ as we noted above in connection with Figure 5.4. Perhaps the easiest of the two models to visualize is that of Figure 5.5, where Z_3 operates completely independently of Z_1 and Z_2. In a simple recursive model we would expect the coefficient of Z_3 to be γ_{33} for *both* the structural and reduced-form equations. In the special case where there is no feedback from X_3 to X_1 and X_2, we have $\beta_{13} = \beta_{23} = 0$, so that Δ reduces to $(1 - \beta_{12}\beta_{21})$, and therefore the coefficient of Z_3 in the reduced form becomes γ_{33} as we would expect. Thus Δ cancels out in the case of Z_3, but not for Z_1 and Z_2 unless the product $\beta_{12}\beta_{21}$ is also zero, in which case we return to the simple recursive model. Also notice that if there is feedback from X_3 to either X_1 or X_2, but if

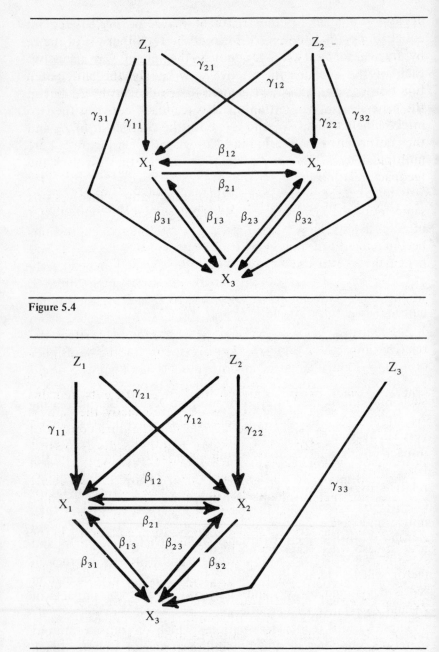

Figure 5.4

Figure 5.5

$\beta_{12}\beta_{21} = 0$, then for the model of Figure 5.5, $\P_{33}$ becomes equal to $\gamma_{33}/\triangle$. If one were to infer the total impacts of the Z_i by tracing forward only, as though the model were recursive, each of the coefficients of the Z_i would be the anticipated functions of the betas and gammas, each divided by $\triangle$. But in the general case, where there is also feedback between the two intervening variables X_1 and X_2, both the coefficient of Z_3 and the coefficients representing the "direct paths" in Figure 5.4 are multiplied by a kind of "correction factor" that involves the feedback relationship $\beta_{12}\beta_{21}$.

It might be argued that since the denominator $\triangle$ involves this same term, the factor $(1 - \beta_{12}\beta_{21})$ compensates for this aspect of $\triangle$ in such a manner that if $\beta_{13} = \beta_{23} = 0$, the two expressions become identical. But in general they will not be equal, and hence the coefficient of Z_3 in Figure 5.5 will not be exactly γ_{33}. We have already noted that for the model of Figure 5.3, when we compare the *relative* impacts of Z_1 and Z_2 their ratios will be the same, regardless of the feedbacks β_{13} and β_{23} from X_3. Feedbacks between X_1 and X_2, however, will affect the relative impacts of the Z_i. Let us focus on the multiplier $(1 - \beta_{12}\beta_{21})$ that appears in both models for Figures 5.4 and 5.5. If there is strong positive feedback between X_1 and X_2, such that an increase in X_1 will increase X_2, further increasing X_1 though by a somewhat lesser amount, and so forth, then a very slight change in either Z_1 or Z_2 may produce a much larger impact on X_1 and X_2 than would have been anticipated on the basis of the γ_{ij} alone. If so, their impacts would be large, relative to those of Z_3 in Figure 5.5. The correction factor $(1 - \beta_{12}\beta_{21})$ would in this instance be positive but less than unity, and hence Z_3 would be "penalized" relative to Z_1 and Z_2. On the other hand, with negative feedback between X_1 and X_2, the sign of $\beta_{12}\beta_{21}$ will be negative and hence the correction factor will be greater than unity.[1] In this instance, a change in X_1 is dampened by X_2, and vice versa, so that the impacts of Z_1 and Z_2 relative to Z_3 are weakened.

These various feedback situations, which of course represent merely a sampling of the possibilities, suggest that feedback models must be handled with care, but that the inferences we would draw on the basis of estimates of the reduced-form parameters will not be misleading. That is, we do not expect to reach conclusions about the relative importance of the Z_i which would differ in fundamental ways from those that would have been inferred on the basis of the full set of structural equations. Translated into practical research terms, this implies that we may safely omit the intervening variables in these instances. In view of other potential complications, some of which will be discussed in the next sections, it is nevertheless recommended that one always construct models involving all variables believed to be of theoretical interest, even where some of these may have to be omitted from the empirical study. One may then trace out the implications of these models before deciding whether or not it is safe to neglect the intervening variables.[2] Such a procedure provides justifications that are based on *theoretical* rather than pragmatic considerations, and it therefore provides the reader with an opportunity to evaluate the adequacy of the entire structural model before being presented with the data and interpretations. One may then introduce other modifications, study their theoretical implications, and thereby interpret the data in light of these changes in the underlying theory.

Why Include Intervening Variables in Our Theories?

We have seen, for the models we have studied, that as long as we confine ourselves to linear additive models, we will not be misled if we omit the intervening variables from the models and simply estimate the relative effects of the exogenous variables from the reduced forms. If the underlying structural parameters could have been estimated from the data, it is true that if we had been able to measure the intervening variables we would have been able to decompose each of the total effects of the Z_i into component paths, thereby adding to our knowledge of the mechanisms involved. But in one sense this would be merely adding frosting to the cake. Given the fact that there will generally be numerous Z_i, each of which needs to be measured with great care, the investigator obviously will never be able to measure *all* of the variables in the theoretical system. Therefore, it would seem to make more sense to concentrate most heavily on the Z_i. We have also seen that as soon as one begins to allow for feedbacks of unknown magnitudes among the X_i, it is likely that many of the equations for the X_i will become under-identified. If so, then *even with perfect measures* of the X_i, it becomes impossible to estimate the structural parameters. In such cases it is obviously unwise to go to the expense of measuring these X_i.

These are indeed important considerations that provide an excellent justification for omitting intervening variables. We have not studied the completely general case, in which there might be several levels of intervening variables, but the principle involved appears to generalize rather simply. The denominators Δ in all such instances will be the determinants of the matrix of the beta coefficients, will be identical for all coefficients of the Z_i, and will not contain any gammas. We also know that the necessary conditions for stability imply that the Δ cannot be zero. At least in the case where there are $k - 1$ intervening variables affected by the Z_i, and where there is a single be-havioral variable X_k, the feedbacks from the X_k to these inter-vening variables never appear in the numerators of the $\P_{kj}$ representing the coefficients in this reduced-form equation for X_k. As soon as one admits the possibility of feedbacks among the intervening variables, however, the situation becomes more complex. Unless one specifies rather carefully what these inter-vening variables are, the assumption of *no* feedbacks among them becomes difficult to justify except on ad hoc, pragmatic grounds.

There is, in addition, one very important consideration that we have thus far neglected. We have assumed that the structural coefficients are constant parameters, at least over the period of investigation. The argument against the reliance on reduced forms, and the necessity of estimating the structural parameters, can be put in the following way: if the structural parameters were to change, we would have no way of predicting what would happen to the $\P_{ij}$. This implies, of course, that the so-called parameters are not really constants, but variables. The common assumption for linear additive models is that all individuals are homogeneous with respect to the parameters. That is, the β_{ij} and γ_{ij} are exactly the same for all individuals. Of course, this is a tremendous oversimplification, but it will be approximately valid as long as there is only random variation about these parameters as measures of central tendency. In other words, we may imagine that there is a distinct β_{ijk} for each of k individuals, but with the expected value $E(\beta_{ijk})$ being the parameter β_{ij}. Individual differences in the parameters are, in effect, cancelled out.

But the parameters may vary systematically from one subpopulation to another, or from one set of conditions to another, which of course means that replications across populations, conditions, or time periods may not give the same results. This implies that it might be fruitful to take the structural "parameters" as functions of other variables and to allow for nonadditive and more complex equation systems. If so, it becomes essential to be able to theorize about these structural parameters and desirable to attempt to measure the intervening variables. Although "subjectivist" social scientists do not generally put the matter in precisely these terms—and perhaps many would even deny that formalization of their arguments is possible or desirable—I believe that their criticisms can be interpreted in this manner. The remainder of this section will be concerned with making this claim a bit more specific.

Subjective Meanings, Definitions of Situations

Ever since W. I. Thomas impressed on sociologists the dictum that situations defined as real by the actors *are* real, there has been the continual warning that subjective interpretations of reality, or the "meanings" persons give to reality, cannot safely be ignored. However, this very general and sensible pronouncement alone in no way enables us to proceed systematically or cumulatively toward the development of testable theory. If it is meant to imply that each individual acts uniquely in an inscrutable way by basically adding a random component to the objective reality, then it would make most sense to aggregate these individuals and thereby cancel out these random components.

If the subjectivist insists on the uniqueness of each individual, without specifying the *conditions* under which subjective definitions vary systematically (with small idiosyncratic elements, to be sure), then he or she is merely asserting the claim that generalization is impossible. If this is true, then there is little or no point in proceeding further. The important task, it seems, is to interpret the subjective factors as implying that objective or situational variables (which we have designated as the Z_i) do not affect all individuals in the same way, but that it is still possible to state lawlike propositions specifying how different kinds of actors will react under various conditions Z_i. In terms of the models we have been considering, this implies that we could take the γ_{ij} as variables that are systematically related to other Z_i or to internal states X_i, that are in turn functions of previous values of certain Z_i.

If we return to the simple model of Figure 5.2, in which Z_1 affects only X_1 and Z_2 affects only X_2, we might theorize that the coefficient linking the situational factor Z_1 (say, the proportion of blacks in the area) to the internal state (say, prejudice of a white individual) is a function of a number of other variables that have not yet been brought into the model. These might include additional situational factors W_i, several additional internal states, and perhaps even Z_2 and X_2. The same might apply to the coefficient linking Z_2 to X_2. For illustrative purposes, we might take the γ_{ij} as the following linear functions:

$$\gamma_{11} = a + b_1 W_1 + b_2 Z_2 + b_3 X_2 + e_1$$

$$\text{and } \gamma_{22} = c + d_1 W_1 + d_2 W_2 + e_2$$

where the e_i indicate idiosyncratic or unexplained factors. If we make the simplifying assumptions (some such *always* being necessary) that $E(e_i) = 0$ and that neither e_i is correlated with any of the independent variables in the respective equations, then we may solve for each of the coefficients if each of the variables has been perfectly measured. Furthermore, we may insert the expected values of the γ_{ij} into the remaining equations and decide the implications.

Such an explicit procedure places the burden of proof on the subjectivist—where it now *should* be placed—to attempt to explain differential interpretations, definitions, or meanings attached to the same objective situations, and to construct alternative models that explicitly build upon the more simplified versions. Thus, it is not enough to point out that different actors may interpret the same situation differently, since we all know this to be the case. The subjectivist is being asked to specify the variables (subjective or objective) that will predict these differential definitions. If this cannot be done, one might as well take the γ_{ij} as constants. Clearly, if one sets out to explain the variable γ_{ij} in this fashion, it is going to be necessary to estimate their numerical values, and we have seen that this will be impossible from the reduced forms alone. If one were willing to accept the very simple model of Figure 5.2, and if one had (nearly) perfect measures of X_1 and X_2, this would be possible because the equations for X_1 and X_2 are identified. But in the more complex model of Figure 5.3, we saw that this would not be possible because of the existence of too many unknowns.

This illustrates an extremely important practical point. One cannot handle too many complexities at once. If, for example, our hypothetical subjectivist wanted to study the behavior of the γ_{ij} under various conditions, he or she could not also allow for feedback among the X_i, as in Figure 5.3, unless he or she were able to modify the model by specifying the time lags or introduce additional variables into these feedback equations. Too often, it seems, there is a tendency to criticize a model as being overly simplistic (as must necessarily be the case) without supplying a more realistic alternative that is also rejectable. In concrete terms, we cannot empirically evaluate a model that purports to explain structural parameters (or the relative importance of variables) which cannot even be estimated from perfectly measured variables. The theorist who constructed the model may appear to be very profound, but this may be only because he or she has not made a sufficient number of simplifying assumptions to make the theory rejectable under the most favorable of circumstances.

Is there a reasonable intermediate position that one may take under the circumstances? I believe there is. One may still construct the theory, taking the γ_{ij} (or other structural parameters) as variables that are functions of other variables in the system. Then one may treat the intervening variables X_1 and X_2 as unmeasured, substitute the functions for the γ_{ij} in the reduced-form equations, and see what this implies about the resulting equations. Let us illustrate in the case of the model for Figure 5.2, where we previously obtained the reduced-form equation

$$X_3 = \frac{\beta_{31}\gamma_{11}}{1 - \beta_{13}\beta_{31} - \beta_{23}\beta_{32}}\, Z_1 + \frac{\beta_{32}\gamma_{22}}{1 - \beta_{13}\beta_{31} - \beta_{23}\beta_{32}}\, Z_2 + \eta_3$$

$$= \frac{1}{\Delta}\, [\beta_{31}\gamma_{11}Z_1 + \beta_{32}\gamma_{22}Z_2] + \eta_3$$

Substituting our equations for γ_{11} and γ_{22}, we get

$$X_3 = \frac{1}{\Delta}\, [\beta_{31}\, (a + b_1 W_1 + b_2 Z_2 + b_3 X_2 + e_1)Z_1 + \beta_{32}\, (c + d_1 W_1$$
$$+ d_2 W_2 + e_2)Z_2] + \eta_3$$

where $X_2 = \beta_{23}X_3 + \gamma_{22}Z_2 + \epsilon_2$

which reduces to a much more complex nonlinear equation of the general form

$$(1 - KZ_1)X_3 = A_1 Z_1 + A_2 Z_2 + A_3 Z_1 Z_2 + A_4 W_1 Z_1 + A_5 W_1 Z_2$$
$$+ A_6 W_2 Z_2 + U$$

Even though we cannot estimate the structural parameters themselves, we may develop a rather weak test by contrasting the explanatory power of this nonlinear equation with the simple linear alternative

$$X_3 = B_1 Z_1 + B_2 Z_2 + B_3 W_1 + B_4 W_2 + V$$

Thus the theory has used subjectivist reasoning to enable us to predict ahead of time a specific kind of nonlinear model that might not have been anticipated without the use of these subjective variables. Although I shall not bother to illustrate this same approach in the succeeding discussion, the same principles can be applied in each instance.

Attitudes Versus Behavior

We have by now become so accustomed to the fact that attitudes do not predict well to behavior that this is often taken as a justification for ignoring attitudes (or other internal states) altogether. But such a rejection of attitude research by some sociologists may be a bit unfair. After all, we rarely find *any* single variable predicting well to *any* behavior of a given individual, unless the predictor is that same variable at an earlier point in time. Sometimes weak correlations between attitudes and behavior are used to bolster the argument that other kinds of "structural" variables must be introduced. It may not even be recognized that weak correlations also could have stemmed from rather half-hearted efforts to measure the attitudes concerned, as for example when one puts together only four or five items to tap a single dimension. In the extreme case, one may even attempt to predict a behavior from a single attitudinal item. It should come as no surprise, under such circumstances, if the measure of association is of the order of magnitude of .2 or .3. But if one applies the same standards of measurement to "situational factors" or "structural variables," say, by using a single item with only three or four levels, one is likely to find that the explanatory power is not much higher.

The important theoretical problem becomes that of explaining the imperfect linkage between attitudes and behavior. In terms of the models we have been considering, this would involve taking β_{31} and β_{32} as variables to be explained by situational factors or other internal states of the individual. For example, if X_1 is degree of frustration and X_3 degree of aggression, we attempt to theorize about the conditions that affect the nature of the relationship between the two. If the perceived source of frustration is too powerful, or if the individual is too closely attached emotionally to that source, we expect aggression toward that source to be low, and perhaps directed toward a substitute target. More generally, if effective social controls are placed on the individual concerned, we expect that he or she will not "act out" these attitudes. As was the case with the gamma coefficients, we might attempt to take β_{31} and β_{32} as functions of certain other variables, including possibly some of the variables already contained in the model. Then, if X_1 and X_2 could not be measured, we could again put these functions into the reduced forms in place of their respective "parameters" and note the implications. Depending on the nature of the specific functions used, we would likely find that X_3 would be a nonlinear function of the Z_i, and this prediction could be specifically tested against the additive model.

Differential Response to Behavior and "Labelling"

It has also frequently been noted that *reactions* to an individual's behavior may play an important part in affecting that person's self-image, attitudes, and expectations. In the field of deviance, so-called "labelling" theory has become a recent version of this old idea. The basic notion is that labelling (or any other form of reaction) is a *selective* process that is not applied uniformly to all individuals. For example, misdeeds perpetrated by a young, black, ghetto male may bring about very different reactions than the very same behavior by a white, middle-class female. What this is in effect saying, then, is that the feedback coefficients β_{13} and β_{23} are not identical for all individuals. Presumably, once more, we would want to theorize about the nature of the variables or factors that affect these feedback coefficients and that make them large under some circumstances and small under others. In particular, we would want to know the circumstances under which such feedbacks are likely to be positive (thereby reinforcing the behavior in question) or negative (and therefore damping it). We could again utilize these

functions for the feedback parameters, put them into the reduced forms, and see what kind of reduced-form function is
implied. Without theories regarding these feedback functions,
we would be at a loss as to how to predict these alternative
forms.

Internal Mechanisms and Balance Theory

Finally, we can take very brief note of various theories that
have been developed to account for internal processes by which
individuals tend to learn to live with potential inconsistencies.
One such theoretical orientation stresses the need to reduce
tensions by "balancing" the attitudes in question so as to make
them appear consistent. There are several alternative theories of
attitude change that postulate somewhat different kinds of
balancing mechanisms, but we need not be concerned with their
specific natures (Taylor, 1973). The essential point is that these
theories deal with the feedback parameters β_{12} and β_{21}
between two (or more) internal states. We would want to be
able to treat these parameters as variables that are functions of
other variables in the system, at least some of which would
presumably be exogenous. Once more, we could eliminate the
unmeasured internal states from the model by substituting these
functions for β_{12} and β_{21} in the reduced-form equations and
noting the implications.

Some General Observations

It should be specifically noted that unless the intervening variables have been measured and the structural parameters estimated, the alternative procedures suggested all provide only
very weak tests of the elaborated theory in question. These tests
have the following characteristic. If they imply complex functional forms that in fact explain quite a bit more of the variance
than the simple linear model, then we have a degree of faith
that a more serious effort to elaborate on the model and
measure the intervening variables is warranted. In order to

justify such an effort, it would of course be wise to rely on *multiple* weak tests of this nature, rather than only one or two. But if the linear additive model proves almost as good as the more complex one, this does not necessarily imply that the more complex model is incorrect, for several obvious reasons. First, the sample selected may be too homogeneous with respect to variables that affect the parameter values γ_{ij} and β_{ij} so that, for the data in question, these *are* for all practical purposes really constants. The implication is that fair tests of these theories may require very carefully selected samples that emphasize extremes.

The second reason is that there may be special cases under which the more complex model *also* predicts a linear additive relationship. As one example of this possibility, which we have not discussed in the present connection, status inconsistency or mobility theory may imply a simple additive relationship between the dependent variable and two status variables *if* the effects of inconsistency or mobility are of approximately equal magnitudes but in opposite directions (Blalock, 1967). Therefore, if one finds that the additive model holds, this does not necessarily imply that there is no inconsistency or mobility effect.

The general import of all of the results we have discussed is that in each specific instance, the theorist-investigator should carefully consider the alternatives that are available and the complexity of the theory that is to be utilized. There will be circumstances under which it is worthwhile to attempt to obtain measures of the intervening variables, even though these measures may be very imperfect. But there will be others in which the postulated feedbacks or other complications will be such that even with perfect measures of these variables, it will still be impossible to estimate the structural parameters or to gain more theoretical insights than would have been attainable without the measures. The essential point is that these decisions should be made *explicitly* on the basis of a theoretical model, and before the data have been collected. If the model is built up ex post facto, as often happens, it is likely that one or two crucial measures will be lacking, in which case little or nothing can be done without a subsequent study.

THE OMISSION OF VARIABLES RELATING
TO PAST EXPERIENCES

We began this chapter by pointing out what appears to be a common practice of justifying the omission of variables on the purely pragmatic grounds that they cannot be easily measured. By now it should be clear that our basic recommendation is that, where variables must be omitted on practical grounds, the investigator should attempt to develop explicit alternative theories that include these variables. If the theoretical assumptions are of certain types, then the omission may be theoretically justified. But if one is not willing to make such assumptions, or if they must be made tongue-in-cheek, then one's interpretations must be modified. In effect, the reader should be told just what the investigator is and is not willing to assume about the relationships between the included and omitted variables.

In this section we turn our attention to a very important class of variables that are practically always omitted from quantitative empirical work in sociology, and often in nonquantitative field work as well. As the title of the section implies, these are the variables that refer directly to the past experiences of the individuals concerned, whether these be persons or macro units. If good time-series data were available, past values of variables could be used to provide this kind of information. But the sociologist or psychologist studying the individual person or small group is rarely in a position to obtain such data except during a relatively brief period, perhaps up to three or four years, but rarely longer. Or where longer-range studies are made, the measurements are typically confined to a very small number of measured items, such as test scores, occupation, income, marital status, and so forth. Detailed day-to-day experiences are lost from sight, except in extremely rare case studies. Where a respondent is studied at a particular point in time, he or she may be asked to provide certain "background" information, typically things like age, sex, race or ethnic identification, religion, father's occupation, mother's and father's formal schooling, size of community during adolescence, and so forth. These background variables are then used as very crude indicators of earlier experiences. Sometimes the individual is asked to recall certain of these experiences in a very general way, perhaps by asking about relationships with parents and siblings, the nature of parental sanctions, or the emphasis placed by parents on education or other desirable or undesirable traits.

Such extremely superficial indicators of past experiences are usually clearly recognized as such, but data analyses are then made as though the measurement errors were negligible. In some cases a reader is left guessing whether, for example, "effects" that are attributed to the biological factors of race, sex, and age are meant to imply a causal chain leading from the biological to the behavioral, or whether the attributes of sex and race, and the continuous variable of chronological age, are merely indicators of other socialization or experience variables. The causal model connecting the two kinds of variables is very often implicit, with the assumption being that the biological factors are causally prior to all other variables. At least this is usually implied in discussions of sex and race differences, though conveniently ignored in instances where the biological influences are not as readily apparent, as for example in the case of inherited intelligence, athletic ability, obesity, and other traits that are not easily separated from environmental influences.

If the true variable of interest is really not the biological attribute of sex or race, but the differential experiences of boys and girls, or blacks and whites, then it is not at all clear that the temporal sequences are unambiguous. Suppose, for example, that the really important differences between men and women occur primarily *after* they have finished their formal educations. Or perhaps sex differences become salient before racial differences in one setting, but much later in another setting. "Education," which is usually measured as years of formal schooling, is often dated as occurring before one enters a full-time occupation. But "education," conceptualized in terms of learning, is obviously a continuous process that cannot easily be dated in time. And the ambiguities in interpreting the effects of "age" and "community background" are certainly equally as great.

It is clear, then, that the insertion of what appear to be very simple and obvious background variables into causal models introduces a considerable amount of specification error into the theory. Yet most of the variables that we would really like to measure are both conceptually elusive and almost impossible to measure, even under almost ideal conditions. We can imagine studies in which one could observe the differential treatments of, say, boys and girls at different ages. But such studies would be extremely time-consuming and therefore not likely to be replicated under a wide variety of circumstances. It is therefore unlikely that we would be able to acquire data for which we had information on both the exogenous variables Z_i that influenced these differential treatments and also adequate measures of the treatments themselves. Nor would we likely have information about the psychic reactions of the boys and girls to these treatments, though it would perhaps be possible to observe their interaction patterns and behavioral responses to these treatments.

In the case of respondents who are presently adults, these pieces of information are usually lost in history. Even were it possible to observe these persons intensively for brief periods when they were very young, considerations of privacy and other matters of research expediency would dictate that follow-ups involve increasingly superficial data as the individuals moved into adolescence and adulthood. In short, it is almost impossible to imagine really detailed longitudinal analyses of the sort that would enable one to obtain systematic information about past histories, except on an extremely limited case-history basis of very atypical persons who would permit such an invasion of their privacy.

There is, of course, the important theoretical stance that since historical factors can only influence present behaviors through *present* states, including memories and expectations based on past experiences, one may neglect the actual past in favor of present characteristics. If one followed this approach, one would want to ask detailed questions about the individual's perceptions of the past, whether factually distorted or not. The theoretical model would then contain *expectations* of behaviors that might be based in part on past behaviors and in part on perceptions of present characteristics. That is, the theory itself would involve only present levels of all variables, but it would allow for the possibility that certain of these levels would, in turn, be based on events of the past. For example, the losers in a war may retain very vivid memories of this war and may predict the future behavior of their adversary on the basis of their (present) perceptions of past events. Certain other features of the environment may also operate to distort these perceptions and expectations. For example, if two parties remain in economic or political competition, this fact may operate to keep alive memories of past interactions and also to distort them in various ways. The essential point is that a truly detailed accounting of present characteristics could substitute for a historical analysis of the actual events.

The obvious ideal resolution is to put the two kinds of formulations together into a more complete model in which actual events in the past affect present perceptions and memories. Unfortunately, we must concern ourselves with what is almost the opposite practice, namely that of ignoring *both* the past events *and* the internal states that incorporate these events in the form of memories and expectations. Suppose we do not know either the detailed set of past events or the internal states, but only have available a rather short list of objective background factors such as sex, race, age, place of birth or childhood residence, group memberships such as religion, and a few parental characteristics such as occupation and education. Under what conditions can we confine ourselves to such variables in models without making invalid inferences? On the face of it, given the extremely complex nature of human experiences, we might expect to be misled quite often. Or, if not misled, we would anticipate finding extremely weak correlations between these background factors and most forms of behavior. This latter anticipation is fulfilled in study after study.

Yet we do find certain instances (e.g., sex differences with respect to criminal convictions, suicides, and occupational distributions) in which the relationships found are rather substantial. In such instances, however, we may also find that the *interpretations* of the mechanisms producing these differences may vary considerably. For instance, if we find a racial difference with respect to school performance, this may be interpreted as being due to biological differences, differences in very early familial socialization, differences within the school settings, peer group influences, differences in expectations based on a perception of adult opportunities, or subcultural language differences. Clearly, without measures of the intervening variables and possible sources of spuriousness, the existence of such differences becomes a source of considerable dispute that cannot easily be resolved. But if such variables are also left out of the *theoretical* model, we often cannot even tell whether or not the disputants are talking past one another. In short, if we have theories that contain the unmeasured variables, we are more likely to become motivated to study the mechanisms involved. Without them, the situation would appear hopeless.

Obviously, then, in order to get hold of this kind of problem we need to put forth some very simple prototype models and study their implications. One such model is given in Figure 5.6. Practically all discussions of so-called background variables presuppose that these variables may be taken as exogenous, though perhaps mutually correlated. At any given point in one's life history, there will certainly be additional exogenous variables Z_i, which will be distinguished from the background variables B_i that are actually measured by the investigator. These B_i and Z_i jointly affect other variables X_i which, in turn, affect internal states and eventually the behavior Y that be-

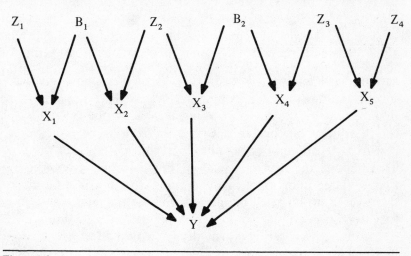

Figure 5.6

comes the ultimate dependent variable at the time of the study.

We might refer to the X_i as situational factors that con-
stituted the objective experiences of the individual at various
times in the past. For example, B_1 might refer to one's sex and
B_2 to race. Several Z_i might refer to cultural variables that
defined how male and female children were socialized, or how
blacks and whites were treated. Other Z_i might refer to the state
of the economy, school variables, or behaviors of peers. The X_i
might then represent various significant events jointly affected
by the B_i and Z_i. The model might have also contained a
number of W_i, taken as dependent on these X_i, referring to
internal states of the individual—memories, expectations, values,
strength of motivations, and so forth. For convenience, we have
omitted the latter set of variables from the model of Figure 5.6.
Presumably, if we were dealing with a rather lengthy time
period, there might be literally thousands of X_i and W_i having
different temporal subscripts.

If all relationships were additive, and if all B_i and Z_i were
perfectly measured, then we have seen that their relative impacts could be estimated without our needing measures of the
numerous intervening situational variables and internal states.
But only a very small proportion of the B_i and virtually none of

the other exogenous variables Z_i will be measured by the investigator. Furthermore, it is very reasonable to assume that a number of the B_i and Z_i will interact to affect the situational factors X_i. For example, it is unlikely that all girls or all blacks will have the same experiences. They are likely to be differentially affected by some of the Z_i, such as those involving subcultural norms or economic variables. This implies, then, that certain of the γ_{ij} connecting the background variables to the X_i will not be constants. Unless the X_i have been measured, it will therefore only be possible to make weak tests of the type discussed in the previous section. Furthermore, given the extremely large number of likely Z_i and X_i that would be operative over a prolonged time period, this type of indirect testing for interaction effects would have to be extremely crude.

An even more serious difficulty, it would seem, stems from the likelihood that important Z_i will be correlated with those B_i that have been measured by the investigator, so that their effects will be hopelessly confounded. If one merely takes the correlations between the unmeasured Z_i and the background variables to be unexplained, as implied by the curved double-headed arrow in Figure 5.7, it will be impossible to infer the effects of the background variables. If all variables in Figure 5.7 were measured, it would be possible to infer both the direct effects of B on Y, and also the indirect effects of B through X. But one could *not* infer the effects of B "through" Z, since the reasons for the correlation between these two variables would be unknown.

The implications are clear. If one wants to infer effects of sex, race, father's occupation, or other background variables while leaving other exogenous variables unspecified because their measurement is impossible, then one must assume something more definite about the relationships between these B_i and the remaining exogenous variables. One possible assumption is that the B_i are completely uncorrelated with all Z_i that have important effects on the behavior Y. Another assumption might be that such Z_i are individually unimportant and sufficiently numerous that their effects cancel out. A third possible assump-

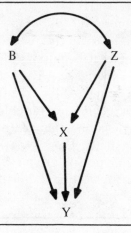

Figure 5.7

tion is that all such important Z_i are *effects* of the B_i in question, as indicated in the prototype model of Figure 5.8. If so, then these omitted Z_i are really another set of intervening variables between the B_i and the X_i. As long as we are willing to assume constant coefficients and an additive model, such Z_i may safely be omitted.

Just how plausible are such assumptions? Obviously, this depends on the nature of the B_i and Z_i. The degree to which one is willing to ignore such assumptions may also depend on one's willingness to confound the effects of the B_i and Z_i. As will be repeatedly emphasized in Chapter 6, whenever we label a given background variable (say, sex, race, father's occupation, or religion), we almost automatically distract the reader's attention from possible confounding variables. Two implications are obvious. First, whenever we suspect the existence of particular Z_i that are unmeasured but that may be confounded with a given B_i, it would seem most honest to use rather general labels to call the reader's attention to this possible confounding. Second, insofar as possible, it is advisable to make explicit assumptions about the causal connections between the B_i and Z_i, particularly if one is going to talk about "sex effects," "religious effects," or "effects of father's occupation."

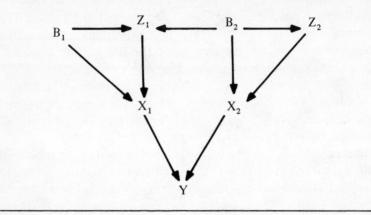

Figure 5.8

The essential point is that such very simple labels are, strictly speaking, only justified if one is willing to assume that the background factor is causally prior to all other Z_i. If they are being used as shorthand expressions for blocks of variables (e.g., all variables correlated with father's occupation), then this should be made explicit. One suspects that it is this latter usage that is intended by most authors, but that the labels are also likely to be used in an ambiguous fashion, sometimes referring to entire blocks and sometimes to specific variables. If so, simplistic explanations of complex processes are likely to result, as for example when one finds certain sex or race differences and jumps to the conclusion that one has found a simple explanatory variable such as "sexism" or "racism."

A truly systematic study of the customary background variables used in survey research is obviously needed. Certain kinds of background variables are more easily disentangled from unmeasured Z_i than others by virtue of the plausibility of the simplifying assumptions one may make. For example, a person's sex will have a negligible relationship with other background factors such as race, occupation, and education of parents, place of birth, and other factors over which the individual has little or no control. Other background factors, such as those that may have been relevant during adolescence, will be less easy to disentangle from one's sex to the degree that boys and girls are differentially exposed to religious experiences, educational programs, peer-group pressures, and the like. Here, it seems to be reasonable enough to assume that one's sex is a cause of such differential exposures and not merely spuriously related to them. If so, then "sex" may be a reasonably purified exogenous variable in the sense that sex differences may be either directly or indirectly attributed to the biological variable.

The case of race is much more complex in that, at least in the United States, one's race is likely to be confounded with both class and subcultural differences. The former may be crudely (but not perfectly) controlled through the use of information about one's father's occupation or education. But the subcultural factors are rarely measured, or are only imperfectly controlled by factors such as region or community size. Therefore, race will be confounded with numerous Z_i. The common assumption among sociologists is, of course, that race in part determines these latter variables. Certainly, the biological factor of race is not caused by these other variables. But the treatment and experiences of different racial groups (e.g., past discrimination) may be partly a cause and partly an effect of these subcultural differences. Therefore, although the biological variable "race" may be taken as a cause of many of the Z_i with which it is correlated, if the investigator is really interested in race as an indicator of discrimination, or differential treatment, this latter will not, in general, be so simply related to the other exogenous variables.

When we come to such background variables as type of home community, region, religious denomination, or any other voluntary group membership criterion, we recognize that such factors are partly *effects* of certain decisions. For example, parents may decide to change communities because of certain Z_i. They may change their religious denominations or other group memberships. In rare instances, a father's occupation may even depend upon certain behaviors of the child. Somewhat less rarely, perhaps, parents may separate as a result of a child's behavior, so that marital status of parents may be partly dependent on this behavior, as well as on numerous unmeasured Z_i.

A background variable such as "education" is perhaps even more complexly related to numerous Z_i. This variable is usually indexed by number of years of formal schooling, since measures of quality of education are rarely available. Most certainly, this kind of achievement background variable is dependent upon numerous unmeasured Z_i that may be confounded with it. In particular, one may find it difficult to find a simple label for such a variable. Is it years of formal schooling, knowledge, ability, "educational status," or what? Likewise, when we talk about the "effects" of "mother's education" (as measured by years of schooling), we may be confounding her formal schooling with numerous socialization and familial variables that are correlated with it.

In Chapter 6 we shall return to this general problem of the confounding of exogenous variables, as well as the practice of using overly simplistic labels. At that point, our concern will be with what appears to be a tendency to use labels, as for example by referring to "SES" effects, for variables that are often correlated with nonstatus variables. Here, we may summarize the general problem by noting the tendency to use the term "effects" in conjunction with rather simplistic and easily measured background variables. As long as one recognizes that the supposed "effects" of "region" or "father's occupation" are much more complex, there is no special harm done. But to the degree that such simplistic labels inhibit us from more serious efforts to specify and measure the remaining Z_i, we will be misled to the degree that these Z_i are important causes in their own right and not related to the customary B_i by simple causal mechanisms.

Omission of Past Values of Independent Variables

Although theoretical arguments often allow for the effects of memories of past events, most cross-sectional research does not take advantage of past levels of independent or exogenous variables. The usual justification, once more, is that of a lack of data. Since respondents' recollections are rightly suspect as indicators of the actual events (though not necessarily of perceptions of these events), it is usually impossible to obtain this information directly except in cases of easily recalled, dramatic events (e.g., one's wedding date, the death of a parent or spouse, or possibly one's own occupational history). The question we must pose again is that of the theoretical justification for such omissions, quite apart from that of the unavailability of data. Under what conditions will the omission of past levels of exogenous or intervening variables be reasonably justified, and under what conditions will serious distortions result? Our argument will again be that a theorist-investigator should attempt to make his or her assumptions explicit, insofar as this is feasible.

Let us begin with a very simple distributed lags model in which there is a single dependent variable Y_t representing, say, an individual's behavior at time t. Suppose that there is a single variable X that affects Y, but that the levels of X have shifted over a period of time, so that we may designate the current level of X as X_t, the level at time $t - 1$ as X_{t-1}, and the level of X at a time $t - k$ as X_{t-k}. For illustrative purposes, X might be a person's relative income at several points in time, or one's occupational prestige, or perhaps a specific kind of treatment by peers over some time period. Since the individual possesses a memory and develops expectations on the basis of past experiences, and may even make projections on the basis of changes in past experiences, we would expect that Y_t might be some reasonably complex function of the Xs at several points in time. In the simplest of cases, we might take Y_t as a linear function of the Xs as follows:

$$Y_t = \beta_0 X_t + \beta_1 X_{t-1} + \beta_2 X_{t-2} + \ldots + \beta_k X_{t-k} + \epsilon_t =$$
$$\sum_{i=0}^{k} \beta_i X_{t-i} + \epsilon_t$$

where for simplicity we have omitted the constant term as well as other causes of Y.

If we had perfect measures of the Xs at all of these points in time, and if the levels of the Xs at successive points in time were not too highly correlated, then we would be able to estimate the β_i parameters associated with the levels of X at the successive points in time. If the changes in X were occurring continuously, rather than discretely in time as implied by the time periods t, t – 1, t – 2, and so forth, then we might postulate some decay function as holding among the beta coefficients. For example, if behavior at time t were most heavily influenced by immediately past levels of X and only weakly influenced by events in the distant past, one might use an exponential decay function. Since this function would have only a relatively small number of parameters, one might be able to estimate it with data collected at perhaps four or five points in time, with "redundant" information for other periods being used to test the goodness of fit of the data to the model. Such an approach, however, would presuppose equally good measurement of X at all time periods and also reasonably large changes in X between successive time periods—conditions that are not likely to hold in realistic research.

Let us modify even this very simple two-variable distributed lags model by assuming that Y_t is influenced by X_t and by only the immediate past level X_{t-1}. But we must allow for a relationship between the X levels at these two points in time. We admit that the unknown exogenous variables that affect X are not likely to shift their levels rapidly, so that in the absence of a knowledge of the underlying mechanisms that produce stability in X, we may take X_t as a function of X_{t-1}. Causally, this does not provide us with any theoretical insights, but from the standpoint of *prediction,* it is a reasonable procedure. Suppose, however, that there is an explicit and known cause of X, namely Z, that shifts levels, so that we may take X_t as a function of X_{t-1} and Z_t, as well as a contemporary disturbance term. We would then have the following (linear) equations:

$$Y_t = \beta_0 X_t + \beta_1 X_{t-1} + \epsilon_{1t}$$
$$\text{and } X_t = \gamma_1 X_{t-1} + \gamma_2 Z_t + \epsilon_{2t}$$

If we were willing to assume that the historical dates are irrelevant, so that the same processes and coefficients that hold for time t also apply to t – 1 and to earlier periods, then we could also write the equations:

$$Y_{t-1} = \beta_0 X_{t-1} + \beta_1 X_{t-2} + \epsilon_{1t-1}$$

$$\text{and } X_{t-1} = \gamma_1 X_{t-2} + \gamma_2 Z_{t-1} + \epsilon_{2t-1}$$

We might, of course, write similar equations for X and Y at still earlier points in time.

In order to see the implications of this very simple set-up, let us imagine that the equation for Y_t is misspecified in that the value of X at time t – 1 is simply ignored, so that β_1 is erroneously assumed to be zero. We might write the incorrectly specified equation for Y_t as

$$Y_t = \beta'_0 X_t + \epsilon'_{1t}$$

where the new residual term ϵ'_{1t} actually contains the effects of X_{t-1}. If we were to use OLS to estimate the effects of X_t on Y_t, we would therefore obtain a biased estimate of the true slope because of the fact that the residual ϵ'_{1t} of the incorrectly specified equation will be correlated with X_t, the independent variable in that equation. This is true because ϵ'_{1t} contains X_{t-1} which is correlated, by assumption, with X_t. The degree of bias in the estimate will depend upon the strength of the correlation between X_t and X_{t-1}, which in turn will depend upon the relative magnitudes of the variations in X_{t-1} and Z_t, as well as the parameters γ_1 and γ_2.

If Z varies erratically from one time period to the next, then the values of X at successive time periods will not be as highly correlated. If there are numerous Z_i instead of just a single Z, and if these are not highly intercorrelated, then we might anticipate that changes in partizular Z_i might cancel out those in other Z_i so that X remained relatively stable. If so, then our estimates of the effects of X_t from the misspecified equation may be seriously biased. And if we used the correctly specified

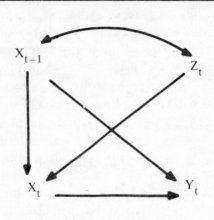

Figure 5.9

equation involving both X_t and X_{t-1} we would encounter problems of multicollinearity. The same principles will obviously apply if the correctly specified equation involves earlier time periods, whereas the incorrectly specified equation omitted certain of these variables.

The above equations may be represented as in Figure 5.9, in which we have allowed for the possibility that Z_t and X_{t-1} are intercorrelated. In fact, this is highly likely, since X_{t-1} is a function of Z_{t-1} and we would expect Z to be correlated with itself at an earlier point in time. Therefore, we may in general anticipate that the level of Z will be correlated with the earlier level of X. But it does not necessarily follow that the *change* in Z will be correlated with previous values. We see, however, that in order to say very much about the seriousness of the bias in our estimates of the effects of X_t on the basis of the misspecified equation that omits X_{t-1}, we need to know or assume something about the factors that are producing changes in X at different points in time.

What are the practical implications of this rather abstract exercise? First, we must recognize that individuals may differ with respect to the relative magnitudes of the beta coefficients. That is, some individuals may have much more rapid memory decays than others, or for other reasons their reactions may be much more sensitive to contemporary events than others. For these individuals, then, β_0 may be much greater in magnitude than β_1, which may be much greater than β_2, and so forth. For such individuals, misspecification through the omission of earlier levels of X may not create serious biases. For these persons, no matter what the past histories, we may predict that behaviors Y_t will be very sensitive to changes in the immediate situation. But for persons with "long memories," changes produced in levels of X may produce only minor changes in Y. Short-run studies of the type that we often encounter in laboratory experiments may lead one to infer that X has only a relatively minor effect on Y, whereas actually the effect may be much more important if one were to insert past levels into one's equations.

To the extent that complex processes are at work within individuals to interpret changes and to anticipate them by extrapolating past trends or by developing working theories to account for these changes, our models for explaining behavior should ideally include these internal states as intervening variables. If satisfactory measures of these expectations can be obtained, then it may be safe to exclude measures of past levels of the independent or exogenous variables. For example, a respondent may be asked to recall past events and to state his or her expectancies on the basis of these events. Or questions may be asked tapping the respondent's interpretations or explanations for possible changes. For example, a black respondent accustomed to certain behaviors on the part of white co-workers might be asked how he or she would interpret changes in these behaviors were they to occur. Would he or she, for example, perceive them to be only temporary or based on expediency? The presumption is that the responses to such changes will depend on one's expectations and interpretations, as well as the actual changes themselves. And these expectations may very well depend upon the *consistency* of past behavior and one's working theory or explanation of that behavior.

In more abstract terms, X_t may refer to the behavior of some other party to which the individual concerned is responding. Let this response be Y_t. Then we expect that Y_t will also be a function of the actor's expectations that have been based on past behaviors X_{t-1}, X_{t-2}, and so forth. If the X values over the past periods have been extremely consistent, but if they differ considerably from the present level X_t, then it may be entirely rational for the actor to base his or her response on these earlier levels, rather than on X_t. He or she might assume, for example, that the shift in levels represented a temporary aberration. Thus, the *patterning* or consistency of past levels of X may become an important variable in its own right.

We may illustrate this particular kind of model by Figure 5.10, in which we have inserted the intervening variable I_t to represent some mental state that has been influenced by present and past levels of X. If all of these X levels are approximately the same, then X_t may represent the entire block reasonably well. This would imply, for example, that cross-sectional or comparative data might be used effectively in instances where between-individual X differences were large as compared with those within individuals (across time). In such instances, if one were to work instead with very simple change models, by getting a difference between X_t and X_{t-1} for each individual, one might be much more easily misled. For if these changes were relatively small, they would likely be dominated by random measurement errors. If they were large, however, it would be desirable to have a measure of the internal state I_t in order to assess the individual's theoretical explanation of this change based on previous patterns of change.

Finally, we should note the possibility that if there are multiple X_i that affect Y, and if each of these X_i have had cumulative effects over time, the situation becomes much more complex, not only for the analyst, but also for the actor who is attempting to interpret all of these changes in some meaningful way. We may surmise that many expectancies as to how these levels will change at some future time will ordinarily be based on oversimplified "working theories" that enable the actor to behave in some semirational manner (Blalock and Wilken, 1979). Presumably, the patterning of the X_i at past points in time will affect these working theories. If so, then if a sudden

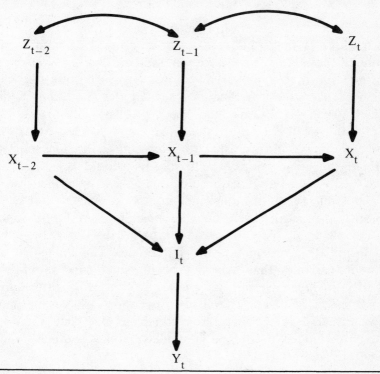

Figure 5.10

change is produced in only one of these X_i at time t, we may anticipate that the actor's reaction is going to depend upon the assumptions made in this working theory. For example, the change may be treated as an exception and ignored. Or the actor may assume that if the other X_i have not changed, then the shift in this particular variable will be only temporary. Still a third possibility is that the actor may believe that this single change is a precursor of future changes in the other X_i, with the possibility that he or she may "overreact" to this single change. Clearly, the more we know about the actor's expectations and working theories used to explain whatever changes are occurring, the more information we shall have in predicting the response.

CONCLUDING REMARKS

Our central concern in this chapter has been with possible distortions or faulty inferences that may result from the omission of variables from a causal system. We have assumed throughout that *some* variables must always be omitted. Our purpose has been to examine a few of the conditions under which such omissions can be justified on theoretical-methodological grounds, rather than on pragmatic ones. The basic argument has been that the omission of variables requires simplifying assumptions which, ideally, should be stated explicitly. Obviously, we have only been able to sample a few of the possible kinds of models and complications that are likely to arise in practice. Therefore, the major message has to be the following: In any particular study involving real data, always try to formulate a reasonably complete model. This model should contain variables that may not be measured, and should explicitly include relevant internal states or other intervening variables, as well as past levels of exogenous variables that may have affected these intervening variables. One may then see what this model (or alternative models) implies and make one's decisions accordingly.

Sometimes we hear blanket statements to the effect that longitudinal data are generally superior to cross-sectional data— or perhaps vice versa. Or one may attempt to argue, rather generally, that it is safe to ignore intervening variables or past values of exogenous variables. It should be obvious from the illustrations in the present chapter that decisions concerning one's design and the variables that should or should not be included need to be based on the nature of the assumptions one is willing to make in a given instance. Therefore, one should be wary of such general assertions unless one is willing to assume *automatically* that there are negligible measurement errors, that structural parameters for unmeasured variables are constants across all subpopulations or time periods, or that memory effects can safely be neglected.

Some such assumptions will have to be made in order to reduce the number of unknowns so as to achieve identification. But the particular kinds of assumptions one is willing to make will depend on the circumstances. If one is confined to a particular set of data or method of data collection—say, a survey at a single point in time—a careful theoretical formulation may make it possible to utilize pieces of information that might not otherwise be suggested. For example, if past events cannot be recalled accurately, it may at least be possible to solicit information about expectations and beliefs about these past events. Certainly, if one is confined to a small number of so-called background variables, and if one also lacks any measures of the intervening variables, the intellectual leap from theory to data, or from data to theory, is going to be exceedingly risky. Even so, given inadequate data, a careful effort to pinpoint the gaps and hidden assumptions should ease the task of the next investigator who may have more adequate resources.

NOTES

1. This will only be true if $|\beta_{12}\beta_{21}| < 1$. If the magnitude of this feedback product is greater than unity, however, the values of X_1 and X_2 will increase or decrease at an accelerating rate. We are assuming here that this will not occur.

2. For feedback models of greater complexity, it may be simpler to rely on procedures discussed in Heise (1975) for reducing the complexity of feedback models by omitting variables.

CHAPTER 6

THE CONFOUNDING OF VARIABLES AND OVERSIMPLIFIED INTERPRETATIONS

Throughout the book we have stressed several major themes. One of these has been that whenever measurement is indirect and certain variables have to be omitted from one's analysis, we will pay a price that becomes increasingly costly to the degree that we wish to generalize across settings or time periods. A second theme has emphasized the importance of homogeneity assumptions that, in regression terminology, permit one to introduce constants into one's equation systems. These "constants," however, are more realistically treated as variables to the degree that the scope of one's generalizations is increased. A third theme has stressed that issues of measurement comparability become increasingly fuzzy and intractable as one moves down the level-of-measurement hierarchy, so that comparability problems are extremely difficult to assess whenever categorical variables have been used. In this connection, it has been argued that attempts need to be made to dimensionalize experience variables, even where these experiences cannot be directly measured.

All of these themes will be relevant to the issues treated in the present chapter, although our immediate concern will be with a fourth theme that was treated briefly in Chapter 5. This fourth theme is that one must be continually alerted to the possibility that unmeasured variables will be *confounded* with the relatively small number of indicators that researchers will have available to them. In this connection, we have argued, it is essential that one pay careful attention to the way our variables become labeled, so that we do not attribute the effects of these unmeasured variables to the indicator variables in a too simplistic and misleading fashion.

The discussion of the previous chapter was highly abstract. In the present chapter we shall elaborate on some of the points made in Chapter 5, while introducing several more. But we shall do so in terms of specific variables of considerable interest to sociologists. For the most part, we shall be concerned with ways in which confounding may occur in connection with variables closely linked to the concept of social status. In Chapter 7 we shall be concerned with confounding that occurs as a result of aggregating operations based upon operationally convenient criteria, rather than criteria that are more easily related to one's theory. In both chapters we shall again stress what is perhaps the most general and important theme of the book, namely that theoretical considerations are inextricably bound to those of conceptualization and measurement.

THE CONFOUNDING OF MEASURED AND UNMEASURED VARIABLES: THE EXAMPLE OF SOCIAL STATUS

The social scientist interested in explaining individual behavior is faced with an obvious and well-known fact. All persons have been exposed to highly complex stimuli that are empirically interrelated and difficult to isolate from one another. Yet the investigator must use only a very small fraction of these stimuli as indicators of others and, furthermore, must admit that the selected stimuli may not be comparable from one setting to the next, or even from one time period to another during the course of a single actor's life. Thus one is faced with several very troublesome decisions. How can one select among these stimuli

in such a fashion as to permit accurate and generalizable findings and theoretical explanations? And what sorts of assumptions can and must be made about those variables that have
necessarily been omitted from one's analysis?

We have already noted that sociologists commonly use group
or category membership variables to represent many of these
stimuli, taking so-called "background variables" as explanatory
factors in causal models. These include factors such as sex, race,
age, region of birth or early childhood, size or type of home
community, religion, occupation and formal education of parents or self, organizational memberships, and the like. Persons
who share these memberships are assumed to have been exposed
to roughly the same experiences and are therefore taken to be
sufficiently homogeneous with respect to these stimuli that
they may be aggregated together so as to compare group means,
rates, or (in some cases) measures of association based on scores
of these aggregates.

One of the most serious dilemmas we shall confront in this
section can be posed either in terms of levels of measurement or
in terms of generalizability. From the former perspective, the
problem is that of deciding whether to treat group or category
membership variables (such as race, religion, or occupation) as
nominal or as ordered along a specific dimension. If they are
conceptualized as nominal, one does not have to make a com-
mitment on the explanatory mechanism, and one may also
"explain" a higher percentage of variance (provided the categories are not collapsed). If the number of unordered categories
is large, it becomes very difficult to make theoretical sense out
of one's findings, however. Even if there are only a few categories (e.g., races or ethnic groups), it is difficult to make much
more than descriptive statements about differences among these
nominal categories. On the other hand, if one commits oneself
to a particular ordering among the groups or categories, this
usually implies the existence of a theoretical variable that, as we
shall see, may very well be confounded with a large number of
other variables that have not been measured. Thus a commit-
ment to a higher level of measurement implies a higher level of

aspiration theoretically, but also a risk of settling prematurely on the wrong theory.

Examined from the perspective of generalizability, it will often be true that the kinds of background factors used in sociological research possess an observable comparability that the less well-measured experience variables do not. Methodists, for example, seem similar to one another across cultures, as do doctors, women, and college graduates. Their *experiences,* however, may vary considerably across societies. Certainly Iranian and American women have very different experiences, as compared to men. Doctors in the United States and the USSR have highly different statuses and dissimilar relationships to their clients and governments. Blacks are treated differently in France, Brazil, South Africa, and the United States. Therefore, if one were to rank a set of categories or groups along specific conceptual dimensions, these rankings might not be the same across settings. Or perhaps the prestige rankings of occupations might be similar, but not the rankings of these occupations with respect to power, job security, or even income.

As we have noted on many occasions, one cannot hope to come to grips with problems such as these without a reasonably clear theoretical formulation that includes conceptual distinctions among important variables, and without an explicit auxiliary measurement theory. In terms of the kinds of issues that will be addressed in the present section, these theories must be concerned with the relationships assumed to exist between the kinds of categorical and group memberships that we commonly refer to as background variables, on the one hand, and the actual experiences of actors on the other. If we lack an explicit theory about these latter experience variables, we may still insert the background variables into regression equations and causal models, but we will neither be able to get a clear handle on issues of generalizability nor shall we able to understand, theoretically, how and why these background variables are linked to behaviors through these experiences.

One further problem addressed toward the end of the previous chapter should again be noted. Experiences occur during various time periods. Some end rather abruptly, as for example when a family moves from one community to the next. Others are more or less continuous throughout life, but may impact on specific behaviors at different times. Still others involve the immediate context rather than some earlier period. Furthermore, the time periods for diverse actors are unlikely to coincide, making it very difficult for the researcher to specify some uniform time intervals appropriate to all actors.

Where the appropriate data are available, some of these problems can be handled in terms of so-called "event history" methodologies, in which the temporal sequences for each actor can be kept straight (Tuma et al., 1979). Often, however, the investigator will not be in a position to obtain these event histories, either because the necessary questions were never asked, because many events cannot be accurately recalled, or because many experiences of a cumulative nature cannot be pinpointed temporally. Regardless of whether or not the appropriate data are available, however, it will always be necessary to make some assumptions about the nature of the relevant temporal processes. Consistent with our earlier positions regarding the theory construction process, we argue that such assumptions should be made as explicit as possible and formally incorporated into one's theory.

How Are Status Effects Inferred?[1]

The notion of "social status" or "prestige" is certainly one of the key concepts in the sociological literature. Although I have not made a systematic canvass of introductory text books—and do not believe that much would be gained from doing so—it seems clear that we have a reasonable degree of consensus on the general meaning of the term, but surprisingly few really serious efforts to disentangle status variables from closely related concepts. It is my impression that relatively more such efforts were made during the 1940s and 1950s than at present, perhaps because we have reached a higher degree of consensus on the operational measures of status, or perhaps because we have simply tired of such abstract theoretical discussions.

The journal literature contains numerous empirical articles oriented to assessing "status effects" of many varieties: general SES effects, mobility effects, status inconsistency effects, or effects of single variables that are given status connotations, such as "effects of occupation" as measured in ordinal terms along a prestige dimension. As a *theoretical* concept, the notion of status is generally given an evaluative connotation, so that the measurement of status would seem to require some kind of assessment of internal states of individual judges. The usual notion of status, I infer, involves the idea that persons evaluate others hierarchically in terms of some combination of their positions, possessions, and behaviors. Hence, status depends upon (1) certain objective characteristics of the individual being rated; (2) the judge's perceptions of these characteristics and how they are evaluated by others; and (3) certain motivational states of the judge that determine his or her own evaluations. There is also the assumption that we expect to find a reasonably high degree of consensus among the evaluators, so that an individual's overall status has generality to it and is not unique to each evaluator.

The early empirical work of sociologists (e.g., Hollingshead, 1949) and the anthropologist Lloyd Warner (Warner et al., 1949) involved direct attempts to measure these evaluations by asking judges to "place" individuals into hierarchically ordered categories according to such overall ratings, with these ratings being compared to results obtained by using so-called "objective" measures involving variables such as income, occupation, education, type of residence and neighborhood, race-ethnicity, or organizational memberships. Probably because of the inherent difficulties with the use of judges, particularly in large cities in which it is manifestly impossible for any one judge to rate more than a small fraction of the residents, the use of judges' ratings of individuals has virtually disappeared from the empirical literature. It is not clear, however, whether or not there is a general consensus that "status" should be given an alternative theoretical definition that relies only on objective properties and not on implicit ratings. My own reading of the literature is that the most commonly used conceptual definitions of status rely heavily on the implication that subjective evaluations are essential ingredients, but that these, in turn, depend upon objective characteristics of the individual being evaluated.

If this is the case, we have a basic model in which objective properties, positions, and behaviors determine in part the sub-jective evaluations which confer status, and that statuses, in turn, may affect the behaviors of both the individual being evaluated (whom we shall call A) and the evaluator, B. Thus "status" becomes an intervening variable in such a model. We shall later elaborate this model by introducing a second inter-vening variable, "power resources," which may be confounded with status. For the time being we confine our attention to those types of intervening variables that are given status labels. We focus on the following kind of possible confusion or con-founding phenomenon. The objective characteristics of the indi-vidual A (say, his or her education, occupation, or race) will have an impact on his or her statuses (evaluation by others), but they will also affect behaviors by numerous other mechanisms that are very often neglected in empirical research. Before constructing some prototype models, let us consider a few illustrations.

We have already commented on the variable "occupation," which is commonly conceptualized as "occupational prestige." Unless an extremely large number of nominal categories is used, it becomes necessary to condense the array to a much smaller number or to use scores of some kind. If the former strategy is adopted, the usual practice is to collapse occupations into categories that are roughly similar according to several criteria that include skill level, income, and prestige. Thus we use the distinction between "skilled," "semi-skilled," and "unskilled" labor, and the grosser dichotomy of "white-collar" and "blue-collar." It becomes clear that we are, in effect, ordering these occupations by prestige (and what else?) even if we do not choose to analyze our data in such a way as to take advantage of these ordinal properties. Otherwise, we might have put together surgeons and farmers because both work with their hands, or lawyers and gamblers because both are concerned with the law. In effect, we are utilizing manifest characteristics of certain types—often those in the minds of those who originally grouped the data for their own purposes—in order to form occupational aggregates.

If we choose to label the resulting groupings as *status* groupings, we may be selecting out only one dimension underlying the aggregating operation while neglecting many others that are correlated with it. For example, occupations that are ordered by status are also likely to be roughly ordered with respect to educational level required, cleanliness, autonomy, job security, power, and many other criteria. In fact, as we shall see, the prestige of the occupation may depend upon certain of these other factors. This in itself comes as no surprise. The difficulty, however, is that since these other factors may *also* affect the behavior in question—quite apart from status mechanisms—we shall have difficulty in sorting out the "status effects" of occupation from the nonstatus effects.

Next, consider "education," which is usually measured objectively in terms of the number of years of formal schooling. To the extent that status or prestige depends on "education" directly, apart from education's effects on occupation or income, we might also wish to have a prestige measure of the schools attended. We presume that in most sections of the country (though to varying degrees), one who has a Harvard A.B. will gain more status than an A.B. from a major state university who, in turn, will have more status than a graduate of a local community college. But presumably, years of schooling plus exposure to "quality education" will affect behaviors through numerous nonstatus mechanisms: the ability to think critically, exposure to the contents of specific courses, exposure to the "milieu" of the college campus, orientation toward work, and conceivably even through a modification of basic values. Thus there will be "education" effects that are not "educational status" effects but that may be highly correlated with them.

Income appears to be much more obviously a status variable, pure and simple. But income buys more than status alone. In particular, it provides economic security for old age, access to better health facilities, recreational opportunities, and access to physical locations that have desirable (nonstatus) characteristics such as beautiful views, open spaces, lower crime victimization rates, and better schools. It is true that one *may* attribute all of these factors to a global type "status" factor, but this would certainly involve a tremendous oversimplification of human motivations. Some persons want acreage simply to get away from others, not to impress them. Others like to look at mountain scenery or to ride horses. Some may even send their children to preparatory schools because they really want them to have an intellectually stimulating environment, and not merely to assure that they will enter a "status" university. The point, again, is that status considerations are likely to be confounded with many of the other factors correlated with income levels.

Finally, let us consider racial or ethnic differences. It is true that such groups may be roughly ranked according to their average statuses, and that an individual's status will be partly determined by such identifications. But again, ethnic and racial groups differ in other ways that do not involve the status dimension directly: in their religious practices and beliefs, in their subcultures, in their modal occupational characteristics, in their deviance rates, and in their political practices. If all of these other dimensions are not *measured* in a given study, and if the block of variables is labeled as "ethnic status," then we encounter the same sort of difficulty as with the other so-called "status" dimensions.

Why belabor these points, since they illustrate nothing more than the well-known methodological principle that before one can attribute a causal significance to a particular variable, one must make every effort to control for possible confounding variables? The essential point is that in fact, sociologists don't make the kind of effort in this regard that one might expect in view of our major interest in status variables as explanatory factors. One obvious reply is that one *cannot* control for such variables, most of which would be exceedingly difficult to measure. This introduces a reasonable pragmatic argument, but it does not imply that their omission is *theoretically* justified, or that merely because it is difficult to separate out status and nonstatus components, that the former should be given the benefit of the doubt in our interpretations of the data. Thus when an investigator talks about the effects of "SES" variables, this imputes a causal importance to socioeconomic *status* components that are supposed to have the effects on the behavior in question. In short, we often act or interpret our data as though the status components had, in fact, been isolated from their correlates.

We shall consider, in turn, two basic kinds of models as represented by Figures 6.1 and 6.2. In the first type of model we imagine that the individual A is given a single overall status S by individuals B_i through a process of evaluating or aggregating his or her various positions, group memberships, and behaviors. This general status S is thus taken as a function of a set of exogenous variables represented by the symbols O_i representing various objective properties, memberships, and behaviors. Both the O_i and S are assumed to affect behaviors Y of either individuals A or B_i. We leave open the question of whether or not the several evaluators B_i use the same criteria for evaluation and can therefore be characterized by the same set of weights W_i given to the various objective characteristics O_i. The basic feature of this type of model is that we assume that there is a *single* overall status measure rather than a number of distinct status dimensions.

In Figure 6.2, in contrast, we assume that the O_i provide separate status criteria S_i that are not combined into a single overall status variable S. According to this second model, the separate status variables or dimensions may individually affect behavior Y. That is, individual A is evaluated in terms of particular statuses: say, first as a black, then as a doctor, and then as the owner of a $200,000 home. In other words, he or she does not receive a single overall status judgment, although he or she may react and be reacted to in terms of a certain

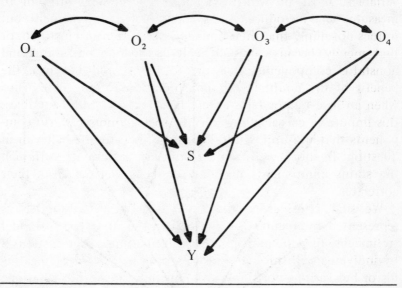

Figure 6.1

configuration of statuses (e.g., a particular pattern of inconsistent statuses). In both models, the status variables S and S_i are conceptualized in terms of evaluations attached to the actor, rather than directly in terms of properties, positions, or behaviors O_i. In a more complex model, some of the behaviors Y that are affected by S and by the O_i may feed back, with lags, to affect the O_i and S at later points in time.

Models such as these suggest that one may "measure" status in several ways, each of which is indirect and deficient in some respect. The first is to rely on the O_i themselves and to bypass the S_i altogether. That is, a variable such as years of schooling, occupation, income, or race is *itself* taken to be status, just as possibly the same kinds of O_i are also sometimes used to "measure" power resources. When these objective measures are used in this manner, however, one must make certain untested and usually implicit assumptions about motivational states, attitudes, and values. For example, being a medical doctor does not automatically confer high status unless members of this profes-

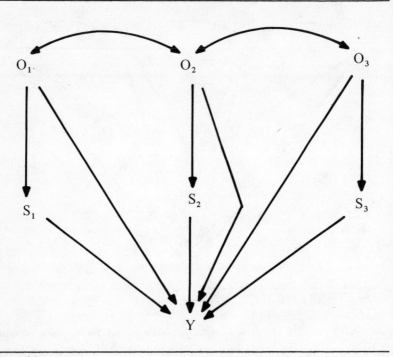

Figure 6.2

sion are valued. If doctors were in oversupply, if they conveyed the impression that they did not really care for the patient, or if reliable functional alternatives (e.g., pills) could be found, then we would expect the average status level of doctors to be lowered. Obviously, if one relies solely on the O_i without ever attempting to assess subjective evaluations, it would be impossible to predict, explain, or even estimate *changes* in status associated with a particular O_i. Often, one merely assumes there have been no such changes, as for example when one compares the "occupations" of fathers and sons as though the same occupations implied the same "occupational statuses."

The second approach is to assess S or the S_i by asking questions of the evaluators, as for example in the case of the well-known North and Hatt (1947) study of occupational prestige. Here one encounters the usual problems of attitude measurement, including the fact that not all evaluators will give the same scores, and that such scores may vary over time, by location, or in accord with how much the evaluator knows about the occupation in question. The essential point is that this approach to measuring the status variables involves some effort to assess the subjective states of the evaluators and relies on the responses of these persons to a specific set of questions posed by the investigator. It thus involves a particular example of attitude measurement for which there are well-known, though less than completely satisfactory, estimation techniques.

The third approach to measuring status is through observations of the Y, or the behavioral responses of the evaluators (and possibly the subject A as well). For example, we might infer a person's status by watching for deference behavior on the part of others or by noting that other persons are seen to interact with him or her under specified conditions in certain ways. The problem with this approach is similar to that encountered with respect to the use of the O_i as measures, namely that of distinguishing behaviors that are primarily due to the status characteristics from those due more to nonstatus factors. For example, suppose we know that individual A is wealthy and B defers to A. Is this because of A's superior status, his or her power, or perhaps something else that may be correlated with wealth, such as the possession of technical knowledge or "culture?" If we merely assume that the behavior in question indicates something about A's status, without even theorizing about alternative causes, we are once more likely to confound status with other variables, particularly power. Some researchers might take the behavior in question to be an indicator of A's status, whereas others might take this same behavior as an indicator of A's power. Both might be right, but perhaps not to the same degree.

Models Involving General Status S

Let us examine models of the first type, as represented in Figure 6.1, in which there is a single status S intervening between the O_i and Y. Here, we imagine that A provides B with certain clues as to his or her objective O_i, these clues not necessarily being accurate ones. We are well aware of the phenomenon of "conspicuous consumption" through which actors try to convey the impression that their income is actually higher than it really is. Similarly, A may put on certain airs in an attempt to convey the impression that his or her education or family background is different from the true state of affairs. The point is that B must react not to the true O_i but to indicators of these O_i. We shall ignore this particular difficulty by making the oversimplifying assumption that B is aware of all of A's characteristics. We shall also deal with the extremely simple situation in which all evaluators B_i evaluate the O_i in exactly the same way, namely by awarding a general status score S by weighting the O_i using the identical sets of weights, W_i. Let us also assume that the implicit weighting scheme is a linear additive one, so that $S = \Sigma W_i O_i$, where the summation runs over all relevant positions, properties, and behaviors of A.

In this simplest of possible cases, we allow for nonstatus effects of each O_i on Y, as represented by the arrows going directly from these O_i to Y. We also have an arrow from each O_i to S, and we assume that this general status S affects Y directly. We wish to infer or measure this "status effect," given the possibility of the nonstatus effects as well. In this model, S is an *exact* linear function of the O_i. These O_i are not so much "components" of S, in the sense that S is *defined* to be an exact function of them. Instead, we are assuming that we have been able to enumerate and measure all of the factors that influence S, so that S is perfectly explained by these O_i. Obviously this is an ideal case, but it is one that we need to examine for its implications. Thus, Y is taken as a (linear) function of S *and* the O_i, and our aim is to estimate the separate coefficients in order to isolate the "status" and several "nonstatus" effects.

Unfortunately, we immediately see that this will be impossible, even in the ideal case, where all O_i are known and perfectly measured. Our estimating procedures will break down because of the exact function connecting S to the O_i, and the equation for Y will be underidentified. To put it succinctly, we have an empirically hopeless situation. Even though we may imagine separate status effects, we cannot isolate them from the other effects of the O_i. Nor could we imagine a situation in which we could hold constant all O_i and still vary S, which is completely determined by these O_i. Our status and nonstatus effects are hopelessly confounded unless we can modify the model in some essential way. For instance, we might be willing to assume a priori that certain of the O_i do *not* affect Y except through status S. That is, there are no nonstatus effects of these particular O_i. We are then imposing additional assumptions on the model, namely that certain of the parameters in the equation for Y are zero. If so, we have some hope of resolving the difficulty, provided that these same O_i are really important sources of variation in S. In other words, we could not take some very minor causes of status, assume that these also have no direct effects on Y, and use such assumptions to resolve the difficulty. We would find that we could vary S while holding the other (major) causes of S constant, but the variation we could produce in S under such circumstances would be so slight that we would obtain extremely large sampling errors in our estimates of the effects of each variable on Y. In effect, S would be extremely highly correlated with the O_i that appear in the equation for Y.

A similar sort of situation will prevail if we are able to find important sources of S that do not appear in the equation of Y but that happen to be highly correlated with other O_i that do have nonstatus effects. If one is willing to assume, a priori, that there are O_i which are (a) important sources of variation in S; (b) do not have any nonstatus effects on Y (i.e., do not affect Y by *any* paths that do not go through S); and (c) are not highly correlated with other O_i that do have nonstatus effects, it then becomes possible to separate out the effects of S from those of the remaining O_i. The resulting model will be similar to that of Figure 6.3, where the symbol U has replaced those O_i that do not have nonstatus effects. It should be noted that if one merely ignores all possible nonstatus effects of the O_i, one is

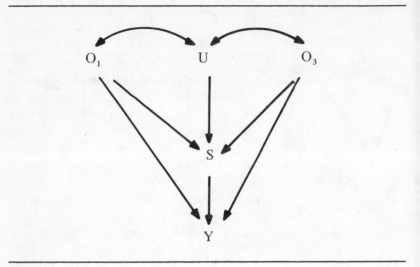

Figure 6.3

making the implicit assumption that they are all *zero*. It may or may not be realistic to assume that they all cancel out in the aggregation process, but without an explicit theory, such an assumption will be difficult to evaluate.

The above approach assumes not only that one is willing to make assumptions (a)-(c) but that one also has an adequate measure of S. If S is derived by asking judges to evaluate A's overall status, then it will not be necessary to have the separate measures of all the relevant O_i included in U. But if the investigator constructs the measure of S by weighting the O_i it will obviously be necessary to use at least some O_i that are assumed to have no nonstatus effects on Y. An alternative resolution to the difficulty is to attempt to specify the mechanisms by which the various O_i affect Y by measuring a set of intervening variables in addition to S. In Figure 6.4, these are labeled as X_i. If we are able to identify and measure *all* of the important intervening variables (one in each simple causal chain being sufficient), and if we are able to control for all such X_i simultaneously, we shall be able to isolate the effects of S. But there is another catch. These X_i cannot be too highly correlated with

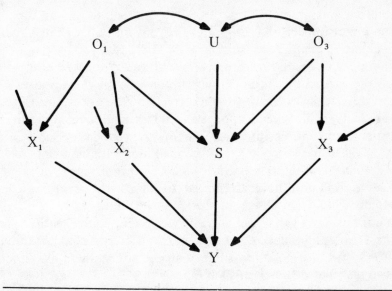

Figure 6.4

the O_i that determine S. If they are, then S will be a nearly exact function of the X_i and we shall again encounter a multicollinearity problem.

Let us examine the model of Figure 6.4 to illustrate a related problem. For simplicity, we confine our attention to two O_i. O_1 is assumed to affect Y by two paths that do not involve S, one through X_1 and the second through X_2. O_3 affects Y through the path through X_3, and we assume that there are additional O_i that produce sufficient variation in S so that S is not too highly correlated with O_1 and O_3. We allow for the possibility that O_1 and O_3 are mutually correlated through unknown mechanisms. With S measured in such a way that it is not a perfect function of O_1 and O_3 we may separate out the effects of S from those of these two objective characteristics. With perfect measures on all variables, we could also test the adequacy of the model. If the model is correct, controls for the X_i and S should wipe out the correlations between O_i and O_3 and the dependent variable Y.

Now suppose that we have either imperfect data or a model that is incorrectly specified. We know that if we have strictly random measurement errors in S, we will tend to underestimate the direct impact of S on Y and that one or more of the X_i will get partial credit for the effects of S. Similarly, random measurement errors in one or more X_i will result in biased estimates of the effects of S on Y. Exactly *which* of the intervening variables receives credit for the effects of the poorly measured variable(s) will depend upon the intercorrelations among these variables. In the limiting case, we might imagine that one of the X_i is measured so poorly that the measured variable would have a zero correlation with the true value. In this instance, we might just as well not have attempted to measure it at all, and its effects will be completely confounded with those of the remaining intervening variables. The implication, of course, is that one must not only have good theories concerning the nonstatus effects but also good measures of all the intervening links if one is to test the adequacy of such models.

There are no new methodological principles here. But we need to examine the implications in the specific context of inferences about status effects. In particular, suppose that one does not have any measure of S, apart from measures of O_1 and O_3. This is indeed likely to be the case if one is using a "two-factor" status index which combines, say, education and income or perhaps education and occupation. With S taken as unmeasured in this model, one might want to infer the status effects by a residualizing operation. The basic idea would be to attempt to list all possible nonstatus effects, to measure the intervening X_i, and then to argue that whatever is *not* due to these nonstatus mechanisms can be attributed to "status effects."

This kind of reasoning is of course legitimate only if all intervening variables have been identified and perfectly measured. If, say, X_2 has been erroneously omitted from the model, and if the effects of O_1 and O_3 on Y, controlling for X_1 and X_3, are inferred to be "status effects," then the effects of S will have been confounded with those of X_2. As the limiting case, if *no* nonstatus effects have been identified and measured, and if all effects of O_1 and O_3 are attributed to the effects of status, then all nonstatus effects will be confounded with those of S. This appears to be the most usual situation in actual practice today in sociology. If this is indeed the case, then an explicit residualizing strategy would seem to be a necessary first step in making us more self-conscious about the operation of nonstatus factors. Presumably, as soon as one begins to specify particular nonstatus channels, other scholars will be motivated to criticize those models by specifying additional routes by which the O_i may affect behavior, and the residuals will more nearly approximate the true status effects.

All of these difficulties, plus the fact that in most situations it will be extremely expensive and impractical to attempt to assess overall status through the use of judges, seem to imply that it would be wise to reject the single status model altogether. Also, if persons are in fact evaluated in some such summary fashion, it will be almost impossible for the persons doing the evaluating to reach a high degree of consensus unless only extremely crude categories are used. It might therefore seem much more sensible to think in terms of distinct status dimensions S_i that are each separately linked to the O_i. We shall see, however, that such a reconceptualization does not really help us avoid the basic methodological difficulty. And we must further recognize that if real-world actors think more in terms of generalized status than in terms of distinct dimensions, then the mere fact that sociologists find it inconvenient to measure such a generalized status will not make their alternative models more realistic or more valid. In other words, we shall not confuse our own convenience with the theoretical adequacy of our underlying models.

Models Involving Differentiated Statuses S_i

We may now be much more brief since we shall not discover any basically new problems or remedies when statuses are differentiated. We begin with a series of O_i such as years of

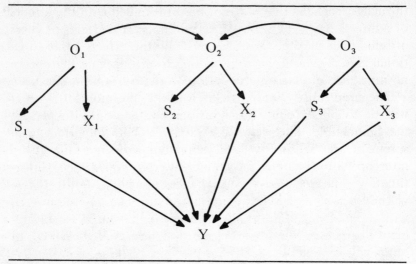

Figure 6.5

schooling, occupational category, income, race-ethnicity, and so forth. We now imagine that there is a separate status dimension associated with each of these O_i. We may refer to these S_i as educational status, occupational status, income status, race-ethnicity status, and so forth. But we again must recognize that years of schooling, occupational experiences, or race-ethnic memberships will have other effects on behavior than through these S_i. For simplicity, let us assume that there is a single alternative path through the intervening variables X_i from each O_i to Y, as indicated in Figure 6.5.

If we knew about each of these X_i and could measure them all perfectly and utilize simultaneous controls, then we could indeed infer the separate status effects. But with imperfect measures of the X_i we will obtain biased estimates of the effects of the S_i, and if we miss certain of the X_i then the paths through these X_i will again be confounded with the paths through the S_i. In the extreme case, if we ignore all nonstatus paths, we will confound all of the effects through the X_i with all of the S_i effects. To the degree that the O_i are intercorrelated, we cannot even be assured that some of the effects through a particular X_i will not be confounded with the effects of a different S_j. For example, certain nonstatus effects of years of schooling may be confounded with the effects of occupational status, even if we were willing to assume that there were no nonstatus effects of occupation on the behavior in question.

The more highly intercorrelated the O_i the more difficult it will be to unconfound these various paths, even with perfect measurement of all intervening variables. With imperfect measurements, the sensitivity to measurement errors increases as the intercorrelations among the O_i increase (Gordon, 1968). Unfortunately, unless we have perfect measurements for the O_i we will not be able to assess the intercorrelations among the true O_i without making assumptions about the nature of the measurement errors and without using multiple measures of each O_i. In other words, if we find relatively low empirical intercorrelations among the *measured* O_i, this is no assurance that there is not a much higher degree of multicollinearity involved.

We may illustrate a related problem by looking at the measurement of occupational status, under the assumption that we shall want to distinguish this S_i from educational and income statuses. Let us take the Duncan (1961) index of occupational status as a measure of this particular variable, although we might have used average ratings based on the North-Hatt scale as an alternative. The Duncan index is based on the finding that these latter ratings, as a criterion, are predicted very well by a linear regression equation involving the average income and educational levels of the individuals in these occupations. One might presume that the evaluators judge an occupation according to these two criteria, so that occupational prestige is causally dependent upon average income and educational levels.

Now suppose we want to distinguish between an individual's status derived from his or her occupation and that person's status derived from his or her *own* education or income. These latter need not coincide with the average levels for his or her occupation, so that the correlation between individual occupational scores and educational levels (years of schooling) or incomes will not be perfect. But these correlations will generally be high, and we again expect to encounter multicollinearity problems. Furthermore, different occupations will have varying degrees of homogeneity with respect to income and educational levels. In the case of many professions, such as medicine or law, we will expect individuals to be extremely homogeneous with respect to number of years of schooling but relatively heterogeneous with respect to income. In other professions, such as public school teaching and social work, both income and educational distributions will be very homogeneous. We may expect a similar homogeneity in the case of occupations at the lower end of the continuum. The point is that persons whose incomes or educations deviate substantially from their occupational averages will *not* be uniformly distributed across all occupations. Put another way, the contributions to the high correlations between incomes, educational levels, and scores on the Duncan index will not be the same for all occupations. And they may also differ according to one's race, sex, or region of employment.

It seems unlikely that many investigators would attempt to separate out the individual status dimensions in this manner unless they were specifically looking for inconsistency effects or peculiar combinations of statuses. The more usual practice is to use a *single* status index, such as the Duncan occupational status index. But then we encounter the same familiar problem. If one finds associations between this index and other variables, one cannot tell whether they should be attributed to an *occupational* status index (as contrasted with, say, an educational status index), to nonstatus characteristics of occupations that are highly correlated with status, or to neither. We do not "unconfound" the effects of several variables by measuring only one of them. Again, this point is well recognized in general terms, but our labels of the variables to which effects are attributed often do not reflect this fact. As Horan (1978) and Udy (1980) have noted, an explanation that relies on a single occupational status score in this fashion contains a number of implicit theoretical assumptions.

Though this assertion is not backed by any quantitative facts, it is my impression that sociologists have been more sensitized to the problem of separating out the possible effects of different status dimensions S_i than to that of distinguishing status from nonstatus effects of the same O_i. If it can be assumed that these nonstatus effects are numerous but not singly important, then it is plausible to assume that they cancel each other out in the aggregation process. But if there are a small number of important nonstatus effects, these will either reinforce or work against the status effects, depending on the signs of the relationships involved. There seems to be one very important kind of nonstatus effect that, in many instances, is likely to operate in the same direction as status effects, namely the effects of power resources based on the O_i. We turn next to a consideration of how power and status effects may be confounded.

The Confounding of Status and Power

In spite of the fact that both status and power are important variables in the sociological literature and are used in explanations of diverse behaviors, the writer has encountered practically no systematic empirical investigations, the aim of which has been to disentangle their presumed effects on these behaviors.[2] Status and power are recognized to be empirically correlated yet analytically distinct. We may easily cite instances of high status and low power, such as the wealthy socialite, the movie star or famous athlete, or even the successful surgeon. Likewise, persons such as ethnic politicians or professional gamblers may have considerable power but low status, at least from the perspective of the average citizen. But such cases are merely exceptions to the general rule that status and power tend to go hand in hand. Perhaps for this reason it may have been implicitly recognized that it will be exceedingly difficult to separate out the effects of each. But since some authors may stress the status effects, whereas others emphasize the power factor, conceptual confusion is likely to result.

The problem is partly a conceptual one that results from the difficulties in measuring either power or status directly. Not only status but also power may be measured in terms of the so-called "reputational approach," in which judges are asked to rate individuals according to either their overall power or their power with respect to specific issue areas. When this is done, we presume that the judges possess a high degree of knowledge about the several individuals and that they are able, through an implicit weighting system of some kind, to arrive at a crude score so as to place each individual at one and only one level on a power or status continuum.[3] If there is a high degree of consensus among the judges, we assume that their implicit weighting systems must be relatively similar and that their knowledge bases are also similar. Presumably, given a sufficiently high degree of knowledge, it would be possible for such judges to produce two separate scores, one for power and the other for status, each of which could then be used as distinct measures of the two variables.

This kind of reputational approach is known to have very definite limitations.[4] In the first place, it is difficult to find judges with a sufficiently good knowledge base to assign scores or ranks to even one of the two variables, to say nothing of the other. If different sets of judges were used to provide the two sets of scores, one would be concerned with whether or not they would be using exactly the same criteria. If the same judges were used for the two sets, there would then be a concern about possible "halo effects." In the absence of a high degree of consensus among the judges, a number of additional questions would arise as to the reasons behind this lack of agreement, particularly whether it was based on differing degrees of knowledge or different implicit weighting systems. The "representativeness" of the judges could be called into question, as would their relative qualifications for judging the two different kinds of variables.

It is not known whether sociologists' tendency to reject these reputational approaches, once their shortcomings have been pointed out, is more a matter of a preference for less costly measurement procedures or whether they believe that the possible biases and distortions produced are in some sense so serious that such approaches must be rejected automatically, quite apart from time and cost considerations. Most certainly, these approaches should be evaluated in comparison with other possible approaches which also have a number of important shortcomings, some of which we have just noted. As a general principle, given that no measures are perfect, it seems wise to employ a variety of different approaches that have defects that are not all similar in nature. But it must be emphasized that multiple measures usually mean multiple confusion and ambiguities unless they are brought together in terms of an explicit theory that includes both the "true" variables and their indicators.

With these remarks in mind, let us return to what seems to be the currently popular approach to the measurement of status and power, namely a reliance on objective properties or positions occupied by the individuals concerned. For status, these include years of formal education, occupation (rated in some fashion), income, race or ethnic background, positions in organizations, and sometimes factors such as type of home, religious preference, and family background. We again represent these objective characteristics by the symbols O_i. In the case of power variables, we have argued elsewhere (Blalock and Wilken, 1979) that these O_i are not automatically transformed into power (as a potential) because of the fact that their use depends upon the motivational structure of other actors. We may represent this fact by taking the power resources R_i as functions of the O_i multiplied by certain weights V_i that need not be constants. That is, the V_i may vary according to the situation or according to the nature of the other relevant actors. If an actor's total power resources can be represented (or approximated) by a sum of his or her separate resources, we might then represent the total resources R as equal to $\Sigma V_i O_i$.

The problem of separating power from status can be seen once we admit to the possibility that many of these same O_i will also appear as determinants of one's overall status S or as a status dimension S_i. For example, income, education, and occupation all would appear to influence both status and power.

Race/ethnicity certainly influences overall status but may or may not affect one's power, depending on the circumstances and nature of power under consideration. Thus we might write total status S as a different function of the O_i, perhaps as $\Sigma W_i O_i$, where the weights V_i and W_i will not be the same. Of course, if they were identical or proportional, assuming linearity, power and status would also be identical except for a constant of proportionality. It would be impossible to distinguish their separate effects.

More realistically, certain of the V_i or W_i will be close to zero, as for example the weighting given to "type of home" as a source of power. But even if the V_i and W_i were very different from each other, to the degree that the O_i were highly intercorrelated, it would still be difficult to disentangle their separate effects. Hence, if "years of schooling" appeared with a large weight in the equation for status but a small one for power, and if "occupational position" were given a near-zero weight in the status equation but a large one in the power equation, then to the degree that education and occupation were highly correlated, it would still be difficult to separate out the effects of status and power because of the resulting high correlation between S and R.

A simplified model of this kind of situation is given in Figure 6.6, in which certain of the O_i are taken as determinants of total power resources R, certain others as determinants of status S, and still others as determinants of both S and R. For simplicity, we now rule out any possible additional effects of the O_i on Y, except through S and R. The model allows for feedback between S and R but not from Y. We may suppose that Y represents the behavior of *other* actors who are reacting to the actor concerned in terms of his or her actual S and R values. More realistically, of course, these other actors' behaviors would more properly be taken as functions of *perceived* resources and status, which might be designated by R' and S' respectively. Figure 6.6 assumes that there is no slippage in this respect, so that $R' = R$ and $S' = S$. In a more realistic model, one might also allow feedback from these behaviors Y to the actor's O_i and therefore his or her R and S scores.

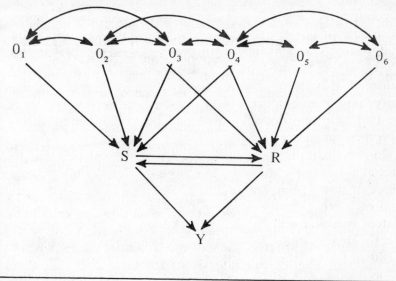

Figure 6.6

This model is of course basically similar in structure to the models that were discussed in the previous chapter, where we were concerned with the implications of omitting intervening variables from a model and assessing whether or not this would affect our inferences concerning the total impacts of the exogenous variables (previously labeled Z_i). Sociologists may be theoretically more inclined to omit intervening variables when these are postulated internal states of persons than when they are status and power, but the methodological principles involved are identical so long as we employ models with the same structural properties. The implications of our previous analysis were that for recursive models one could safely infer the relative effects of the O_i on behavior without ever introducing the notions of status or power.

The student of power or status, we would surmise, is not likely to be very comfortable with Figure 6.6, nor with the thought of omitting R and S from theories or verbal interpretations of the relationships between the O_i and the behavior Y. In line with our previous discussion of intervening variables, one may of course do so by thinking in terms of the status-power block as being a "black box," the contents of which are inscrutable. This also implies that if any of the structural parameters (here the V_i, W_i, and coefficients linking R and S to Y) were to change or vary from one subpopulation to the next, it would not be possible to predict what would happen to the reduced-form parameters linking the O_i to behavior. For example, if "race" were differentially related to either status or power resources, we would not, in general, be able to predict or explain its relationships with behavior Y. Presumably, one would want to take into consideration possible changes in attitudes or values that might affect the V_i or W_i, but this would not be possible on the basis of the reduced-form equations alone. Basically, we would not be able to explain what is going on, nor could we predict the implications of policy changes that might affect some of the structural parameters.

The basic alternative strategies are the same as in the case of other kinds of intervening variables. One possibility is to attempt to obtain "effect" indicators of R and S. One way to do this is to obtain measures of perceived status or resources through the use of judges. Another would be to attempt to find sets of behaviors U_i and Z_j that one is willing to assume, a priori, are dependent on only one of the two intervening variables. If the U_i depend only on S, and the Z_j only on R, then one may use factor analysis to obtain measures of R and S, and one may also make use of multiple-indicator models to provide simple tests of the model. The problem with this strategy of attempting to find "purified" forms of behavior that are affected only by R or only by S is that most forms of behavior, like Y, may be affected by both. If so, we will have too many unknowns in the picture and will be faced by the same kinds of ambiguities that generally arise in the case of nonorthogonal factor analyses.

Another alternative strategy, and one that we tend to use implicitly without recognizing the fact, is to make a series of a priori assumptions regarding the weights V_i and W_i, thereby obtaining unique measures for R and S. One such procedure is to assume certain of these weights to be zero and, for the remaining O_i, to use equal weights, or weights that are normalized so as to correct for differences in standard deviations of the O_i. The simplest possibility would be to use certain of the O_i for R, a completely different set for S, and to exclude altogether those O_i that are assumed to affect both R and S. But this of course imposes a great deal of simplicity on the model and is likely to weaken the correlation between the measured R' and S' values, as contrasted with the true values. For example, we certainly want to assume that income affects *both* status and resources. Certainly, occupation may do so as well. Perhaps race and education do not, but this is undoubtedly open to question. This kind of strategy may provide one with measures of status and resources that are not too highly correlated, but it so oversimplifies reality as to beg most of the theoretical questions that are most likely to interest us.

The only remaining strategy that occurs to me is to attempt to develop more sophisticated theories that involve possible nonlinearities or nonadditive relationships, so that one can make a series of weak tests of the postulated linkages between the O_i and Y, without obtaining any measures of either R or S. For example, if one could predict nonlinear relationships through R but not through S, or if relationships were expected to involve different *forms* of nonlinear relationships for the two paths (say, one with an increasing slope, the other with a decreasing slope), perhaps a series of weak tests could be made. I have discussed this strategy elsewhere, one illustration of which is the possible resolution to the status inconsistency problem by using nonlinear models (Blalock, 1967). However, I am not optimistic that it can successfully be applied in the present kind of situation without considerable refinement of our theories. The alternatives of either attempting to find behaviors that rather simply tap either R or S or relying on judges to provide separate estimates of these intervening variables seem more promising. But in view of the difficulties encountered with all approaches, a strategy that involves multiple measures seems to be our wisest course. Such a strategy, however, will be costly and will require much more careful conceptualization than we have thus far witnessed.

BACKGROUND VARIABLES AND EXPERIENCES
INVOLVING DIFFERENCES OR COMPARISONS

Sociologists and other social scientists commonly stress that human actors base many of their judgments and behaviors on comparisons with others, so that it is relative rather than absolute values that are most significant as causal factors in social interaction. For convenience, we often construct difference scores to represent these comparisons, though in most instances ratio comparisons would be equally plausible. These difference scores are then used as explanatory variables, sometimes along with the component scores as distinct variables, though more often without explicit attention being given to these component scores.

These derived difference (or ratio) scores only require that the component scores be operationalized and therefore do not create special measurement problems. However, if one then wishes to allow for the possibility that both components *and* the difference score may have distinct effects on some dependent variable, say, a behavior, one encounters an identification problem if the equation is a linear one, or a multicollinearity problem if nonlinearities are introduced. Suppose, for example, that a behavior Y is to be explained by two independent variables X_1 and X_2, along with a third "independent" variable $X_3 = X_1 - kX_2$, which is an exact linear function of X_1 and X_2. It will be impossible to obtain an ordinary least-squares solution to the equation $Y = \alpha + \beta_1 X_1 + \beta_2 X_2 + \beta_3 X_3 + \epsilon$ and, in fact, it will be impossible to estimate the three regression coefficients by *any* means unless a priori assumptions are made concerning one or more of these coefficients. For instance, if one is willing to assume that the coefficient of X_1 is zero, or that the coefficients of X_1 and X_2 are identical to each other, one may then estimate each of the unknowns. But without some such assumptions, the situation is hopeless in the sense that an indefinitely large number of possible sets of values of the coefficients will be equally compatible with one's data.

The Confounding of Variables

In order to illustrate the generality of the problem, let us briefly list and discuss a number of substantive variables that presumably would be indirectly measured in terms of such difference measures or some other index involving a comparison operation.

Status Inconsistency. The so-called "status-inconsistency" problem has probably received more thorough methodological discussion than similar notions because of the fact that early investigators made an explicit attempt to distinguish status-inconsistency effects from the main effects of two or more separate statuses.[5] The essential idea is that individuals' experiences and behaviors are not only influenced by their separate statuses, such as educational levels, incomes, occupational prestige, or ethnic status, but that whenever these statuses are strikingly different or "inconsistent" (in some sense), this is also likely to have a distinct impact on the individual concerned. For instance, the black doctor or the highly educated ditch digger may have cumulative experiences of a frustrating or ambiguous nature. Whereas the black doctor may wish and expect to be treated as a doctor, actual treatment may be primarily in terms of that actor's *lower* status, namely as a black. Or those whose achieved statuses are much lower than their ascribed statuses may develop intrapunitive tendencies that show up as higher levels of symptoms of stress, such as psychosomatic difficulties of one sort or another (Jackson, 1962). Persons who experience these status inconsistencies may, however, also tend to blame "the system" and express this tendency in more liberal voting records than would be predicted on the basis of an additive model involving only the several status variables taken individually.

Social Mobility. It has also been argued that social mobility—say, inter- or intragenerational occupational mobility—will also have effects on behaviors over and above the effects of the two component statuses. Thus, sons of blue-collar workers who experience upward mobility may be predicted to have relatively low prejudice scores, whereas those experiencing downward mobility may be predicted to have higher prejudice, perhaps through the mechanism of frustration or relative deprivation (Bettelheim and Janowitz, 1950). Mobility is thought to produce certain kinds of strains in the individual, perhaps because learning experiences that were adequate in one setting are no longer so in another, or perhaps because of changes in expectations brought about by the change in one's set of peers. The "nouveau riche" individual is stereotyped as "gauche," too much interested in conspicuous display, and lacking in the "proper" credentials necessary to admit him or her into elite circles.

Geographic Mobility. A change of location in physical space might, of course, be measured as a difference in purely spatial terms, though usually our operationalization of geographic mobility will be in categorical terms. Nevertheless, we often claim that spatial movement per se causes an uprooting and a series of adjustments to a new environment that affects both attitudes and behaviors. For this reason, one may wish to distinguish between effects due to the prior location, the present one, and the fact that the actor has experienced geographic mobility. There may have been frustrations, ambiguities to face in the new setting, the necessity of "negotiating" new roles and establishing one's credentials, and perhaps the learning of a new set of skills more appropriate to the new setting.

Differences Between Expectations and Aspirations. In studies of high school students, one commonly finds measures that compare career or educational aspirations with what the youths actually expect to attain, with the difference between the two being used to measure anticipated frustrations or perhaps the "realism" of the students concerned. Similar measures may be obtained to infer deprivation gaps of one kind of another, or the degree to which one's current status differs from some idealized level. Both the gap measure and the current level may then be used to explain such things as learning behaviors, deviance, the need for escape mechanisms, or attitudes toward other kinds of actors.

Relative Deprivation. A very similar kind of difference measure may be obtained by comparing oneself with some other set of actors, as for example one's immediate peers, members of the opposite sex, one's siblings, members of another racial or ethnic group, and so forth. Here, the comparison is with another set of actors rather than between the real and the ideal, but similar notions of frustration, possible self-degradation, and motivation may enter into the explanatory theories. The notion is that one does not compare oneself in some absolute sense with a fixed standard, but that one's reference point will usually be one's perceptions of levels being experienced by other actors. Needless to say, these other actors may shift over time or may differ from one individual to the next. That is, actor A may compare himself or herself with B, whereas actor C may make comparisons with D or possibly A. One's behavior, then, may conceivably be influenced by both these relative comparisons and also the absolute levels themselves. We usually assume, however, that A's behavior will be affected by A's own levels and by the difference between A and B, but not by B's levels as well (Blalock and Wilken, 1979, ch. 7).

Age–Period–Cohort Effects. Efforts to separate so-called cohort effects due to common experiences of an age cohort from those due, on the one hand, to contemporary influences at the time the data are collected and, on the other, to the aging process itself have encountered a similar difficulty. If cohort effects are indexed by the year of birth and period effects by the year of data collection, then clearly the respondent's age will be the exact difference between the two. One cannot hold constant year of birth and time of interview and still vary the respondent's age, just as one cannot hold constant both father's and son's occupational prestige and still vary the mobility score. In a linear model, this of course implies the impossibility of distinguishing age, period, and cohort effects unless a priori restrictive assumptions are made on the coefficients.

Growth Rates. On both the micro level of the individual and the more macro level of groups, we are often interested in distinguishing the effects of growth from those of either the initial or final levels. Thus if one attributes certain problems among prison inmates to very recent prison growth, an alternative explanation may be given in terms of existing or past levels,

230 Conceptualization and Measurement in the Social Sciences

rather than growth per se. Is discrimination toward a minority primarily due to factors deriving from early history, events that are occurring contemporarily, or to *changes* in customs, relative population sizes, densities, or patterns of behavior? The analogy to the age-period-cohort problem is obvious. Again, one often finds that theorists will tend to stress either one or two of the three factors, but seldom all three, suggesting the implicit assumption that one of the coefficients may be safely assumed to have a zero value. Someone wishing to allow for the operation of all three factors, however, will encounter the same kind of identification problem.

Deviancy Effects in Contextual-Effects Models. Sometimes one wishes to distinguish among the effects of some individual characteristic X_{ij} of the ith individual in the jth group, a group mean $\bar{X}_j$, and the deviation of X_{ij} from $\bar{X}_j$, representing the degree to which the ith individual deviates from the group mean. Again, there will be only two empirical quantities—in this case X_{ij} and $\bar{X}_j$—but three distinct terms in the regression equation, making it impossible to estimate the three regression coefficients uniquely without the imposition of further assumptions. As long as one wishes to allow for "deviancy effects" in these contextual models, this implies the need to make simplifying assumptions about one or the other of the two remaining coefficients. If, for example, one is willing to assume no contextual effects apart from the deviancy effect term, one may set the coefficient of the $\bar{X}_j$ term equal to zero and solve for the remaining two coefficients.

Comparisons Among Means of Nested Groups. Although much less common in contextual-effect models, one may also wish to make comparisons not only of individual scores with group and subgroup means, but also of subgroup means with means of the larger groups in which they are embedded. Thus if one has individuals who are members of departments or committees within some larger organization, one may want to form such difference terms as $X_{ijk} - \bar{X}_{jk}$, $X_{ijk} - \bar{X}_k$, and $\bar{X}_{jk} - \bar{X}_k$, where we are referring to the ith individual within the jth subgroup of the kth group. Models of this type are discussed in

Blalock and Wilken (1979) and involve essentially the same difficulties, though in a more complex form. Studies that involve comparisons across several levels of aggregation are very likely to require measures of this type.

Differences Among Expectations of Others. An actor placed in a setting in which two or more others have very different expectations regarding that actor's performance may be expected to undergo certain strains and to experience ambiguities and frustrations that are due primarily to this inconsistency. Of course, not all contrasting sets of expectations can be measured in terms of a simple difference notion, but where this is possible—as for example by measuring two actors' expectations regarding how much time a faculty member should devote to teaching as compared to research—we may also imagine interest being focused on trying to assess how important this difference in expectations is, as compared with the effects of each of the expectations considered separately. Here, we are trying to assess the importance of inconsistency, incompatibility, or some such notion, as distinct from that of the *levels* of the distinct expectations.

Exposure to Distinct Cultures: The Marginal Man. Much more difficult to conceptualize is the notion of "marginality," but it is clear that this concept—as discussed in Stonequist's (1961) classical work, for example—involved the idea that the individual who is brought up in two very different cultures is likely to be subjected to a wide variety of stresses that, in effect, involve different sets of expectations, socialization skills, and status inconsistencies that produce high levels of frustrations and confusion. No doubt the concept of "marginality" is multidimensional and therefore in need of being broken down into component dimensions, some of which have been previously discussed. If this could be done, and if efforts were also made to separate out the effects of marginality from the individual effects of the two distinct cultures, we would expect to encounter basically the same kinds of problems.

Cognitive Imbalances. As noted by Taylor (1973), various social psychological theories, such as Heider's (1958) balance theory, Newcomb's (1968) A,B,X theory, and Festinger's (1957) theory of cognitive dissonance all involve the idea that individuals tend to experience strains or discomforts whenever there are cognitive inconsistencies among their beliefs, provided that these are perceived as relevant to each other. For instance, in Newcomb's theory, if actor A likes actor B, but if A and B have opposite attitudes toward some object X, there is an "inconsistency." This may be resolved (in the case of A) either by changing the attitude toward B to that of dislike, modifying the attitude toward X, or perhaps by getting B to reverse his or her attitude. As Taylor notes, these variant versions of cognitive consistency theory can be formulated in terms of difference scores and also involve the same kinds of indeterminacies as do the other examples we have been discussing.

As implied, there are several strategies for resolving the impasse created by introducing difference measures alongside their component variables as explanatory factors, say, of a particular form of behavior. The first two strategies will be noted only in passing, since they are not really relevant to the kinds of conceptualization problems under discussion in the present chapter. The first such strategy, which is often an implicit one, is to place restrictions on the coefficients of the "main effects" of the component terms. Hope (1971, 1975), for example, attempts to resolve the status-inconsistency problem by constructing a single index for the status variables, thereby making a priori assumptions about the relative magnitudes of the coefficients. If one constructs a "general status" measure, say, by forming a weighted average $W_1 X_1 + W_2 X_2$, then by selecting values for W_1 and W_2 (e.g., setting W_1 equal to kW_2), the effect is to remove one of the unknowns from the equation. But this of course sidesteps the problem of assessing empirically the magnitudes of all three slope coefficients.

A second strategy is to work with highly specific nonlinear models, relying on substantial departures from linearity to resolve the identification problem. This is essentially the strategy explored in one of my own studies, without very encouraging results. Mason et al. (1973) employ a variant of this same strategy, though perhaps in a disguised fashion. They recommend placing restrictions on certain coefficients by assuming—in the case of age-period-cohort effects—that the coefficients for two (or more) adjacent cohorts might be set equal to each other. This amounts to imposing a very particular kind of nonlinearity assumption to the effect that cohort differences are negligible across several adjacent cohorts, whereas this is not the case with respect to the remaining ones.

Both of these strategies seem arbitrary unless justified on substantive grounds. Indeed, there are indefinitely many ways in which one may estimate the coefficients, given a set of restrictive assumptions, but the prior question is obviously the *theoretical* one of justifying these restrictive assumptions in the first place. It would indeed be unfortunate if empirically inclined investigators were to use either of these approaches without benefit of such a theory (Glenn, 1976). For instance, the notion of "cohort effects" is totally vague unless one can identify a set of variables that are systematically linked to the calendar dates. Why should one assume a similarity between persons born between 1925 and 1930 but not for those born between 1930 and 1935?

The third alternative strategy is much more difficult, both in terms of its demands on our theoretical apparatus and also of the data needed to employ it. This approach is to reconceptualize one's variables so that it becomes possible to replace the difference variable by a more direct measure of the experience variable(s) it is assumed to tap. In the case of the inconsistency or mobility example, this might involve more direct measures of strains due to inconsistency or mobility. One would then replace the inconsistency (or mobility) terms by the strain variable. Or, in the case of the difference between achievements and aspirations, one might obtain a more direct measure of the frustration experienced. In the case of "age" effects, one might want to reconceptualize the variable as "maturation," "amount of experience," or some other variable that is both more directly relevant to one's theory and also only moderately correlated with chronological age. Needless to say, reconceptualizing either (or both) of the component variables might also be appropriate. Precisely what is a "cohort effect" or a "period effect?" In what sense can a calendar date adequately represent the relevant experiences?

This third approach involves the necessity of modifying one's data *collection,* practically always in the direction of obtaining much more detailed information and often requiring the use of subjective or "soft" data involving the recall of past events or perceptions of current ones. The first two alternatives can be used at the data analysis stage and obviously involve considerably less effort in terms of the need for additional data and also from the standpoint of requiring a less careful conceptualization of one's theoretical variables. It is no wonder, then, that the first two avenues appear to have had considerably more appeal. But it does not follow that they will have any greater payoff. Certainly, if we wish to make use of formulations involving such closely interrelated independent variables, we must expect serious complications that will require a number of different avenues of attack.

NOTES

1. The remainder of this section is a revised version of the writer's article, "The Confounding of Measured and Unmeasured Variables: The Case of Social Status," *Sociological Methods and Research* 3 (May 1975): 355-383. Reprinted with the permission of the publisher.

2. Rather recently, critiques of the status attainment literature have, however, focused on the power dimension of occupations in order to increase the explanatory power of "occupation" as a predictor of income. See especially Wright (1978), Wright and Perrone (1977), and Kalleberg and Griffin (1980).

3. The writer is unaware of efforts to assess the transitivity or consistency of such judgments using pair comparisons or triads of individuals.

4. The reputational approach was stimulated by Hunter's (1953) classic study of Atlanta but severely criticized by Dahl (1958, 1961) and several of his students (Polsby, 1959, 1962; and Wolfinger, 1960). There is no need to review this debate here except to note that one of the issues raised centered on whether power should

be conceived of as "potential," or whether it can only be measured in its kinetic form, as power in action. See also Blalock and Wilken (1979), chs. 8 and 9.

5. See especially Lenski (1954), Goffman (1957), Jackson (1962), Jackson and Curtis (1972), Hope (1971, 1975), and Wilson (1979).

CHAPTER 7

AGGREGATION AND MEASUREMENT ERROR IN MACRO-ANALYSES

An examination of macro-level sociological research, plus con-
versations with colleagues and graduate students working in this
area, leaves me with the impression that macro-level measurement is for the most part opportunistic and atheoretical.
Lacking the necessary resources to collect their own data,
investigators have usually searched for available indicators without adequately spelling out the assumed connections with the
variables they are intended to measure. Very frequently, macro-
level researchers are forced to rely on derived measurements
that have been based on decisions made by persons whose
purposes are very different from those of the investigators.
Therefore, it becomes essential to examine very carefully just
how these derived measures have been constructed, what homogeneity assumptions have been made, and how they are to be
linked to the important constructs in macrotheories.

In particular, we need to pinpoint more precisely the similarities and differences between aggregation on the micro- and
macro-levels. Psychologists are of course engaged in an aggrega-

AUTHOR'S NOTE: This chapter represents a revised version of the writer's article,
"Aggregation and Measurement Error," *Social Forces* 50 (December 1971): 151-165.
Published with the permission of the University of North Carolina Press.

tion process whenever they put together behavioral acts deemed to be "similar" in certain respects. In fact, in constructing tests or attitude scales, psychologists attempt to make the individual engage in repeated acts that are assumed to have similar causes. For example, a child may be asked to take a test consisting of a number of items all designed to tap mathematical reasoning ability rather than a conglomerate of abilities or attitudes. After subjecting these repeated acts to certain consistency tests, the investigator makes a decision as to whether or not to aggregate them into a single score tapping a single "factor." Similarly, in a controlled experiment the psychologist attempts to manipulate a single causal stimulus, or at most two or three, so as to elicit behaviors that can be assumed to be similar with respect to this presumed cause. If they are deemed similar, then they may be aggregated into a single score.

The essential point is that the notion of "similarity" is basic to the process of aggregation. But similar with respect to what? In causal analyses it is certainly to our advantage if individual items can be aggregated according to common causes or effects. But whenever items are aggregated on the basis of admin-istrative convenience, rather than on theoretical grounds, they are likely to be put together on the basis of manifest content or some other criteria that may confuse one's theoretical analysis. This problem occurs on the micro-level, as for example where criminal acts are classified according to manifest properties (e.g., murder, burglary, arson, forgery) or according to serious-ness (e.g., misdemeanor versus felony). But it is perhaps most common in the case of macro-level measurement, if only be-cause the limited resources of the social scientist force one to make much greater use of secondary data sources. Furthermore, macro-level social scientists are rarely in a position to conduct quasi-experiments in which the subject is forced to act re-peatedly under standardized conditions.

Aggregation according to manifest characteristics is of course absolutely essential in terms of economy of thought. It would obviously be impossible to reclassify each murder committed in New York City according to a single cause, even assuming that the actual perpetrator had been caught and subjected to a thorough psychiatric examination. We must admit a number of diverse kinds of murders—those resulting from drunken brawls, those committed in the act of robbery, those resulting from jealousy, and so forth. To some extent, these diverse causes are recognized in legal terminology (e.g., first- versus second-degree murder) and in differential prison sentences. But the "measurement errors" involved are substantial. No special analytical problems will arise as long as murder rates are not taken as an indicator of some presumed cause (e.g., alienation or frustration). But whenever one is interested in raising the level of abstraction by connecting several such indicators to underlying causes, all sorts of ambiguities will arise.

Two alternative approaches seem possible in such instances. The first is to try and purify the data, either by gaining access to the unaggregated data or by searching for different indicators that have been aggregated according to simpler causal criteria. The second is to learn to live with data that have been aggregated with other purposes in mind, and to attempt to correct for distortions by developing a relatively complex auxiliary theory of measurement that incorporates the presumed disturbing influences. The first alternative is obviously preferable when feasible, but the second will often be necessary as a practical expedient. The worst practice from the standpoint of scientific integrity, however, is to work with unpurified data that have been aggregated in poorly understood ways and then to pretend that resulting measurement errors are negligible.

In the remainder of the chapter I shall discuss four kinds of aggregation problems that can be conceptualized in causal terms and that are especially relevant in macro-level research where the focus is on *groups* as units of analysis, but where measures often require the aggregation of characteristics or behavioral acts of persons. In each instance, some kind of causal relationship will be postulated between unmeasured variables and their indicators. The assessment of measurement error depends on the equations we write connecting the unmeasured variables with their indicators, but each such question must be justified in terms of a set of assumptions we are willing to make concerning the real-world processes connecting the two.

AGGREGATING EFFECT INDICATORS

Ever since Durkheim's (1951) ambitious attempt to infer global group properties on the basis of suicide rates, sociologists have been intrigued with the possibility of this kind of indirect measurement. Yet the problem remains as elusive as ever because of the large number of plausible rival explanations for each empirical finding. Durkheim attempted to eliminate as many such alternatives as possible given the limitations of his data, but in the process found it necessary to invoke several different "types" of suicides. In effect, his argument boiled down to postulating three basic causes of suicide, namely "anomie," "egoism," and "altruism." Unfortunately, the several types could not be distinguished on the basis of behavioral differences (e.g., method of committing suicide), and therefore Durkheim was left with a single indicator of more than one unmeasured variable.

The basic strategy was nevertheless sound and is essentially similar to that invoked in attitude measurement and testing theory, where we have just noted that the aim is to induce standardized behaviors that are presumed to be similar with respect to underlying causes. In the ideal case, the behavioral indicators can be grouped according to common causes as indicated in Figure 7.1. Each indicator or measured variable X_i is taken to be an effect of one or more unmeasured "factors" or exogenous variables F_i plus other variables e_i that produce idiosyncratic variation. Thus, any covariances among the responses X_i are attributed to the unmeasured factors rather than to possible direct (or indirect) effects of the indicators on each other. In the simplest case, there will be distinct sets or blocks of indicators, each of which is affected by a single factor, so that the indicators in each block may be weighted to produce an estimate of the factor or unmeasured variable affecting that block.

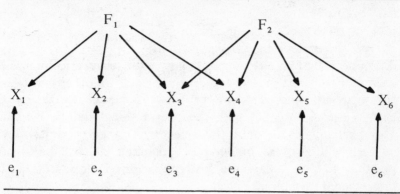

Figure 7.1

When behavioral acts occur in natural settings, our models must be more complicated, but we may still retain the basic idea that the measured variables are to be taken as effects of unmeasured variables, plus perhaps certain of the earlier acts. For example, we may admit that a successful delinquent act may in itself influence the next act. The general strategy in aggregating behaviors in natural settings is to construct as realistic a model as possible and then to note its implications in terms of the kind of aggregate measure(s) that should be constructed. Let us turn to the example of homicides and suicides for illustrative purposes.

Although it has already been implied that it will be theoretically most useful to aggregate behaviors in terms of simple causal models, it is often helpful to look carefully at manifest characteristics. Considering homicides and suicides, the two kinds of acts are obviously similar with respect to an important manifest characteristic: the taking of (human) life by means of a voluntary act. Therefore, we might want to add suicide and homicide rates to obtain a measure of "lethal aggression" (Gold, 1958; Whitt, 1968). But before we do so, we should also ask how the acts *differ*. They obviously differ with respect to choice of target, and one is naturally led to the question of why aggression is sometimes directed against others and sometimes toward the self.

More generally, behavioral acts or any other kinds of "similar" items will not be identical, and before the aggregation process takes place one should, in effect, ask why they should *not* be aggregated. In putting them together, we obscure any differences that may exist, not only with respect to manifest characteristics *but underlying causes as well.* In other words, in the aggregation process we can always expect to confound certain causal variables with the one(s) being studied. We will also partially cancel out the effects of other variables. But without a theory as to what is happening, we will be in no position to give meaningful interpretations in terms of these unmeasured variables.

When we say that both homicide and suicide are forms of aggression, and if we add the assumption that aggression is produced by frustration, then we may wish to add the two rates together (or obtain a weighted average) in order to obtain a more complete indicator of frustration. If we could list and measure all forms of aggression, weighting them with respect to intensity, we could obtain a still better indicator. If Figure 7.1 is valid, then this simple procedure would indeed make sense. But which other variables might be confounded with frustration, and which variables might be cancelled out in the aggregation process? If the remaining causes of each act are idiosyncratic, then the aggregation process will reduce their variance in accord with the law of large numbers, while in other instances it will not.

First, suppose that one act of aggression stimulates responses that lead to other acts. If the victim attempts to resist, he or she may be "marked" for later attacks. He or she may be murdered in the extreme case, not because of frustration but as a purely utilitarian act. Where acts of different individuals are being aggregated, the risk of this particular possibility is not too great, but we recognize that other kinds of contextual variables may be operative in addition to those acting through frustration. Certain aggressive acts may be instrumental in keeping a minority in its place or in regulating police behavior. These possibilities are all obvious. The point is that they should be incorporated into one's decisions about aggregate measures and their relationships with unmeasured variables.

To illustrate in terms of the homicide-suicide example, the fact that there are manifest differences as well as similarities should aid in the search for variables affecting choice of target. One important kind of variable that has been suggested in the literature, and that would be extremely difficult to measure directly, is the degree to which group norms and socialization practices result in intrapunitive, as contrasted with extrapunitive, tendencies. Where degree of frustration is roughly constant, such a factor may be used to account for the inverse relationship that is often found between homicide and suicide rates (Whitt, 1968).

Let us suppose that the micro-level or social-psychological theory can be represented as in Figure 7.2, where each "case" is a single person characterized by a certain probability (y_1) of committing homicide and a different probability (y_2) of committing suicide. These probabilities are influenced by the amount of frustration experienced by the individual (x_1) and by his or her internalized extrapunitiveness (x_2). The latter two variables are influenced in turn by two macro-level or system variables, namely system frustration (X_1) and system extrapunitiveness (X_2), respectively. Perhaps system frustration is itself a result of a number of environmental factors impinging on the individual, such as unemployment, family pressures, the impossibility of fulfilling unrealistic objectives, and so forth. Perhaps system extrapunitiveness is a result of a set of shared values and norms that emphasize that blame for failure is to be directed toward specific targets other than oneself. (Notice that variables appropriate to individuals have been designated by lower-case letters, whereas the system or aggregated variables are designated by capital letters.)

Let us now imagine that we aggregate individuals who are assumed to have been exposed to similar environmental stimuli, perhaps those belonging to a common occupational category or the same geographic community. We assume that homicide *rates* (Y_1) will be a simple function of the summed probabilities of

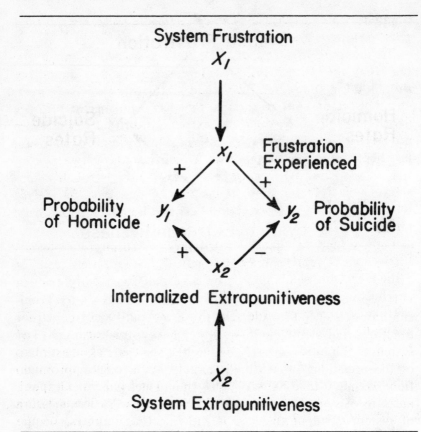

Figure 7.2

homicide; for example, that $Y_{1j} = k_1 \sum_i y_{1ij}$, where the subscript j denotes the jth aggregated unit (e.g., the jth community), and where we sum over all of the i individuals in the jth aggregated unit. We make a similar assumption with respect to suicide rates (Y_2) for the various macro-units. If we likewise assume that the aggregated experienced frustrations will be an almost exact (linear) function of system frustration (X_1), and also that the aggregated internalized extrapunitiveness scores will be an almost exact function of X_2, then we may shift to the macro-level model in Figure 7.3. Let us suppose that both homicide and suicide rates are available on the macro-level, but that X_1 and X_2 are taken as unmeasured variables that we wish to estimate from their "indicators," Y_1 and Y_2.

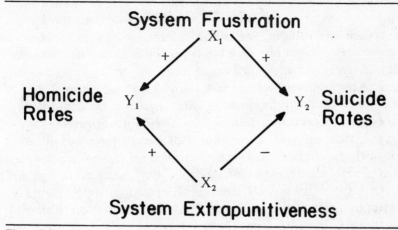

Figure 7.3

If we knew the true coefficients in the equations for homicide rates (Y_1) and suicide rates (Y_2), we could easily construct functions that would eliminate either system frustration (X_1) or system extrapunitiveness (X_2) using the aggregate as an estimate of the remaining unmeasured variable. As a rough approximation, we might take $X_1' = Y_1 + Y_2$ (homicides plus suicides) as a measure of system frustration and $X_2' = Y_1 - Y_2$ as a measure of system extrapunitiveness. If the true (but unknown) equations linking the indicators to the unmeasured variables were as follows:

$$Y_1 = b_{11}X_1 + b_{12}X_2 + e_1$$
$$Y_2 = b_{21}X_1 + b_{22}X_2 + e_2$$

with b_{22} negative, then we would have

$$X_1' = Y_1 + Y_2 = (b_{11} + b_{21})X_1 + (b_{12} + b_{22})X_2 + (e_1 + e_2)$$
$$\text{and} \quad X_2' = Y_1 - Y_2 = (b_{11} - b_{21})X_1 + (b_{12} - b_{22})X_2 + (e_1 - e_2)$$

To the degree that any of the (compound) coefficients approached zero, we would effectively remove the corresponding independent variable from the equation.

Unfortunately, since both X_1 and X_2 will be unmeasured, and since our theory will provide only the *signs* of the b_{ij} but not their magnitudes, we cannot count on eliminating one or the other unmeasured variable from the measure of the other. But if we could find *additional* indicators of both frustration and extrapunitiveness, and if we could assume a knowledge of the signs of the relationships, then perhaps we could obtain more satisfactory indicators of each variable. Suppose, for example, that we used several kinds of assault rates as indicators of both frustration and extrapunitiveness. Likewise, suppose that several other forms of deviance (e.g., drug addiction and certain types of mental disorders) were negatively related to extrapunitiveness but positively related to frustration. Referring to those m indicators positively related to extrapunitiveness as Y_{1i} and those n indicators negatively related to extrapunitiveness as Y_{2j}, we might take as our indicator of system frustration the quantity

$$X_1' = \frac{1}{m} \sum_{i=1}^{m} Y_{1i} + \frac{1}{n} \sum_{j=1}^{n} Y_{2j}$$

and as our indicator of system extrapunitiveness the quantity

$$X_2' = \frac{1}{m} \sum_{i=1}^{m} Y_{1i} - \frac{1}{n} \sum_{j=1}^{n} Y_{2j}$$

In the case of the expression used to measure system frustration, the coefficient of system extrapunitiveness X_2 would not be exactly zero, but it would be dominated by the coefficient of X_1 since all of the b_{ij} in the case of the latter would be positive. If our theory provided us with only the signs of the coefficients, but if we were to assume a reasonable distribution of the magnitudes of these coefficients, then we would expect that the more indicators used, the closer the approximation to a zero coefficient for X_2 in the case of the measure X_1' and, conversely, an approximately zero coefficient for system frustration X_1 in the case of our index of system extrapunitiveness X_2'.

The above approach obviously has a lot in common with factor analysis, though it should be noted that in the case of

Figure 7.3, we in effect have two "factors," each of which may be related to *all* of the indicator variables. In general, one should first construct a plausible model, taking into consideration not only the unmeasured variable(s) one is attempting to measure, but also others that may be confounded with them. If the resulting model is such that factor analysis or related techniques are appropriate, then they may be effectively utilized. If not, then causal approaches to measurement error may be adapted to the model at hand. The essential point is that a theoretical model will be necessary in order to justify whatever aggregation procedure is used. The more explicit this theory is, the easier it will be to criticize and improve one's measurement of global macro-level concepts.

AGGREGATING CAUSE INDICATORS

If all indicators of unmeasured variables could be taken as effects of these variables, then our conceptual problems would be relatively simple. Many macro-level variables have been so vaguely defined that it is indeed difficult to specify clearly just how they are to be linked with operational procedures. Sociological jargon contains many "weasel words"—such as "symptoms," "correlates," "aspects," "facets," "syndromes" and "subsumed under"—which enable the theorist to gloss over difficult measurement problems without ever facing up to the ambiguities involved. For example, what do we mean by saying that something is an "aspect" of urbanization? If one claims that crime in the streets is a "mere symptom," does he or she mean a simple effect or something else? If several indicators are "correlates" of a theoretical variable of interest, how is this known when the latter is not measured? And how is validity to be assessed when the criterion variable is unmeasured?

In terms of measures involving aggregation, we sometimes attempt to measure a variable by summing across factors that each contribute to this variable. Suppose, for example, that one wants to measure the amount of communication in a society, linking this on the one hand to technology, urbanization, or industrialization, and on the other hand to aggregated response measures such as the Communist vote, domestic violence, or political stability. Although formidable aggregation problems will be encountered in connection with the measurement of each of these variables, let us confine our attention to "communication" and assume perfect measurement of all other variables in the system.

How should total communication be measured? Obviously, conceptual clarification will be necessary to decide which indicators should be included in the total, not to mention the weights each should receive. Rather than merely restricting oneself to readily available indicators such as railroad mileage, number of automobile registrations, numbers of TV sets and radios, and newspaper circulation, one should also include other means of communication, such as word of mouth, that cannot be measured with available resources.

The next step is to construct a causal model containing all of the indicators, including those that cannot be obtained, together with the remaining variables in the theoretical system. Let us suppose that the model of Figure 7.4 is used as a first approximation, with the several modes of communication X_i each taken as affecting "total communication," which is unmeasured. The variable "technology" (W) is assumed to affect most types of communication directly, rather than total communication, which is conceived as an aggregate. In a more realistic model one would also want to allow for the effects of each type of communication on the others, since some are clearly alternatives for others (e.g., automobiles versus trains, TV versus radio), so that resources allocated to improving one form of communication may be taken away from another. The model also allows for several unmeasured forms of communication U_i that affect total communication and that may or may not also be linked to technology. Finally, the dependent variable Y (say, political participation) is taken as a direct effect of technology and total communication, rather than specific types of communication. Thus, technology is assumed to influence the dependent variable by paths in addition to that through communication, and the empirical task may be that of comparing the direct effect of technology with the effect through communication.

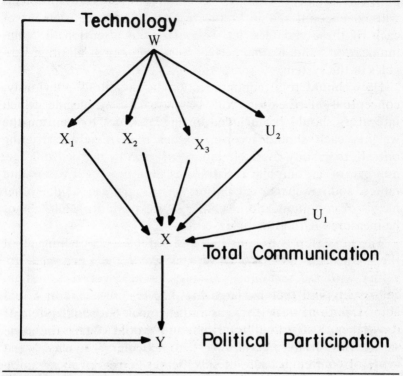

Figure 7.4

If all components X_i have been perfectly measured (for the time being ruling out possible U_i), and if there is no specification error in the model (e.g., if there are no other causes of Y that are also systematically related to X and W), then we may correctly estimate the effects of W on Y using the multiple regression of Y on all of the X_i and W. The partial slope relating Y and W will provide a measure of the "direct" effects of W on Y through paths other than through the sources of communication, and the partial correlation $r_{WY.X_1X_2X_3}$ can be interpreted in the usual way. Furthermore, if the model is correctly specified, the proper regression weights will be given to the several X_i. Of course, if these types of communication are highly intercorrelated, as is likely, then the resulting multi-

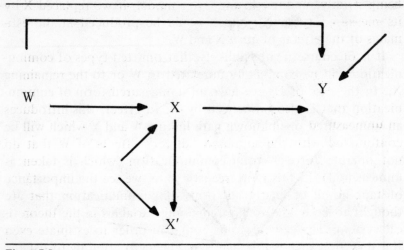

Figure 7.5

collinearity will produce large sampling errors, so that it would be preferable to treat the X_i as a single block (Gordon, 1968). If it were not for sampling errors, one would obtain the same weights for the X_i regardless of the particular Y inserted in the model. However, because of specification error involving ambiguities in the notion of "total communication," such a simple result should not be expected. Ideally, if one obtained different weights using different dependent variables, it might be possible to gain insights into such ambiguities.

Now suppose that there is another type of communication U_1 that we have neglected, and that U_1 is completely unrelated to W (and any other variables in the system aside from X and Y). Although this will introduce measurement error in X, it can easily be seen that it will not systematically affect our estimate of the direct effects of W on Y. The situation is the same as though we had an additional source of variation in X that is unrelated to W. This will weaken the *correlation* between Y and our imperfect measures of X (controlling for W), but will not introduce biases in the slope estimates involving the X_i. This situation is in contrast to that of the model of Figure 7.5, where X' is taken as an *effect* indicator of X, with measurement error being strictly random. In the latter model, if we replaced X by its measured value X′, biases would be produced in the estimates of the effects of *both* X and W.

It is of course highly unlikely that omitted types of communication will be completely unrelated to W or to the remaining X_i. In the case of U_2 we have an unmeasured form of communication that is also influenced by W. In effect, this introduces an unmeasured or unknown path linking W and Y which will be confounded with the supposed "direct" effects of W that do not operate through total communication (which is taken as unmeasured). In this more realistic case, we see the importance of tapping all or nearly all forms of communication that are thought to be linked to the remaining variables in the theoretical system. The general point is that in order to estimate even the direction of possible biases, we need to attempt to list the causal indicators that have not been tapped and to construct theories as to their possible relationships with the other variables. Merely ignoring them will not enable us to grapple systematically with these sources of error.

Perhaps the major lesson to be drawn from the above illustration is that even when we are attempting macro-level analyses, we need better micro-level formulations concerning the causal processes involved. The more adequate our understanding of how various types of communication processes affect individual decision processes, the better position we shall be in to construct macro-level measures that combine indicators in a reasonable way (Converse, 1969). Without such theories, our measurement procedures are likely to continue to reflect ad hoc decisions that make macro-level causal interpretations difficult at best and highly misleading at worst. Economists in particular have been highly critical of quantitative research in sociology because it lacks a base in behavioral theory. I would infer that they have in mind theories analogous to those involving utility and cost functions that provide at least some basis for a theory as to how aggregate measures should be constructed. This is another illustration of the interplay between theory and measurement: in this instance the need for micro-level theories in order to construct macro-level measures.

AGGREGATING BY GEOGRAPHIC PROXIMITY

Certainly the most common type of aggregation problem that sociologists face is that in which individuals have been grouped according to geographic proximity, by block, census tract, SMSA, county, state, or nation. Yet the relationship of the grouping "variable" W to the other variables in almost any theoretical system is likely to be very poorly understood whenever simple location is used as a grouping criterion. In effect we will have confounded together the diverse effects of common regional cultures and subcultures, group norms, effects of locally applied sanctions, early socialization patterns, networks of communication, friendship choices, family patterns, and selective in- and out-migration. The criterion for grouping will thus almost surely be related to most of the remaining variables in the system, but because of its complexity it will be extremely difficult to theorize very precisely about such relationships. In grouping by proximity, we seem to have almost the perfect example of how *not* to aggregate one's data, and yet surprisingly little serious thought has been devoted to this important subject in the sociological literature.

Ever since Robinson's (1950) classic study on so-called "ecological correlations," the problem has been well-known, although as Hannan (1971) has pointed out, our attention has been focused primarily on the practical problem of *disaggregating* (inferring individual characteristics from macro-level ones) rather than the logically prior problem of aggregation. It is almost as though sociologists have resigned themselves to a completely passive role in the data collection and measurement processes, assuming that aggregation by proximity will always be undertaken for the sake of administrative convenience rather than as an aid to theoretical simplifications.

To be sure, whenever the geographic territories have a sociological or political unity, it is convenient to obtain summary measures for each such unit so that socioeconomic "indicators" of income, educational, occupational, and housing characteristics can be obtained. Furthermore, since aggregation is in terms of a simple manifest property—location in physical space—one does not need a theory in order to carry out the aggregation. The same aggregated data may be used by many different scholars for very different purposes. Thus, economy is achieved. But it would be naive to assume that one can economize so easily without paying a price, and the price seems to be that of confounding the effects of many of the variables we most want to disentangle. I am suggesting that the price may be much too high, and that furthermore, our uncritical use of such aggregated measures may be one of the major contributing causes of the lack of integration of micro- and macro-level theoretical analyses.

Hannan (1971) suggests the heuristic device of explicitly designating the aggregating variable (here, proximity) by a symbol (W) and then introducing such a variable into one's theoretical model. It has previously been shown (Blalock, 1964) that if we can reasonably assume that W causes X but not Y, and if we are concerned very simply with the effects of X on Y, assuming a recursive model, then in grouping by W we will not systematically affect our estimate of the slope relating Y to X. But we will generally increase the correlation between the two variables because of the fact that in grouping by W, which does not relate to the remaining causes of Y, we tend to cancel out their effects. It is well-known that individual-level correlations that are extremely weak can be inflated dramatically by such a simple grouping operation. But this bivariate situation is far too simple, and as soon as we attempt to study the interrelationships among as few as five or six variables, it becomes totally unreasonable to assume that only the most causally prior among these variables will be directly affected by such a complex "variable" as geographic proximity. If we ignore W altogether, as is common practice, we will have absolutely no way of assessing the distortions produced. To be sure, we can think generally in terms of "contextual effects" or "structural effects," but such blanket terms can only mask our ignorance of the true causal processes.

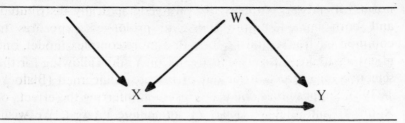

Figure 7.6

If we begin our analyses with data that have already been aggregated according to a theoretically complex block of variables indexed by geographic proximity, it would seem almost impossible to infer what is taking place. In effect, we will be in the hopeless position of trying to disaggregate (in order to infer micro-level processes) without any adequate theory of the aggregation process. We will be putting the cart before the horse. Hannan is certainly correct in noting that we must first understand the aggregation process, which has fortunately been well studied by econometricians. If there is one lesson this literature teaches us, however, it is that aggregation requires *linear* models of relatively simple kinds, and that the formulae used to construct the aggregates must be explicit and simple.

In practice, economists usually try to aggregate items that they are willing to assume *behave* similarly in terms of whatever theoretical variables appear in their systems. They would not aggregate by geographic region without assuming such homogeneity. Yet it is rare that sociologists are willing to assume any real degree of homogeneity within even a single community, to say nothing of an entire state or larger region. We group individuals together suspecting a certain homogeneity with respect to some variables of interest, but we are often not very sure which ones. I rather suspect, moreover, that only the most crude hypotheses of this sort have been made explicit in macro-level sociological research.

In order to make these points more specific, it is necessary to consider particular models of relatively simple types. In Figure 7.6, it is assumed that W affects both X and Y through various unknown mechanisms: common socialization patterns and norms, friendship patterns that are geographically distributed, and both immediate pressures and prolonged exposures to common environmental factors. In a more complex model, one might also take W as an effect of X or Y, thus allowing for the selective migration into or out of the area concerned (Blalock, 1979b). Suppose that one is interested in inferring the effects of X on Y, and that W is not of immediate interest. We wish, however, to control for W in order to separate its effects from those of X. If we were to conduct a micro-level study within a single geographic area, we might be willing to assume a constant W for each individual, and if similar results were obtained within several diverse geographic areas (e.g., cities of different types in widely scattered regions) we might be willing to infer a rather general relationship between X and Y. The argument can of course be generalized to multiple X_i, each of which could be expected to be correlated with both W and Y.

But if we group individuals by proximity W, we do the very *opposite* of controlling for W; we further confound it with X. One way of seeing this is to consider that we have grouped by a cause of a dependent variable, thus confounding X with other causes of Y. I have already stated this argument elsewhere (Blalock, 1964) in terms of simple groupings by Y. Let me therefore consider it in somewhat more general terms. If W affects Y by paths other than through X, we might represent these as through the unmeasured variables U_i, as indicated in Figure 7.7. Because of their common cause W, the U_i will in general be correlated with X unless W is held constant (as within a single geographic area). Of course, X and the several U_i will also have other causes, represented by the side arrows. When we group together individuals according to proximity, we tend to cancel out the effects of these idiosyncratic factors, thereby increasing the correlations between X and the U_i. If we consider the incorrectly specified equation

$$Y = \alpha + \beta X + \epsilon$$

and wish to estimate the effects of X on Y, we wish the disturbance term ϵ containing the effects of the U_i to be

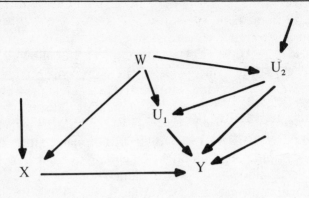

Figure 7.7

uncorrelated with X. But if we have grouped by proximity, we increase the correlation of the U_i (and therefore ϵ) with X, thereby confounding with X a whole host of effects of other variables. The more causes of Y that are causally connected to the proximity variable W, and the larger the size of the groupings, the more serious this effect will be. Therefore, we are likely to attribute to X the effects of numerous variables also associated with the grouping criterion.

We may examine this same model from a slightly different perspective. It can be shown that in grouping by W we approximate the results that would be obtained by using W as an "instrumental variable" to estimate the effects of X on Y (Blalock et al., 1970). If we are willing to assume that W affects X but that it does not belong in the equation for Y, then the estimate $b^* = \Sigma wy/\Sigma wx$, where all variables have been expressed in deviate form, will be a consistent estimator of β (i.e., it will have negligible large-sample biases). But if there is specification error, and if W belongs in the equation for Y, then the bias of the instrumental-variable estimator b^* will be greater than that for ordinary least squares. In particular, if the correct model is

$$Y = \alpha_1 + \beta_1 X + \beta_2 W + \epsilon_y$$

and $X = \alpha_2 + \beta_3 W + \epsilon_x$

where ϵ_y is uncorrelated with W and X and ϵ_x is uncorrelated with W, then the large-sample bias of the instrumental-variable estimator will be approximately β_2/β_3, whereas the least-squares bias will be approximately $(\beta_2/\beta_3)\,[1- \sigma_{\epsilon_x}^2/\,\sigma_x{}^2]$. Thus, in grouping by W and in approximating the bias of the instrumental-variable estimator, we introduce a greater bias than if we had merely ignored W and estimated Y from X using individual-level data. The greater the direct effect of W on Y (as measured by β_2) relative to the effect of W on X, the greater the relative bias of the grouping procedure. To the degree that we could be sure that we were incorporating into the equation all of the mechanisms through which W affects Y, the less we would need to worry about this kind of aggregating procedure. But in the multivariate case, we must remember that grouping by W is likely to increase the intercorrelations between X and other independent variables introduced as causes of Y, thereby producing a multicollinearity problem.

The problem may also be examined from the standpoint of what has been termed "aggregation bias." Hannan and Burstein (1974) argue that under most circumstances, aggregating by a criterion such as geographic proximity will *amplify* any specification biases that may exist in one's micro-model (see also Burstein, 1978). In the case of Figure 7.7, for instance, if one were unaware of the existence of U_1 and U_2, and if in a micro-model one simply related X and Y without controlling for W (say, community of residence), this would produce a certain specification bias. But if one were to use a macro-model in which data had been aggregated according to the criterion W, this specification error would be amplified by an additional aggregation bias, basically for the reasons we have just outlined above.

Irwin and Lichtman (1976), as well as Langbein and Lichtman (1978), have noted that there *may* be occasions under which a macro-model contains less specification error than a micro-model, and that the proper question to ask is whether the micro- or the macro-model is better specified, in the sense that assumptions made about omitted variables are more nearly correct. In the special case where a micro- and macro-model have both been correctly specified, neither will involve a systematic bias. Conceivably, one may have a poorly specified micro-theory—perhaps due to variables that could not be measured—but a much better specified macro-model, in which case there might be an aggregation *gain*. Firebaugh (1978) introduces still another way to look at the aggregation situation by showing that if $\bar{X}$ belongs in the micro-equation for Y, aggregation will amplify biases.

What all of these complementary formulations clearly imply is that the assessment of aggregation and specification biases requires a series of theoretical assumptions not only about micro-level processes, but also about how the criterion for aggregation (here, proximity) fits into this theory. Without such a theory, one will have no way of deciding whether the micro-theory is better specified than the macro-, or vice versa, or whether $\bar{X}$ belongs in the correctly specified micro-equation for Y.

Of course, some sociologists may claim that they have little or no theoretical interest in the micro-level relationships between variables such as X and Y, and that the geographic units should be studied in their own right. If so, however, it will be extremely difficult to integrate the two levels of analysis. As we have just seen, macro-level measurement decisions often require adequate micro-level formulations as underpinnings. To the degree that social analysts see basic causal mechanisms in the motivations and behaviors of human individuals, however aggregated, it will be impossible to achieve definitive results without paying attention to these problems. Even where one adopts a strictly positivist and atheoretical stance, relying solely on the magnitudes of correlation coefficients and estimates of slope coefficients, one is likely to be continually frustrated by the fact that intercorrelations among "independent" variables are likely to be high and also very dependent upon the choice of the unit of aggregation.

The obvious alternative is to gain access to the unaggregated data, so that various groupings can be made (e.g., using larger and larger geographic units or using same-sized units but with differing sets of boundaries), and so that the aggregated and unaggregated data can be compared in terms of specific causal models. There is a considerable amount of important research that could be conducted, for example, with one-in-a-thousand census data on individuals—provided that information concerning geographic location is supplied. Geographic proximity undoubtedly influences behavior according to many diverse mechanisms that vary not only in terms of duration of time (some immediate, some delayed, some continuous) but also in terms of the size of the spatial unit. Friendship patterns and informal social controls may operate only within a very small neighborhood, whereas there may be common political influences over a much wider area. A threat posed by a large minority may have different implications within a neighborhood than within the larger SMSA or county. Larger spatial aggregates will in general be less homogeneous than smaller ones, but the differences in relative homogeneity may depend upon the variables under consideration as well as the kind of area involved (e.g., rural versus urban).

In addition to forming various combinations of geographic units using real data, it may also prove valuable to attempt to simulate certain kinds of causal processes likely to have a geographic base (e.g., political controls stemming from a single center, or diffusion processes produced by friendship networks). The advantage of constructing one's own data with known processes is that the results of different grouping procedures can be compared. The disadvantage is that one can only guess as to the correspondence between the real-world processes and those produced in the simulation. The obvious point is that if sociologists are forced by the realities of data collection limitations to continue using data aggregated by geographic units, then for many kinds of problems in which they are most likely to be interested, a large number of simplifying assumptions are going to be necessary. Yet one cannot make rational decisions concerning the relative priorities of these assumptions without making them reasonably explicit.

AGGREGATING SAMPLES OF VARIABLES FROM BLOCKS

Finally, we turn to a problem that appears to be even more difficult to conceptualize than that of aggregating by proximity. We often find ourselves talking about large sets or blocks of variables that, on the surface, might be expected to be highly intercorrelated but that have not been clearly distinguished or measured. For example, when we speak of the way children have been socialized, we may have in mind a very large number of behavioral sequences involving parents, siblings, friends, teachers, and other adults that have culminated in a particular constellation of attitudes. As a practical research device, however, we may find it necessary to ask only ten or twenty questions about parental behavior, reactions of teachers and friends, and so forth. We may then combine the responses to these items into one or more indicators of socialization. Or perhaps we may be able to obtain ten or twenty measures of industrialization, considering these as a sample of a much larger number of possible indicators.

Whenever we speak about certain "aspects" or "facets" of a phenomenon, I rather suspect that we have this kind of sampling operation in mind. Being modest, we know that we cannot measure all aspects of socialization or industrialization. If we are fortunate, we may have on hand a relatively explicit definition of a complex variable that suggests a very limited number of kinds of measures that might be used. For example, suppose we are given a definition of "socialism" as a form of government that involves *both* governmental control of the means of production and democratic control over the decision-making apparatus. This definition would suggest two distinct "aspects" of socialism, though each could be measured in a number of different ways. Furthermore, the two aspects might interact nonadditively on certain dependent variables, thereby making it advantageous to treat them as distinct dimensions or variables in their own right.

What can be done in the absence of a more explicit theory interrelating variables within such a block? In many instances, an investigator will find it impossible to obtain more than four or five measures for each block and yet will be faced with practical decisions as to how to weight them and as to whether or not he or she can legitimately use them to "stand for" the entire block. A similar problem arises within the field of attitude measurement, where one must necessarily sample from some larger universe of possible items presumed to tap the entire block.

The question seems to be unanswerable in the absence of a theory interrelating the variables in the block. Therefore one should try to list other variables or "aspects" that have not been measured and construct a rudimentary theory as to how the omitted variables may differ from those included, both in terms of their relationships with the dependent variable(s) and with each other. Such a preliminary theory may suggest a division of the block into several components, some of which are expected to be more closely related to the dependent variable than others. Some form of empirical dimensional analysis, such as factor analysis, may be of value at this initial stage. The essential point is that one should attempt to include in one's working theory not only the measured indicators, but others that might conceivably be measured under more ideal conditions.

In the absence of an explicit theory that has been adequately tested, it may nevertheless be desirable to weight the indicators of one or more blocks in order to simplify the analysis. One way of doing this is to factor analyze the indicators, using the factor loadings as weights and attempting to name the factors according to the indicators most highly correlated with them. This procedure has the important advantage of using weights that do not depend on the particular dependent variable under investigation, but it implies a particular kind of causal structure within the block. The "factor" within each block is presumed to affect each of the indicators (plus perhaps indicators of other blocks as well) which are *not* functions of each other. Given that the true causal structure is unknown, this approximation may be suitable for exploratory purposes, as long as the factors are not reified.

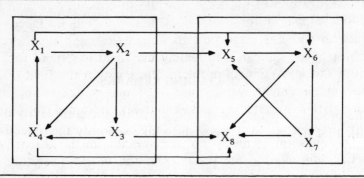

Figure 7.8

An alternative approach essentially involves weighting the indicators according to their correlations with the dependent variable.[1] This procedure has the advantage of maximizing the "explained" variance in the dependent variable but the disadvantage that the weights will shift with each dependent variable used. Conceptually, we might imagine a complex network of causal interrelationships within the block, together with unknown multiple causal connections between the separate variables and the dependent variable. For example, if we were studying the effects of urbanization on domestic violence, we would recognize that the many "aspects" of urbanization influence individuals in slightly different ways that are obscured in the aggregation process. But these influence patterns may also have differential effects on various forms of behavior, so that the weight given to a particular indicator in affecting voting behavior may not be the same as its weight in connection with participation in a riot.

According to this line of reasoning, there is no direct effect of the "block" itself on each dependent variable. Instead, the block merely represents a set of highly intercorrelated variables, some of which are causally related to the dependent variable(s) directly, and others only indirectly. This way of conceptualizing the interrelationships is illustrated in Figure 7.8. For each dependent variable, the total influence of each block may be assessed using a multiple-partial correlation (Sullivan, 1971), even though it may be meaningless to estimate the separate slopes for each indicator because of the high intercorrelations within each block.

CONCLUDING REMARKS

The preceding examples should illustrate the complexity of the task that lies ahead if we wish to take seriously the objective of improving our aggregate measures. The problem is both technical and theoretical, and only gradual progress can be expected in view of the number of unknowns that are involved. But there are also practical difficulties, as sociologists are well aware. Hopefully, sociologists will become increasingly self-conscious concerning present inadequacies in available data sources so that, as a profession, we will coordinate our research more effectively, standardize our measuring instruments, and make a greater effort to influence not only the collection of data but the ways in which these data are aggregated and made available for scientific use. The political and ethical implications involved in making unaggregated data more readily available must also be squarely faced so that respondents and informants are fully protected.

In the absence of really adequate measuring instruments, it seems obvious that we must rely on multiple indicators obtained by using diverse data collection procedures. The notion of "triangulation" has been emphasized by Webb et al. (1966) and by Denzin (1970) as a way of proceeding by indirect measurement to eliminate plausible rival explanations to individual empirical findings. I would emphasize, however, that "triangulation" (which derives from a mathematical concept) is impossible without an explicit and rather precise theory concerning the properties of triangles. Likewise, the major thrust of our argument through this book has been that multiple measures without a theory will only lead to chaotic results. Whenever indicators are combined into aggregate measures of any kind, either an implicit or an explicit theory is being used. Our initial efforts at making such theories explicit and increasingly realistic will certainly be discouraging and entirely inadequate, but without such a self-conscious attempt, it is difficult to imagine how we can systematically improve upon existing ad hoc procedures.

NOTE

1. For a somewhat similar discussion of a rationale for measurement according to effects on dependent variables, see Coleman (1964).

APPENDIX

ASSESSING COMPARABILITY WITH MULTIPLE INDICATORS

Unless one is willing to make highly restrictive and therefore unrealistic assumptions that in effect amount to automatically *imposing* comparability on at least some of one's indicators, the empirical assessment of comparability may become both difficult and risky unless one has available not only multiple indicators of each variable but also information about at least three different settings.

The purpose of this brief appendix is to illustrate a strategy of attack on the comparability problem, although simultaneously pointing up the necessity of carefully stating just what assumptions one is willing to make about the variances of both the true values and also the measurement-error components across several settings. We shall see that under certain circumstances, it becomes possible to make a limited number of testable predictions that may then be assessed in terms of their correspondence with one's actual empirical results. We must emphasize at the outset, however, that our intent is merely that of outlining a strategy of attack that will need to be modified according to the nature of the number of indicators and settings studied and also the complexity of whatever multiple-indicator models one is attempting to assess.

Recall that our definition of equivalence of indicators across settings requires that for any indicator X_i, we must have identical deterministic equations linking X_i to X across settings *and* a disturbance term that has identical variances across these settings (as well as identical covariances with other variables in the system). Clearly, this is a very strong set of conditions that we rarely expect to be approximated in the real world. Furthermore, with a single indicator of X, it will be impossible to test these assumptions empirically unless, of course, the true value of X is known. We will have sample estimates of $\sigma_{x_i}^2$, but all three of the quantities b_i σ_x^2, and $\sigma_{e_i}^2$ will be unknown. However, with multiple indicators it becomes possible to make some indirect or weak tests,

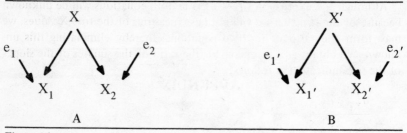

Figure A1

provided we are willing to make certain simplifying assumptions. Let us examine two specific cases to see what they imply.

Unequal Variance in X_i Across Settings

If it is expected or determined that indicator variances will be very different across settings, and if one has available data for at least three settings, one may develop a test criterion for the equivalence assumption. Consider the two-indicator model given in Figure A1, which we may assume to be a portion of a larger model. The equivalence assumption requires that $\sigma_{e_1}^2 = \sigma_{e_1'}^2 = k_1$ and similarly $\sigma_{e_2}^2 = \sigma_{e_2'}^2 = k_2$. The variable X has been written as X' in B to emphasize that the variances in X may differ across settings. We may therefore write

$$\sigma_{X_1}^2 = b_1^2 \sigma_X^2 + \sigma_{e_1}^2 = b_1^2 \sigma_X^2 + k_1$$

and

$$\sigma_{X_1'}^2 = b_1^2 \sigma_{X'}^2 + \sigma_{e_1'}^2 = b_1^2 \sigma_{X'}^2 + k_1$$

Since the unstandardized slope b_1 is assumed to be invariant across settings, we may eliminate k_1, representing the measurement-error variance, by subtraction getting

$$\sigma_{X_1}^2 - \sigma_{X_1'}^2 = b_1^2 (\sigma_X^2 - \sigma_{X'}^2)$$

Similarly, for X_2 we will have

$$\sigma_{X_2}^2 - \sigma_{X_2'}^2 = b_2^2 (\sigma_X^2 - \sigma_{X'}^2)$$

Although the expression $(\sigma_X^2 - \sigma_X^2{}')$ in both equations will be unknown because of the fact that we will not have measures of the true X values, we may form the ratio of the two equations, thereby eliminating this unknown. We obtain an expression for the ratio of the squares of the slopes of the two indicators as follows:

$$\frac{\sigma_{X_1}^2 - \sigma_{X_1}^2{}'}{\sigma_{X_2}^2 - \sigma_{X_2}^2{}'} = \frac{b_1^2}{b_2^2}$$

With only two settings there will be no way to test the model (unless the slope ratio is assumed a priori), but if we had data available in a third setting C, and if we were willing to assume equivalence for both X_1 and X_2 across all three settings, then we could compute a similar ratio for the settings A and C, expecting the two sets of ratios to be approximately equal.

A note of caution is appropriate, however. If the differences between the two indicator variances $\sigma_{X_i}^2$ and $\sigma_{X_i}^2{}'$ are small, then the ratios of these differences will approach indeterminacy, implying very large sampling errors. Therefore, in addition to all of the remaining assumptions, one must have rather substantial differences in indicator variances across settings in order to apply this particular kind of test criterion. Where such differences are substantial, it should be noted that the typical sorts of path-analytic comparisons, using standardized measures, must be made with extreme caution.

Proportional Equivalence

With multiple-indicator models it may be possible to relax the equivalence assumption somewhat, while still being able to develop test criteria designed to evaluate the reasonableness of such weaker assumptions. We illustrate with a very simple two-variable, two-indicator model, indicated in Figure A2, in which we assume that the errors in all four indicators are strictly random. Both correlation coefficients and unstandardized regression coefficients have been inserted in the diagrams, with primes being used for the variables and coefficients appropriate to setting B. Costner (1969) has shown that a test criterion may be used to evaluate the adequacy of this simple model, namely the prediction

$$r_{X_1Y_1}r_{X_2Y_2} = r_{X_1Y_2}\, r_{X_2Y_1}$$

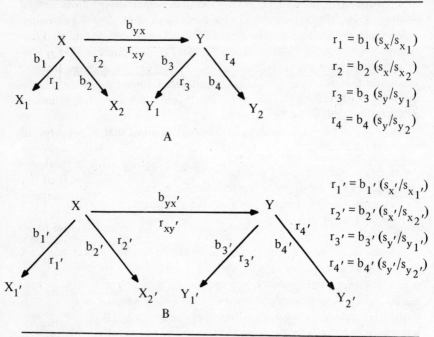

A

$$r_1 = b_1 \, (s_x/s_{x_1})$$
$$r_2 = b_2 \, (s_x/s_{x_2})$$
$$r_3 = b_3 \, (s_y/s_{y_1})$$
$$r_4 = b_4 \, (s_y/s_{y_2})$$

B

$$r_1{'} = b_1{'} \, (s_x{'}/s_{x_1}{'})$$
$$r_2{'} = b_2{'} \, (s_x{'}/s_{x_2}{'})$$
$$r_3{'} = b_3{'} \, (s_y{'}/s_{y_1}{'})$$
$$r_4{'} = b_4{'} \, (s_y{'}/s_{y_2}{'})$$

Figure A2

If there are sources of nonrandom error that produce additional covariances across indicators of the *different* variables X and Y, this condition will not be satisfied. If, however, an extraneous variable were to affect both indicators of X (or of Y), this would not be detectable with this particular test criterion. With three indicators of each variable, one may detect this second type of source of nonrandomness, as well as the possibility that X directly affects one of Y's indicators, or vice versa. It is assumed that the reader is familiar with the essentials of Costner's argument. Basically, as Costner and Schoenberg (1973) point out, one may construct a series of two-indicator submodels to check for cross-variable nonrandom errors, and then use three-indicator submodels to search for additional sources of nonrandom errors.

If we were trying to make comparisons *across* settings, here A and B, what kinds of expectations would seem reasonable? Given that variances of X and Y, (as well as of sources of measurement errors) are unlikely to remain constant, one would not ordinarily expect *correlations* or standardized path coefficients to be equal or even proportional across several settings. In particular, we would not expect r_{XY} and r'_{XY} to be equal, even where the corresponding unstandardized slopes are identical. Likewise, we would probably not want to impose the assumption that $r_i = r_i'$ or even that ratios of correlations remain invariant across settings. Instead, it would be much more plausible to impose assumptions about the relative magnitudes of unstandardized slope coefficients, the expected values of which do not depend on variances.

Our equivalence of indicators assumption requires that $b_i = b_i'$ for all equivalent indicators. Notice that we are *not* assuming equivalences *across* indicators, say X_1 and X_2, within the same setting. Our equivalence assumption also requires equal variances (for the same indicators) of the measurement-error terms, but it does *not* require equality across settings with respect to variance in *true* values of X or Y. Thus, even if all $b_i = b_i'$ and all corresponding measurement-error variances in A and B were identical, because of possible differences in σ_x^2 and σ_y^2, we would not expect that the corresponding correlations would also be equal. Of course, in the very special (and restrictive) case where variances in the true values were also equal across settings, we would then expect equalities among the correlations as well.

Clearly, one must find ways to relax some of these very stringent requirements so that reasonable comparisons can be made across settings. Without a priori assumptions about variables that produce differences in variances across settings, however, it seems totally unreasonable to impose assumptions about the relative values of correlations. In order to see what these might imply, however, we shall begin with a particular kind of assumption that we may later modify so as to work with unstandardized slopes rather than correlations. The assumption that we shall make is that the *relative* adequacy of two or more indicators remains invariant. We begin by working with indicators of one of the variables, say Y, assuming that the ratio r_3/r_4 remains constant. That is, we assume

$$r_3/r_4 = r_3'/r_4' \text{ or } r_3 r_4' = r_3' r_4.$$

Such an assertion is of course not directly testable, since none of the correlations involving X or Y can be computed. Instead, we will have available the six correlations among indicator variables in setting A, along with an additional six correlations in setting B. Suppose we select one of the indicators X_1 of the measured variable (X) for which we have *not* imposed this proportionality assumption. We will have available the correlations of X_1 with each measure of Y in both settings and may use the test criterion

$$r_{X_1 Y_1} \, r_{X_1'Y_2'} = r_{X_1'Y_1'} \, r_{X_1 Y_2}$$

to evaluate the reasonableness of the proportionality assumption regarding the Y indicators. A second test may then be made using the second (and additional) indicator(s) of X.

To justify the above criterion, we may note that one may multiply both sides of the (assumed) equation $r_3 r_4' = r_3' r_4$ by the product of four correlations, namely the two correlations between X and Y (r_{XY} and r_{XY}') and the two correlations of X with X_1 (r_1 and r_1'). Carrying out this multiplication and arranging terms we get

$$(r_1 r_{XY} r_3) \, (r_1' r_{XY}' r_4') = (r_1' r_{XY}' r_3') \, (r_1 r_{XY} r_4)$$

$$\text{or } r_{X_1 Y_1} \, r_{X_1'Y_2'} = r_{X_1'Y_1'} \, r_{X_1 Y_2}$$

The corresponding test criterion using X_2 is

$$r_{X_2 Y_1} \, r_{X_2'Y_2'} = r_{X_2'Y_1'} r_{X_2 Y_2}$$

Had we also assumed a similar invariant ratio for the indicators of X, namely $r_1/r_2 = r_1'/r_2'$, we would have obtained two additional test criteria by using Y_1 and then Y_2, as follows:

$$r_{X_1 Y_1} \, r_{X_2'Y_1'} = r_{X_1'Y_1'} \, r_{X_2 Y_1}$$

and

$$r_{X_1 Y_2} \, r_{X_2'Y_2'} = r_{X_1'Y_2'} \, r_{X_2 Y_2}$$

As suggested above, it does not seem plausible to impose the assumption of invariant ratios of *correlations* among two or more indicators because of the fact that correlations are affected by variances that cannot be expected to remain stable across settings. However, it seems much more reasonable to assume that the corresponding ratios of slopes connecting indicators to true values remain constant, even where their individual values may not. That is, even though $b_i \neq b_i'$ we may wish to make the slightly less restrictive assumption that the ratios of slopes for either or both variables X and Y do remain constant. Indeed, this seems an appropriate meaning for the assertion that the indicators retain their relative "validity" across settings in which variances are not invariant.

For instance, if both X_1 and X_2 are subject to bias, as measured by their respective slopes, the assumption would amount to asserting that their relative biases do not change from one setting to the next. If so, we could assume that $b_1/b_2 = b_1'/b_2'$. A similar assumption might be made for Y, giving a cross-product equation $b_3 b_4' = b_3' b_4$. Although the algebra is now somewhat more complex because we must consider ratios of standard deviations, it can easily be shown that the previous prediction criteria can still be stated in terms of products of correlations among measured indicators, each modified by a product of two standard deviation terms. If we impose the ratio condition for the Y indicators, the modified predictions become

$$r_{X_1 Y_1} \, r_{X_1' Y_2'} \, [s_{Y_1} s_{Y_2'}] = r_{X_1' Y_1'} \, r_{X_1 Y_2} \, [s_{Y_1'} s_{Y_2}]$$

and

$$r_{X_2 Y_1} \, r_{X_2' Y_2'} \, [s_{Y_1} s_{Y_2'}] = r_{X_2' Y_1'} \, r_{X_2 Y_2} \, [s_{Y_1'} \; s_{Y_2}]$$

The corresponding predictions in the case of the ratio condition for the X indicators are

$$r_{X_1 Y_1} \, r_{X_2' Y_1'} \, [s_{X_1} s_{X_2'}] = r_{X_1' Y_1'} \, r_{X_2 Y_1} \, [s_{X_1'} s_{X_2}]$$

and

$$r_{X_1 Y_2} \, r_{X_2' Y_2'} \, [s_{X_1} s_{X_2'}] = r_{X_1' Y_2'} \, r_{X_2 Y_2} \, [s_{X_1'} s_{X_2}]$$

Obviously, in realistic cases, even the multiple-indicator models that have been pruned of noncommon indicators will be more complex than any of the simplistic models we have been discussing. Where there are sources of nonrandom errors, additional assumptions about the comparability of the coefficients involving these disturbing influences will have to be made. Where differences in the variances of these sources of nonrandom errors can be expected, we may once again need to work with unstandardized coefficients. Overall goodness-of-fit tests using LISREL can be utilized, along with the kinds of submodel explorations of the types suggested by Burt (1976) and by Costner and Schoenberg (1973).

In such explorations, however, one must be mindful that common indicators, merely because they are operationally nearly identical, cannot automatically be assumed equivalent. Therefore, one must be exceedingly cautious about the nature of the restrictions one imposes on the values of coefficients across settings. In particular, one must not automatically use common indicators as reference indicators, since this will impose a common metric on true values when in fact the slope coefficients should not be treated as identical.

REFERENCES

Akers, Ronald and Frederick L. Campbell
  1970   "Size and the Administrative Component in Occupational Associations."
          Pacific Sociological Review 13: 241-251.
Baumol, William J.
  1970   *Economic Dynamics* (3rd Ed.). New York: Macmillan.
Bettelheim, Bruno and Morris Janowitz
  1950   *The Dynamics of Prejudice,* ch. 4. New York: Harper & Row.
Blalock, H. M.
  1964   *Causal Inferences in Nonexperimental Research.* Chapel Hill: University
          of North Carolina Press.
  1967   "Status Inconsistency and Interaction: Some Alternative Models."
          American Journal of Sociology 73: 305-315.
  1968   "The Measurement Problem: A Gap Between the Languages of Theory
          and Research," in H. M. Blalock and Ann B. Blalock (eds.) *Methodology
          in Social Research.* New York: McGraw-Hill.
  1969   *Theory Construction: From Verbal to Mathematical Formulations.*
          Englewood Cliffs, NJ: Prentice-Hall.
  1974   "Beyond Ordinal Measurement: Weak Tests of Stronger Theories," in
          H. M. Blalock (ed.) *Social Science Measurement.* Chicago: Aldine.
  1975   "Indirect Measurement in Social Science: Some Nonadditive Models," in
          H. M. Blalock, A. Aganbegian, F. Borodkin, R. Boudon, and V. Capecchi
          (eds.) *Quantitative Sociology.* New York: Academic Press.
  1976   "Can We Find a Genuine Ordinal Slope Analogue?" in D. R. Heiss (ed.)
          Sociological Methodology 1976. San Francisco: Jossey-Bass.
  1979a "Dilemmas and Strategies of Theory Construction," in W. E. Snizek,
          E. R. Fuhrman, and M. K. Miller (eds.) *Contemporary Issues in Theory
          and Research.* Westport, CT: Greenwood Press.
  1979b "Measurement and Conceptualization Problems: The Major Obstacle to
          Integrating Theory and Research." *American Sociological Review* 44:
          881-894.
Blalock, H. M., Caryll S. Wells, and Lewis F. Carter
  1970   "Statistical Estimation with Random Measurement Error," in Edgar F.
          Borgatta and George W. Bohrnstedt (eds.) *Sociological Methodology
          1970.* San Francisco: Jossey-Bass.
Blalock, H. M. and Paul H. Wilken
  1979   *Intergroup Processes: A Micro-Macro Perspective.* New York: Free Press.

273

Blau, Peter M.
   1977   *Inequality and Heterogeneity: A Primitive Theory of Social Structure.*
           New York: Free Press.
Burstein, Leigh
   1978   "Assessing Differences Between Grouped and Individual-Level Regression
           Coefficients: Alternative Approaches." *Sociological Methods and
           Research* 7: 5-28.
Burt, Ronald S.
   1976   "Interpretational Confounding of Unobserved Variables in Structural
           Equation Models." *Sociological Methods and Research* 5: 3-52.
Campbell, Donald T. and D. W. Fiske
   1959   "Convergent and Discriminant Validation by the Multitrait-Multimethod
           Matrix." *Psychological Bulletin* 56: 81-105.
Campbell, N. R.
   1928   *An Account of the Principles of Measurement and Calculation.* London:
           Longmans, Green.
Christ, Carl
   1966   *Econometric Models and Methods.* New York: John Wiley.
Cohen, Morris R. and Ernest Nagel
   1934   *An Introduction to Logic and Scientific Method.* New York: Harcourt
           Brace Jovanovich.
Coleman, James S.
   1964   *Introduction to Mathematical Sociology,* ch. 2. New York: Free Press.
Converse, Philip E.
   1969   "Survey Research and the Decoding of Patterns in Ecological Data," in
           Mattai Dogan and Stein Rokkan (eds.) *Quantitative Ecological Analysis
           in the Social Sciences.* Cambridge, MA: MIT Press.
Coombs, Clyde H.
   1953   "Theory and Methods of Social Measurement," in Leon Festinger and
           Daniel Katz (eds.) *Research Methods in the Behavioral Sciences.* New
           York: Dryden Press.
   1964   *A Theory of Data.* New York: John Wiley.
Costner, Herbert L.
   1969   "Theory, Deduction, and Rules of Correspondence." *American Journal
           of Sociology* 75: 245-263.
Costner, Herbert L. and Ronald Schoenberg
   1973   "Diagnosing Indicator Ills in Multiple Indicator Models," in Arthur S.
           Goldberger and Otis Dudley Duncan (eds.) *Structural Equation Models in
           the Social Sciences.* New York: Seminar Press.
Dahl, Robert A.
   1958   "A Critique of the Ruling Elite Model." *American Political Science
           Review* 58: 463-469.
   1961   *Who Governs?* New Haven, CT: Yale University Press.
Denzin, Norman K.
   1970   *The Research Act,* chs. 3 and 5. Chicago: Aldine.
Duncan, Otis Dudley
   1961   "A Socio-economic Index for All Occupations," in Albert J. Reiss (ed.)
           Occupations and Social Status. New York: Free Press.
   1975   *Introduction to Structural Equation Models.* New York: Academic Press.

Durkheim, Emile
1951   *Suicide.* Glencoe, IL: Free Press.
Festinger, Leon
1957   *A Theory of Cognitive Dissonance.* Palo Alto, CA: Stanford University Press.
Firebaugh, Glenn
1978   "A Rule for Inferring Individual-Level Relationships from Aggregate Data." *American Sociological Review* 43: 557-572.
Fisher, Franklin
1966   *The Identification Problem in Econometrics.* New York: McGraw-Hill.
Freeman, John H. and J. E. Kronenfeld
1973   "Problems of Definitional Dependency: The Case of Administrative Intensity." *Social Forces* 52: 108-121.
Fuguitt, G. V. and Stanley Lieberson
1974   "Correlation of Ratio or Difference Scores Having Common Terms," in Herbert L. Costner (ed.) *Sociological Methodology 1973-1974.* San Francisco: Jossey-Bass.
Gibbs, Jack P. and Walter T. Martin
1964   *Status Integration and Suicide.* Eugene, OR: University of Oregon Books.
Glenn, Norval D.
1976   "Cohort Analysts' Futile Quest: Statistical Attempts to Separate Age, Period, and Cohort Effects." *American Sociological Review* 41: 900-904.
Goffman, Irwin W.
1957   "Status Consistency and Preference for Change in Power Distribution." *American Sociological Review* 22: 275-281.
Gold, Martin
1958   "Suicide, Homicide, and the Socialization of Aggression." *American Journal of Sociology* 63: 651-661.
Goldberger, Arthur S. and Otis Dudley Duncan (eds.)
1973   *Structural Equation Models in the Social Sciences.* New York: Seminar Press.
Gordon, Robert A.
1968   "Issues in Multiple Regression." *American Journal of Sociology* 73: 592-616.
Guttman, Louis
1944   "A Basis for Scaling Qualitative Data." *American Sociological Review* 9: 139-150.
Hannan, Michael T.
1971   *Aggregation and Disaggregation in Sociology.* Lexington, MA: Lexington Books.
Hannan, Michael T., and Leigh Burstein
1974   "Estimation from Grouped Observations." *American Sociological Review* 39: 374-392.
Hargens, Lowell L.
1976   "A Note on Standardized Coefficients as Structural Parameters." *Sociological Methods and Research* 5: 247-256.
Hauser, Robert M. and Arthur S. Goldberger
1971   "The Treatment of Unobservable Variables in Path Analysis," in Herbert L. Costner (ed.) *Sociological Methodology 1971.* San Francisco: Jossey-Bass.

Heider, Fritz
    1958   *The Psychology of Interpersonal Relations.* New York: John Wiley.
Heise, David R.
    1975   *Causal Analysis.* New York: John Wiley.
Hildebrand, D. K., J. D. Laing, and H. Rosenthal
    1977   *Prediction Analysis of Cross Classifications.* New York: John Wiley.
Hollingshead, A. B.
    1949   *Elmtown's Youth.* New York: John Wiley.
Hope, Keith
    1971   "Social Mobility and Fertility." *American Sociological Review* 36:
            1019-1032.
    1975   "Models of Status Inconsistency and Social Mobility Effects." *American
            Sociological Review* 40: 322-332.
Horan, Patrick M.
    1978   "Is Status Attainment Research Atheoretical?" *American Sociological
            Review* 43: 534-541.
Hunter, Floyd
    1953   *Community Power Structure.* Chapel Hill: University of North Carolina
            Press.
Irwin, Laura and Allan J. Lichtman
    1976   "Across the Great Divide: Inferring Individual Level Behavior From
            Aggregate Data." *Political Methodology* 3: 411-439.
Jackson, Elton F.
    1962   "Status Consistency and Symptoms of Stress." *American Sociological
            Review* 27: 469-480.
Jackson, Elton F. and Richard F. Curtis
    1972   "Effects of Vertical Mobility and Status Inconsistency: A Body of
            Negative Evidence." *American Sociological Review* 37: 701-713.
Johnston, J.
    1972   *Econometric Methods* (2nd Ed.) New York: McGraw-Hill.
Jöreskog, Karl
    1970   "A General Method for the Analysis of Covariance Structures." *Bio-
            metrika* 57: 239-251.
    1973   "A General Method for Estimating a Linear Structural Equation Sys-
            tem," in Arthur S. Goldberger and Otis Dudley Duncan (eds.) *Structural
            Equation Models in the Social Sciences.* New York: Seminar Press.
Jöreskog, Karl and D. Sörbom
    1978   "LISREL IV: A General Computer Program for Estimation of a Linear
            Structural Equation System by Maximum Likelihood Methods." Chi-
            cago: National Educational Resources.
Kalleberg, Arne L. and Larry J. Griffin
    1980   "Class, Occupation, and Inequality in Job Rewards." *American Journal
            of Sociology* 85: 731-768.
Kasarda, John D. and Patrick D. Nolan
    1979   "Ratio Measurement and Theoretical Inference in Social Research."
            Social Forces 58: 212-227.
Kim, Jae-On and G. Donald Ferree, Jr.
    1981   "Standardization in Causal Analysis." *Sociological Methods and Research*
            10: 187-210.

Krantz, David H., R. Duncan Luce, Patrick Suppes, and Amos Tversky
  1971   *Foundations of Measurement, Vol. 1: Additive and Polynomial Representations.* New York: Academic Press.
Langbein, Laura Irwin and Allan J. Lichtman
  1978   *Ecological Inference.* Beverly Hills, CA: Sage.
Lazarsfeld, Paul F.
  1954   "A Conceptual Introduction to Latent Structure Analysis," in Paul F. Lazarsfeld (ed.) *Mathematical Thinking in the Social Sciences.* New York: Free Press.
Lazarsfeld, Paul F. and Neil W. Henry
  1968   *Latent Structure Analysis.* Boston: Houghton Mifflin.
Lenski, Gerhard E.
  1954   "Status Crystallization: A Non-Vertical Dimension of Status." *American Sociological Review* 19: 405-413.
Long, Susan
  1980   "The Continuing Debate over the Use of Ratio Variables: Facts and Fiction," in Karl F. Schuessler (ed.) *Sociological Methodology 1980.* San Francisco: Jossey-Bass.
Lord, Frederic M. and Melvin R. Novick
  1968   *Statistical Theories of Mental Test Scores.* Reading, MA: Addison-Wesley.
MacMillan, Alexander and Richard L. Daft
  1979   "Administrative Intensity and Ratio Variables: The Case Against Definitional Dependency." *Social Forces* 58: 228-248.
Mason, Karen O., William M. Mason, H. H. Winsborough, and W. Kenneth Poole
  1973   "Some Methodological Issues in Cohort Analyses of Archival Data." *American Sociological Review* 38: 242-258.
McKinney, John C.
  1966   *Constructive Typology and Social Theory.* New York: Appleton-Century-Crofts.
Namboodiri, N. Krishnan, Lewis F. Carter, and H. M. Blalock
  1975   *Applied Multivariate Analysis and Experimental Designs.* New York: McGraw-Hill.
Newcomb, Theodore M.
  1968   "Interpersonal Balance," in R. P. Abelson, E. Aronson, W. J. McGuire, T. M. Newcomb, M. J. Rosenberg, and R. H. Tannenbaum (eds.) *Theories of Cognitive Consistency: A Sourcebook.* Chicago: Rand McNally.
North, C. C. and Paul K. Hatt
  1947   "Jobs and Occupations: A Popular Evaluation." *Opinion News* (Sept. 1).
Northrop, F.S.C.
  1947   *The Logic of the Sciences and the Humanities.* New York: Macmillan.
Polsby, Nelson
  1959   "The Sociology of Community Power: A Reassessment." *Social Forces* 37: 232-236.
  1962   "Community Power: Some Reflections on the Recent Literature." *American Sociological Review* 27: 838-841.
Przeworski, Adam and Henry Teune
  1970   *The Logic of Comparative Social Inquiry.* New York: John Wiley.
Pullum, Thomas
  1975   *Measuring Occupational Inheritance.* Amsterdam/New York: Elsevier.

Robinson, William S.
1950   "Ecological Correlations and the Behavior of Individuals." *American Sociological Review* 15: 351-357.
Schoenberg, Ronald
1972   "Strategies for Meaningful Comparison," in Herbert L. Costner (ed.) *Sociological Methodology 1972*. San Francisco: Jossey-Bass.
Schuessler, Karl
1973   "Ratio Variables and Path Models," in Arthur S. Goldberger and Otis Dudley Duncan (eds.) *Structural Equation Models in the Social Sciences.* New York: Seminar Press.
1974   "Analysis of Ratio Variables: Opportunities and Pitfalls." *American Journal of Sociology* 80: 379-396.
Sears, Francis W., Mark W. Zemansky, and Hugh D. Young
1980   *University Physics* (5th Ed.) Reading, MA: Addison-Wesley.
Shepard, Roger N., A. Kimball Romney, and Sara Beth Nerlove
1972   *Multidimensional Scaling, Vol. 1: Theory.* New York: Seminar Press.
Stonequist, Everett
1961   *The Marginal Man.* New York: Russell & Russell.
Sullivan, John L.
1971   "Multiple Indicators and Complex Causal Models," in H. M. Blalock (ed.) *Causal Models in the Social Sciences.* Chicago: Aldine.
Taylor, Howard F.
1973   "Linear Models of Consistency: Some Extensions of Blalock's Strategy." *American Journal of Sociology* 78: 1192-1215.
Thurstone, L. L.
1947   *Multiple Factor Analysis.* Chicago: University of Chicago Press.
Trimmer, John D.
1950   *Response of Physical Systems.* New York: John Wiley.
Tuma, Nancy B., Michael T. Hannan, and L. Groeneveld
1979   "Dynamic Analysis of Event Histories." *American Journal of Sociology* 84: 820-854.
Udy, Stanley H.
1980   "The Configuration of Occupational Structure," in H. M. Blalock (ed.) *Sociological Theory and Research.* New York: Free Press.
Warner, W. L., M. Meeker, and K. Eels
1949   *Social Class in America.* Chicago: Science Research Associates.
Webb, Eugene J., Donald T. Campbell, Richard Schwartz, and Lee Sechrest
1966   *Unobtrusive Measures: Nonreactive Research in the Social Sciences.* Chicago: Rand McNally.
Whitt, Hugh P.
1968   *A Synthetic Theory of Suicide and Homicide.* Ph.D. dissertation, University of North Carolina.
Wiley, David E.
1973   "The Identification Problem for Structural Equation Models with Unmeasured Variables," in Arthur S. Goldberger and Otis Dudley Duncan (eds.) *Structural Equation Models in the Social Sciences.* New York: Seminar Press.

Wilken, Paul H. and H. M. Blalock

    1981   "The Generalizability of Indirect Measures to Complex Situations: A Fundamental Dilemma," in Edgar F. Borgatta and George W. Bohrnstedt (eds.) *Social Measurement: Current Issues.* Beverly Hills, CA: Sage.

Wilson, Kenneth L.

    1979   "Status Inconsistency and the Hope Technique, I: The Grounds for a Resurrection." *Social Forces* 57: 1229-1247.

Wolfinger, Raymond

    1960   "Reputation and Reality in the Study of 'Community Power.' " *American Sociological Review* 25: 636-644.

Wright, Erik Olin

    1978   "Race, Class, and Income Inequality." *American Journal of Sociology* 83: 1368-1397.

Wright, Erik Olin and Luca Perrone

    1977   "Marxist Class Categories and Income Inequality." *American Sociological Review* 42: 32-55.

INDEX

Age - period - cohort effects, 229, 233
Aggregation, 41, 126-127, 260-264
   of behaviors, 104-106
   biases in, 253-258
   of cause indicators, 247-251
   of effect indicators, 240-247
   of manifest characteristics, 238-239
   by proximity, 252-259
Akers, Ronald, 55n, 273
Attitudes, 172-173
Auxiliary measurement theories, 25-27, 59-68

Background variables,
   confounding of, 182-186
   and experience dimensions, 135-144, 226-234
   omission of, 176-186
Balance, cognitive, 150, 174, 231-232
Baumol, William J., 158, 273
Behaviors,
   alternative, 99-106, 119
   versus attitudes, 172-173
   categorization of, 27
   choice, 130-135
   responses to, 173-174
Bettelheim, Bruno, 228, 273
Biases, 106-107
   in aggregation, 253-258
   in OLS, 157
Blalock, H. M., 25, 31n, 61, 74, 81, 89, 95, 116, 122, 127, 130, 158, 221, 229, 235n, 255, 273
Blau, Peter M., 73, 274
Blocks, of variables, 260-263
Burstein, Leigh, 257, 274, 275
Burt, Ronald S., 84, 271, 274

Campbell, Donald T., 93, 274, 278
Campbell, Frederick L., 55n, 273
Campbell, N. R., 35, 274
Carter, Lewis F., 273, 277
Categorical variables, 27
   and choice behaviors, 130-135
   and collapsing decisions, 120-127
   constraints on, 127-130
   cutpoints for, 118
   interpretations of, 115-120
   multidimensionality of, 110-115, 126
Christ, Carl, 151, 274
Cohen, Morris R., 35, 38, 274
Coleman, James S., 40, 43, 264n, 274
Collapsing categories, 120-127
Common indicators, 62, 74, 76-85, 271
Comparability, of measures, 29
   of alternative behaviors, 99-106
   and categorization, 109-145
   and complexity of settings, 94-106
   and generalizability, 62-68, 72-76
   and intercepts, 91-94
   meaning of, 57-59
   multiple indicators, 76-85, 265-272
   and slopes, 85-91
Complexity, 27-31, 61, 75
   of settings, 94-106
Concatenation, 35, 37-43
Conditional probabilities, 122-124
Confounding,
   in aggregation, 242, 249-250, 255-256
   of background variables, 182-186
   of measured and unmeasured variables, 198-219
   of status and power, 219-226
Contextual effects, 230-231

Converse, Philip E., 251, 274
Coombs, Clyde H., 34, 47, 48, 50, 51, 53, 135, 274
Costner, Herbert L., 84, 107n, 267, 268, 271, 274
Counting, 41-46
Curtis, Richard F., 235n, 276

Daft, Richard L., 55n, 277
Dahl, Robert A., 234n, 274
Denzin, Norman K., 263, 274
Derived concepts, 38-39, 226-234
Difference variables, 226-234
Dimensionality, assessment of, 46-54
Discrimination, measurement of, 95-99
Duncan, Otis Dudley, 107n, 135, 151, 217, 218, 274, 275
Durkheim, Emile, 240, 275

Ecological correlations, 252
Edwards, Alba, 119
Eels, K., 278
Effect indicators, 95-99
Equivalence, in multiple indicators, 266-271
Errors, and redundant information, 46-54
Event histories, 201
Expectations, 179, 191-193
Experience dimensions,
    and background variables, 135-144
    involving differences, 226-232
Extensive measurement, 35-46

Factor analysis, 52-53
Feedbacks, 195n
    and omitted variables, 155-176
    and stability, 158-159
Ferree, G. Donald, 107n, 276
Festinger, Leon, 232, 275
Firebaugh, Glenn, 258, 275
Fisher, Franklin, 157, 275
Fiske, D. W., 93, 274
Freeman, John H., 55n, 275
Fuguitt, G. V., 55n, 275
Fundamental measurement, 33, 35-46

Generalizability, 199-200
    and comparability, 29, 62-68, 72-76
    and parsimony, 27-31, 61
Geographic proximity, 252-259
Gibbs, Jack P., 137, 275
Glenn, Norval D., 233, 275
Goffman, Irwin W., 235n, 275
Gold, Martin, 241, 275
Goldberger, Arthur S., 83, 107n, 275
Gordon, Robert A., 31n, 217, 250, 275
Griffin, Larry J., 234n, 276
Groeneveld, L., 278
Guttman, Louis, 34, 47, 53, 275
Guttman scaling, 47-48

Hannan, Michael T., 127, 252, 253, 254, 257, 275, 278
Hargens, Lowell L., 107n, 275
Hatt, Paul K., 208, 217, 277
Hauser, Robert M., 83, 107n, 275
Heider, Fritz, 231, 276
Heise, David R., 195n, 276
Henry, Neil W., 52, 277
Hildebrand, D. K., 145n, 276
Hollingshead, August B., 202, 276
Homogeneity properties, 28, 38, 45
Hope, Keith, 232, 235n, 276
Horan, Patrick M., 114, 218, 276
Hunter, Floyd, 234n, 276

Identification problems, 157, 160-162, 167, 210-213, 222
Inclusiveness, of measures, 72-76
Indicators,
    background variables as, 176-186
    common, 62, 74, 76-85, 271
    equivalent, 70, 74, 81
    identical, 70, 74
    multiple, 67, 76-85, 265-272
    reference, 71, 80-85, 107n
Indirectness of measurement, 20-27, 72-76
Instrumental variables, 256-257
Intercepts, 91-94
Intervening variables,
    omission of, 148-176, 181, 223-224
    of status and power, 219-226
Irwin, Laura, 127, 257, 276

Jackson, Elton F., 137, 227, 235n, 276
Janowitz, Morris, 228, 273
Johnston, J., 151, 276
Jöreskog, Karl, 83, 87, 107n, 276

Kalleberg, Arne L., 234n, 276
Kasarda, John D., 55n, 276
Kelvin, Lord, 7
Kim, Jae - On, 107n, 276
Krantz, David H., 34, 35, 38, 39, 40, 41, 277
Kronenfeld, J. E., 55n, 275

Labelling, 173-174
    of variables, 198
Lags, distributed, 188-189
Laing, J. D., 276
Langbein, Laura Irwin, 257, 277
Latent structure analysis, 52
Laws, 22-23
Lazarsfeld, Paul F., 34, 52, 277
Lenski, Gerhard E., 137, 235n, 277
Lichtman, Allan J., 127, 257, 276, 277
Lieberson, Stanley, 55n, 275
LISREL, 83, 87, 271
Long, Susan, 44, 55n, 277
Lord, Frederic M., 70, 277
Luce, R. Duncan, 34, 277

MacMillan, Alexander, 55n, 277
Marginal distributions, 120-127
Martin, Walter T., 137, 275
Mason, Karen O., 233, 277
Mason, William M., 277
McKinney, John C., 129, 277
Measurement errors, 14-17
Measurement by fiat, 19, 31
Meeker, M., 278
Memory decays, 187-191
Multicollinearity, 14-17, 31n, 211-214, 217, 222, 249-250
Multiple indicators, 67, 76-85
    and comparability, 265-272
Multiplicative models, 88-91, 104-106, 171, 174-175
Multitrait-multimethod approach, 93

Nagel, Ernest, 35, 38, 274

Namboodiri, N. Krishnan, 89, 107n, 151, 153, 277
Nerlove, Sara Beth, 278
Newcomb, Theodore M., 232, 277
Nolan, Patrick D., 55n, 276
Nominal Scales, see Categorical variables
Nonlinear relationships, 86-88, 171, 174-175, 225
North, C. C., 208, 217, 277
Northrop, F.S.C., 109, 277
Novick, Melvin R., 70, 277

Omission of variables,
    independent, 186-193
    intervening, 148-176, 214-215
    past experiences, 176-186
Operationalism, 61
Ordinal measurement, 36-37, 47-51
    and categorical variables, 114-120, 133-135
    and status variables, 199-204

Pair comparisons, 48
Parsimony, 27-31, 61, 75
Perrone, Luca, 234n, 279
Polsby, Nelson, 234n, 277
Poole, W. Kenneth, 277
Power,
    measurement of, 220-221, 234n
    and status, 219-226, 234n
Precision, of measurement, 27-31
Prediction logic, 145n
Properties, of systems, 22-24, 26
Przeworski, Adam, 62, 277
Pullum, Thomas, 118, 277

Ratio scales, 40-41
Ratio variables, 44-45
Recursive models, 151-155
Reduced forms, 153-168
Redundant information, 46-54, 188
Reference groups, 141
Reference indicators, 71, 80-85, 107n, 271
Responses, 22-24
Robinson, William S., 252, 278
Romney, A. Kimball, 278
Rosenthal, H., 276

Scaling, 47-54
Schoenberg, Ronald, 80, 84, 107n, 268, 271, 274, 278
Schuessler, Karl, 55n, 278
Schwartz, Richard, 278
Scope, of measures, 72-76
Sears, Francis W., 7, 278
Sechrest, Lee, 278
Shepard, Roger, 34, 52, 278
Simplicity, 27-31, 75
    of settings, 61, 94-106
Slopes, and comparability, 85-91
Smallest-space analysis, 52-53
Sörbom, D., 87, 276
Stability, in feedback systems, 158-159, 195n
Standardization, 107n
Status inconsistency, 137, 227, 232, 235n
Status variables, 198-226
    differentiated, 206-207, 215-219
    measurement of, 201-209
    and power, 219-226
Stimuli, 22-24
Stonequist, Everett, 231, 278
Structural parameter, 153-168
Subjective meanings, 168-172
Sullivan, John L., 262, 278
Suppes, Patrick, 34, 277
Systems, 22-26

Taylor, Howard F., 174, 231, 232, 278

Tests, of theories, 30
Teune, Henry, 62, 278
Thomas, William I., 168
Thurstone, L. L., 34, 278
Transformations, mathematical, 71-72, 107n
Transitivity, 36-37, 48
Triad comparisons, 48
Trimmer, John D., 23, 278
Tuma, Nancy B., 201, 278
Tversky, Amos, 34, 277

Udy, Stanley H., 114, 119, 218, 278
Unfolding technique, 51

Validation of measurements, 40

Warner, W. Lloyd, 202, 278
Webb, Eugene J., 263, 278
Wells, Caryll S., 273
Whitt, Hugh P., 241, 243, 278
Wiley, David E., 80, 107n, 278
Wilken, Paul H., 61, 95, 97, 130, 192, 221, 229, 231, 235n, 279
Wilson, Kenneth L., 235n, 279
Winsborough, H. H., 277
Wolfinger, Raymond, 234n, 279
Wright, Erik Olin, 114, 234, 279

Young, Hugh D., 278

Zemansky, Mark W., 278

ABOUT THE AUTHOR

Hubert M. Blalock, Jr. received his Ph.D. in sociology from the University of North Carolina in 1954. He is a past President of the American Sociological Association and Fellow of the American Statistical Association, and has been elected to the National Academy of Sciences and the American Academy of Arts and Sciences. The author of a number of books, including *Social Statistics, Theory Construction,* and (with Paul H. Wilken) *Intergroup Processes: A Micro-Macro Approach,* he is currently Professor of Sociology and Statistics at the University of Washington, having previously taught at the University of Michigan, Yale University, and the University of North Carolina.